MW01284518

ROOT FOR THE CUBS

Root for the Cubs

Charlie Root and the
1929 Chicago Cubs

Roger Snell

WIND PUBLICATIONS

Copyright © 2009 by Roger Snell. All rights reserved. Printed in the United States of America. No part of this book may be reproduced in any manner, except for brief quotations embodied in critical articles or reviews. For information address Wind Publications, 600 Overbrook Drive, Nicholasville KY 40356.

International Standard Book Number 978-1-893239-95-1
Library of Congress Control Number 2009924270

First edition

The front cover is a collage of photographs from Della Root Arnold's private collection and the Catalina Island Museum collection, design by Roger Snell and the publisher.

This book may be purchased from local bookstores or from on-line booksellers such as Amazon.com or BN.com. The author and publisher may be contacted at the following websites respectively: rootforthecubs.com, and windpublications.com/books.

Acknowledgements

Ted Sloan was my sounding board and a volunteer editor, blending his shared love of baseball with his exacting detail for the written word. Most importantly, he is a friend.

Peter Golenbock saw an early draft of the manuscript and offered detailed advice as a baseball author. Golenbock is today's oral historian of baseball, and "Wrigleyville" is just one example of his outstanding work. Check out his other books about the "Bums," the Mets, the Cardinals, St. Louis Browns and so much more.

Clifton Blue Parker offered similar help, including important enhancements. What a joy it is to talk baseball and writing with the author of the best book about Hack Wilson, "Fouled Away." Parker's most recent work is about two brothers of the same era, Paul and Lloyd Waner, in "Big and Little Poison."

Also standing at the top of these baseball biographies is Charles Alexander's "Rogers Hornsby." If you can't be a baseball player, then the next dream job is what Alexander has carved out—college professor of baseball history.

In my own writing career, my list of newsroom influences includes Gale Baldwin, Mike Berens, Bonnie Bolden, Bob Dreitzler, Mark Ellis, Terry Ganey, Everett Kennell, Marvin Jones, Jim Leickly, David Lore, Joanne Myers, Mike O'Brien, Doug Oplinger, Randy Sissell, Bill Southerland, Stuart Warner, Keith White, Steve Wilson and Andy Zajac.

Special thanks also to Anne Bernini, daughter of 1929 spring training tryout Eddie Lautenbacher, Valerie Edgeworth, Karla Hoyt, Kirk Kandle, Bryan Laubaugh, Craig Starner and Stephen White. To all members of the Root family who are winners just like Charlie, especially Nancy Arnold Wade who is the Smithsonian of Root family photos, "The Nancesonian," as her mother Della calls her. To Tony Gaier who kept pushing for this story to see the light of day, to Richard and Lizz Taylor of Poor Richard's Books in Frankfort, Kentucky., and to publisher Charlie Hughes who has collaborated on the dreams of more than 60 authors.

Many thanks also to the welcoming hosts at Catalina Island, especially my Cub-loving tour guide for the day, Joe Saldana, and his wife, Trudy, owners of Coyote Joe's restaurant on the island. Special thanks to Lolo Saldana who is Joe's brother and the barber of Avalon, innkeeper Susan Griffin who watches over the beautifully preserved home of William Wrigley Jr. high atop Mt. Ada, Catalina Museum curator Jeannine Pedersen who made the search for 1929 photos effortless, and Casino and island tour guide Chuck Liddell and museum manager John Baraggina who keep this Cub story alive for tourists.

The *Chicago Daily News* photographs used here are from the archives of the Chicago History Museum.

Thanks to John H. Meyer of Carmel, California, who converted the Nikolas film to digital images, and to Cathy Koch of St. Charles, Illinois, grandaughter of George J. Nikolas, Jr. (1892-1968), Chicago businessman and life-long Cubs fan, who filmed portions of the first game of the 1929 World Series using a 16-mm home-movie camera.

Thanks to Kirk M. Kandle of Lousiville, Kentucky, who supplied the photo of Babe Ruth taken from a 16-mm home movie shot by his great-grandfather, Matt Kandle, Sr., the only known film of the Babe hitting his famous "called shot" in the 1932 World Series.

Photo by Roger Snell

Della Root Arnold, age 90, shows a photo of herself
at age 10 with her family during 1929 spring training
at Catalina Island.

Dedication

To Della Root Arnold, whose father, Charlie Root, taught her about winners.

To the memory of Berlyn "Trader" Horne, the Arcanum, Ohio, neighbor who made his dream come true for a season and who sparked my dream in journalism with that first interview in 1978.

To family, friends and the memory of Roger Toppins, a defending World Champion who ran our computer baseball league for 24 seasons and whose last baseball trip was to Wrigley Field with me after being diagnosed with a terminal illness. He died in May 2004, never seeing the final manuscript. He was like a brother to me. His last e-mail message, two nights before he died, was devoted to baseball.

To Robert Gorman and David Martin, who walked the same hallowed ground one hot summer day in Middletown as we discovered Root's birthplace, the vacant lot where he first pitched as a child, and the burial place of his parents.

And to family and friends who supported my dream, especially Linda, Rachel, Hannah, a father who never tired of playing ball with his son, and a mother who tolerated a lawn of well-worn base paths and windows of shattered glass.

Contents

Photographs

Tables

Introduction

The Boston Red Sox ended their 86-six-year drought with a World Series championship in 2004. But Cub fans have suffered even longer since their last championship in 1908.

The season of 1929 started with the realistic hope of reaching the World Series. There was every reason to consider the Cubs the best team in baseball—or perhaps second only to the New York Yankees. Many of the national baseball writers chose the Cubs to win it all because of their strong pitching staff, obvious sluggers, and the move over the winter to acquire Rogers Hornsby.

Manager Joe McCarthy had never played a day in the majors, a rarity for baseball at the time, but he had carefully tapped the minors for the hidden talent now at the center of this 1929 club. Cub pitching ace Charlie Root was one of McCarthy's key recruits.

Root is the thread that ties together the story of the 1929 season, as told by an eyewitness and loving daughter, Della Arnold, who turned 90 on February 21, 2009, and lives in California. She was a 10-year-old girl watching her Dad on center stage at the greatest moment in his life and career.

Because of Della, the daily sports reports of Edward Burns, and boxes of yellowed news clippings, this is so much more than a baseball story.

The story begins with spring training of 1929 and with Chicago's Al Capone as the prime suspect in the Saint Valentine's Day Massacre, a gangland shooting in a warehouse just blocks away from the Roots' apartment and Wrigley Field.

It is a love story about a wife who insisted that Root should let nothing stop his dream, overcoming his Dad's disgust about his pursuit of a child's game.

It is the powerful tragedy of Hack Wilson who grew up without parents who loved or wanted him. When he found a father figure in

1

baseball who understood, the childhood scars were washed away powerfully but only briefly.

This is also a personal story of my own Moonlight Graham. Just like in the movie "Field of Dreams," Berly Horne got one chance to make the major leagues when he reported to Catalina Island for spring training in 1929. Over twenty-five years, I have told friends about this quiet and kindly gentleman who lived just down the street from my childhood home.

One friend, caught up in the story as much as I, was David Martin, and yet he never met Horne. Martin tracked down minor league records and newspaper stories. Martin also wrote to the Hall of Fame and retrieved one scrap of paper, a survey that Horne filled out when he retired from professional baseball.

Horne was asked if he would do it all again, he wrote, "Absolutely" and added a bold exclamation mark.

Martin even tracked down minor league baseball cards and some old team photos. We were excited when we learned that Horne pitched more than 20 years in the minors, 12 years before reaching the Cubs in 1929 and 10 years after.

Despite all this material, there still wasn't enough material for a book, and I was snagged. Then I met Ohio appeals court judge Robert Gorman of Cincinnati, a nephew of Root. That is how I found Della Root.

Della devoted hundreds of hours of interviews to help me and shared a 166-page personal account that she had written for her daughter and Charlie Jr.'s children, called "Life with Charlie." Della gave enthusiastically of her time, looking forward to our weekend phone conversations because they took her back to 1929, when she was a 10-year-old girl and the world revolved around her father.

The fans, box scores and records tell what a winner Root was. Della's story goes beyond the numbers to tell the more significant story about what her dad was like off the field, spiced with stories of some true characters who loved baseball when it was just a game.

In the summer of 2002, Martin, Gorman, and I walked through Root's childhood neighborhood in Middletown, Ohio. Several blocks away, Gorman felt compelled to drive into an old cemetery. He apologized for wasting our time, but I told him to go even farther into the cemetery. Just as we were ready to leave, Martin turned and saw a "Root" gravestone. With no lead or plans at all, we had driven to the burial place of Root's mother and father. Everything about that trip was like walking on hallowed ground. John Bombatch, sports editor of the local newspaper, even took time from his busy schedule on a Saturday to help us and then hurried to be at a wedding on time.

The epilogue also details the story of one of baseball's most controversial moments—Babe Ruth's alleged "called shot" off Root.

Root would win more games in a Cub uniform than any pitcher in club history, including Grover Cleveland Alexander and Ferguson Jenkins. Yet today Root is remembered more for one pitch to Babe Ruth in the 1932 World Series than for his 201 wins and almost 3,200 innings pitched.

"If that big fat guy had pointed, you think we would have seen it," said Della, who was only a few rows behind home plate when Ruth hit his second homer of the game. Details of the controversy, discovery of the only photographic record, thorough research of all of the same-day news accounts, and new insights are at the end of this book.

Now we go back in time, to 1929, when Della takes us to one of the greatest Cub seasons ever.

Photo by Roger Snell

Della Root Arnold with photos of her parents,
Dorothy and Charlie

Last Chances

Spring training trips do not always produce news for fans. Outside of speculation on the class of a few rookies, there sometimes are very few fan problems to be settled by training camp developments. But Catalina should be different, perhaps to a greater degree than any training camp of recent years.
— Edward Burns, *Chicago Tribune*, February 1929.

Charlie Root steps to the mound as the warm breeze gently stirs the eucalyptus trees lining the fence from third base to left field.

Catalina Island is sunny as usual for late February, much warmer than the Chicago weather to which Root is accustomed. But today is cooler than the typical 70 degrees, and the locals are grumbling about that.

Gabby Hartnett is not complaining. Unlike Root, who now lives in California in the winter, Hartnett had left freezing, dreary Chicago behind at Union Station and brought his new bride here for their honeymoon.

Root kicks at the dirt on the mound, raises his glove to his face, breathes in the musty smell of the leather, and looks toward Hartnett who is smiling, settled into his crouch behind the plate, watching Root trying to get loose by wind-milling his right arm. Root is good at hiding his emotions, trying unsuccessfully to get rid of the pain and popping that never used to be in his elbow.

Root has what appears to be a smooth, effortless side-arm or three-quarter overhand pitching motion, and he repeatedly whips the arm with the force of a slingshot, pitch after pitch and inning after inning. His pitching hand and the ball are disguised and seem to jump out of his uniform, leading into a graceful, powerful follow-through.

Root will be thirty on March 17, usually the peak of a pitcher's career. He has used this arm to pitch hard and regularly for half his life. There are no relief specialists in professional baseball at this time. A starter is expected to finish. Charlie has thrown more than 300 innings each season in the minors and close to that every year in the majors.

Charlie didn't attend high school, which was typical for kids of his time. Poor families needed everyone working for the extra income, and it didn't matter that those unskilled, backbreaking jobs were in factories and mills. Baseball had rescued Charlie from such hard labor in Middletown, Ohio. Cub teammates Hack Wilson and Gabby Hartnett escaped textile mills because of their baseball skills.

Root family archives

Charlie Root

Charlie went to work in the noisy, dirty, fiery hot Armco Rolling Mill when he was thirteen. His entire wage from the steel mill went to his dad, and Charlie got a weekly allowance of twenty-five cents in exchange.

Any first-time visitor to a steel mill is intimidated by the noise, heat and fire. Massive cauldrons of molten iron hang overhead. When they are tipped to pour the liquid steel into molds, the splash of fiery darts burns through clothes to leave tiny scars on workers' arms. This workplace is the devil's own workshop.

Armco, the largest factory anywhere near Cincinnati, with tens of thousands of employees, had a gigantic pool from which to select quality players for the company baseball team. Employees were often hired because of their playing ability. The competitiveness and quality of some company teams surpassed baseball's own minor leagues in many cities.

A baseball player could have desire, deep love of the game, heart, spirit and a tremendous work ethic. But a professional career also hinged on how tendon, muscle, bone and sinew all held together. Pitch

6

by pitch and inning by inning, Root was excelling, but at the same time adding tremendous strain to his arm.

By age twenty-two, Root had pitched Armco to several championships, and he was pitching for several semi-pro teams on the side for $5 a game. His big break came while pitching an afternoon game for Armco in 1921 against the touring St. Louis Browns. The Browns would finish third in the American League that season, behind an offense led by .371 hitter George Sisler.

Root baffled the pros, shutting them down on a three-hitter. He was signed immediately and ordered to report to Terre Haute, Indiana, for the remainder of the 1921 season.

By 1929, everything is riding on Root's right arm—a comfortable life and more money than any of his friends back home could make, including the most educated ones.

His arm supports two growing kids, his wife, Dorothy, and himself. Della would turn ten on February 21 and Charlie Junior five on February 27, while the family is together at Catalina Island.

His arm provides for a better downtown apartment than before in Chicago, a maid to help Dorothy around the house, and the chance for her to be a full-time mother.

They are making plans to move from their rented home in Los Angeles and buy their own place there. Last season, they got a much better summer home—their apartment in Chicago. They talk of buying a California ranch someday and taking cruises to Hawaii and Australia, without a second thought to the cost.

Root and his teammates all have an indulgence that tips off their previous poverty and current wealth. They compete against each other to have the classiest suits and ties.

As a boy, Charlie was used to wearing out shoes and having to wait on repairs from a cobbler. He only had one pair. Today, as an established and well-paid baseball star, Root's closet is full of countless, expensive, polished shoes.

Sometimes Charlie felt guilty about the money, knowing how hard others were working for so little. And he was getting paid to play a game that he loved.

Charlie would never have reached this point if he had listened to his dad, who thought this was a frivolous dream to chase while trying to raise a family.

Dorothy and Charlie jokingly referred to his dad as "The Kaiser" for his rough demeanor and his stubborn insistence in speaking his native German in the home.

Nobody messed with the Kaiser and certainly didn't talk back to him—except Dorothy. Without Dorothy, Charlie probably never would have left Middletown.

At times, Charlie shared his father's doubts. But all he knew was baseball.

These doubts were far stronger on this February day in 1929 as spring training began. And only Dorothy and

Charlie knew why. Their marriage was a powerful bond. They formed a humble, humorous, dignified team that the other Cubs recognize and are drawn toward.

The young, single players are either missing home or trying to get away from miserable lives, and Dorothy loved cooking for them. The Root home is where the Cubs go for a home-cooked meal, to play cards, or to test another practical joke, gag gift or magic routine.

Could this all come to an end, Dorothy wondered, as Charlie threw his first warm-up pitch to Gabby? She tried to dismiss the thought.

Only weeks before today's arrival at Catalina, Root saw Doc Spenser in St. Louis. Cubs owner William Wrigley Jr. made the arrangements and considered Spenser the best.

"Doc Spenser recommended surgery on dad's elbow, which somehow had become encased in a muscle or tendon. Whatever it was, it was really bad news," his daughter, Della, wrote years later. [1]

---

[1] All personal details of the Roots in this chapter are derived from interviews with Della Root Arnold and from her journal.

"We had moved to a classier neighborhood to a larger apartment where Mom and Dad had their first private bedroom. Junior and I slept on a pull-down Murphy bed in the living room. It was to that apartment Dad returned after his St. Louis visit with Doc Spenser. I can see Dad yet, sitting in a big overstuffed chair, completely dejected. He began to cry."

"'Dorothy, the doc says I'm through and I'll never pitch again.'"

"He covered his eyes and great sobs racked his body. It's a terrible thing to see your dad cry."

This was the only time that Della ever saw her quiet, reserved father cry.

"Mom put her arms around him and said, 'Now Charles, you know that's ridiculous. Of course you'll pitch again and be better than ever.'"

Charlie still had his doubts. They decided against surgery, nervously anticipating spring training at Catalina. There was every reason to believe his career was over, but Dorothy refused to accept it.

Beginning with Catalina in 1929, Dorothy, Della and little Charlie Junior would massage Charlie's arm before and after every game, just as they were taught by club trainer Andy Lotshaw.

"The greatest trainer in the world worked on Charlie's arm and, at night, a five-year-old boy, a 10-year-old girl, and a devoted wife would rub it, too. I don't know, nor can I imagine, how much physical help we were, but I think at least it re-sparked Dad's remarkable determination," Della wrote.

Back on the mound at Catalina, Root reaches for his cap, tips it slightly, just as he always does before the first pitch of any game when Dorothy is in the stands. This is the first time he's done this in practice, but he knows his wife is watching even more closely today.

Berly Horne sees Root tip his cap to Dorothy as he throws easily along the foul line in left field with aging catcher Mike Gonzales.

Manager Joe McCarthy always matches his rookie pitchers with veteran catchers to see what they really have.

Everything rides on spring training for Horne. Like Root, Horne also turns thirty in the spring, on April 12. Horne had signed his first minor league contract in 1917, nearly twelve years earlier. He is running out of time to make the majors.

Although Root and Horne are only a month apart in age, the distinction between established veteran and old rookie is huge.

Horne's arm feels as strong as when he pitched for the auto parts factory in Dayton, Ohio, as a teen. But he is competing against kids like Eddie Lautenbacher, who is already showing off his young, live arm, and also was invited to Catalina for the first time.

Horne is here because of his previous season in Jersey City, easily his best in the minors. He overcame his shyness and pushed the minor league club to shop his name around the majors.

McCarthy still has great contacts in the minors from when he managed in Louisville, and Horne's numbers caught his eye—three shutouts and a 3.01 ERA for Jersey City in the tremendous hitters' International League.

The real numbers that matter to McCarthy are the ones proving Horne is a workhorse. He pitched 266 innings, completed 24 games and won 16 games for a dead-last team. McCarthy allows himself to dream about what Horne might do with an offense led by Rogers Hornsby, Hack Wilson, Kiki Cuyler, Riggs Stephenson and Gabby Hartnett.

McCarthy thinks good coaching can overcome Horne's wildness. He walked 140 hitters while striking out 137 the previous year.

Both Horne and McCarthy are realistic. The Cubs already have one of the best pitching rotations in baseball, with Charlie Root, Pat Malone, Sheriff Blake, and Guy Bush. Behind them are Hal Carlson, Art Nehf and Mike Cvengros.

Just like everyone else in baseball, Veeck and McCarthy are always looking for an arm that can deliver solid innings, maybe mop up in a blowout, or start when the hot summer and travel begin wearing down the aces.

Horne, a little guy, showed no signs of wear and tear in Jersey City.

Horne feels the pressure but welcomes his big chance. With only eight teams in each league, a new pitcher has to be better than the 80 best and strongest arms in all of America to anchor a major league rotation. There were thousands waiting in line, mostly farm boys and factory workers who had played on semi-pro teams from small towns.

Adding to the pressure, the short spring training season was intended to get the stars into playing shape.

Horne might get to appear very briefly, only once a week, and one bad outing, even a few bad pitches, could erase his dreams.

Photo from Root family archives — first appeared in the *Chicago Evening American*.

Dorothy traveled on the train with Charlie to most of his games, chasing off groupies who followed the team. They played cards frequently and Charlie was just as competitive as on the field.

St. Valentine's Day

"The train left on schedule from the Dearborn Street station at 1:35 o'clock this afternoon. No one of the scheduled party of 28 missed the train and all of the pitchers and catchers were at the station more than an hour before the caravan pulled out. At all stops west in Illinois there were delegations at the depots to catch a glimpse of the athletes. The extent of these demonstrations set a precedent in the matter of off season baseball interest, it is said."

—Edward Burns, Chicago *Tribune*, February 14, 1929.

Rookies Berly Horne and Tom Angley would never forget Thursday, February 14. They nervously wait to meet the other pitchers and catchers, scheduled for the three-day train ride that will take them to their first spring training.

Yesterday, they reported to Manager Joe McCarthy's office at Wrigley Field with the required fresh haircuts and baggage ready for Trainer Andy Lotshaw to haul to Union Station.[2]

In Los Angeles, Dorothy Root packs the last items in a large wardroom trunk. She used to sew new outfits for Della and Junior, but now they have the money for the finest clothes this spring. If the *Tribune* takes their pictures again this year, she says, they're not going to look like they fell off the turnip truck.

Charlie calls the cartage company that will haul the trunk to the Wilmington pier for the trip to Catalina Island. Dorothy is ready to join

---

[2] *Chicago Tribune.*

her friends, the wives of Clyde Beck, Sheriff Blake, Charlie Grimm and Johnny Moore.[3]

Al Capone starts Valentine's Day with a dip in the swimming pool at his Florida mansion, where he is spending the winter. He eats a huge breakfast and dresses impeccably as usual. His chauffeur drives him in his Packard downtown to the county solicitor's office in Miami, where Capone is to be questioned as a suspect in other crimes.[4]

Back in Chicago, a light snow is powdering the city, and brisk winds are whipping off the lake.

Bugs Moran, a gangster crowding Capone's territory on Chicago's North Side, is expecting a delivery at 10:30 a.m. at his warehouse at 2122 North Clark Street, several blocks south of where Clark passes Wrigley Field.

Seven friends are waiting to meet Moran at the warehouse, having received a call about a great deal on prime whiskey. They are wearing heavy coats and hats in the unheated warehouse. Moran is running late.[5]

Edward Burns makes a final stop at the *Tribune*. He can't resist razzing the unlucky stiffs in the newsroom with his fake complaints about how horrible his upcoming working conditions are going to be, stranded on an island, baked by sun and heat, and forced to watch baseball while everyone else enjoys the brisk winds, snow and ice of Chicago.

He doesn't have a story to write until this afternoon, from the train. Burns worked out plans with Western Union where he would type his copy on the swaying Pullman and drop it off at a depot with a telegraph operator. The story would get to the sports desk well before tonight's deadline.

---

[3] Della Root Arnold.
[4] Pg. 229, Kobler, John, *Capone: The Life and World of Al Capone.*
[5] Pg. 308, Bergreen, Laurence, *Capone: The Man and the Era.*

Burns sits down at the desk that he hardly ever used in the *Tribune* newsroom to read today's paper, checking whether the copy editors had mangled his prose of yesterday. "You might say that the 1929 National League pennant race will be well under way today," Burns read.

He fanned the controversy about whether the Cubs' new second baseman would get along with anyone. "Every day or so, we shall emphatically deny rumors, started in pool halls and smoke shops, that Manager McCarthy and Rogers Hornsby have engaged in fisticuffs in the Avalon clubhouse. Once a week, probably Tuesdays, we'll tell how Charlie Root has regained the hop on his fast one."

The "Pullman gabfest on the train" today will have the players convincing themselves of an undefeated spring training record for starters before the first pitch is thrown, Burns wrote.

As Burns and Horne prepare to head to Union Station and Capone answers questions in the Miami prosecutor's office, hit men dressed as cops are driving to Moran's warehouse. Bugs, unknowingly, is only about a minute behind them.

Moran isn't just crowding into Capone's North Side turf. He has hijacked Capone's trucks loaded with booze, traveling between Detroit and Chicago. He stole the entire Capone cargo of whiskey from a Canadian ship docked at Lake Michigan.[6]

Moran's warehouse is a one-story, red-brick building previously used as a repair garage. The floors are stained with oil and grease. Tall, wide doors in the rear are perfect for unloading trucks inside and out of view.

Three empty trucks are parked against the side walls. A fourth is jacked up in the center of the floor while ex-safecracker Johnny May, 40, makes repairs. His dog, Highball, is tied to the truck's axle. May brought some scraps of meat for him in a paper bag. A coffeepot percolates on an electric plate.

---

[6] Pg. 227, Kobler.

Six others at the warehouse are Frank and Pete Gusenberg, James Clark (Moran's brother-in-law); Adam Heyer; Albert R. Weinshank; and Reinhardt H. Schwimmer.[7]

The Gusenberg brothers plan to drive two of the empty trucks to Detroit at noon to pick up some smuggled Canadian whiskey.

Heyer is a college graduate and accountant who has served prison time for embezzlement. He keeps Moran's books. Heyer owns the cartage company, served several prison sentences since 1908 for robbery and con games, and is "the brains of the Moran mob." He also owns a dog racing track and is carrying $1,399 in his pockets.

Weinshank is the newest gang member and the muscle that got Moran into protection money for dry cleaners and laundries. He also looks a lot like Moran, and triggers the mistaken signal from the hit men that Moran has arrived. He also is the cousin of a former state representative.

Schwimmer is called "Doc," but he isn't an eye doctor. He simply fits people for glasses. He has no criminal record but is like a mob groupie who boasts about being in the alcohol racket, hints at being able to get people killed and pretends to have all kinds of power through association with Moran.

About twenty blocks away, a black Cadillac touring car sideswipes a truck driven by Elmer Lewis. Lewis is amazed when the "policemen" wave him on, smiling.

The "police car" reaches the warehouse just before Moran arrives and Moran drives on, thinking there is a raid or shakedown. The target of the hit misses dying at the warehouse by that much.

Witnesses report what they thought was the chatter of a drill and then two blasts like a car backfiring. Two women in apartments looking down on the warehouse hear howling from the dog inside.

Two civilians came out with their hands raised. Two men behind them are wearing police uniforms, holding pistols to the backs of the civilians. The fifth man must have been a plainclothes detective, the witnesses thought.

---

[7] All details about the victims come from Kobler's book and from the same-day accounts of the *Chicago Tribune.*

One of the women sends a boarder to check on why the dog is howling. He returns, running from the warehouse, yelling, "They're all dead."

Moran's henchmen were executed along the wall by machine gun fire, sweeping first at their heads, then chests and then stomachs. "Two of the executioners were in police uniform and the seven men thought they were facing only arrest, yielding to disarming and obeying orders to stand in a row facing the wall," police told the *Tribune*. One victim managed to stagger toward the alley entrance of the garage before he collapsed over some chairs.

May took machine gun fire to the back, but his face was gone from a shotgun blast. Highball, was still frantically barking by his side as the real police arrived.

Al Capone mug shot.

Frank Gusenberg survived fourteen bullet wounds just long enough to tell a questioning detective at Alexian Brothers Hospital, "Nobody shot me."[8]

Moran told friends, "Only Capone kills like that."

Burns knows Alphonse "Scarface" Capone well from his crime reporting days. More recently, he saw Capone as a fan at Wrigley Field, wearing his gray fedora, sitting in the front row near the screen behind home plate.

Burns started as a police reporter and thought he had the best beat at the *Tribune*—until he moved to sports to cover the Cubs.[9]

Some days he envied the current police reporter, James O'Donnell Bennett, who was dominating the front page repeatedly.

---

[8] Pg. 234, Kobler.
[9] Pg. 181, Grimm, Charlie, *Jolly Cholly.*

16

Bennett had worked most of the winter months investigating organized crime and political corruption in the city. His five-part series was called "Gangland: The True Story of Chicago Crime." [10]

Bennett's warning of escalating gangland wars was just as impeccable as his timing. *Tribune* editors planned the massive series for five consecutive Sundays, the day when readership is highest, beginning on February 3rd. Chicago readers would get an unprecedented look at organized crime and the rise of Capone:

> This crew ran dozens of breweries and thousands of stills, and it made millions of dollars. Its corruption funds were enormous. It bribed policemen, police officers, federal deputies, and prohibition agents.
>
> What it could not accomplish by bribery it accomplished by terrorism, with the results that the leaders of boozedom did pretty much as they pleased in the fifth city of Christendom for nearly a decade.
>
> How they did it, what pitiless energy, what real genius for organization, what ruthlessness of heart, and what shamelessness of soul they brought to bear forms one of the most amazing chapters in the annals of big city crime, and the blackest chapter in the annals of bogus prohibition.
>
> I must note the leaders of boozedom are lying low. Nobody can say how much further they would have gone if the abused city had not risen last year and turned out of office a feeble officialdom that had shown itself incapable at times of coping with this new form of criminality and at times unwilling.
>
> But boozedom is only marking time. It is only waiting for the first sign of weakness or of stupidity in the new regime in the state's attorney's office and in the police department to resume operations. One slip and the leaders of boozedom will be up from their villas in Florida and down from their hunting lodges in Wisconsin and on this town's neck again, and the terrorists and corruptionists will be as active as they were in 1923, '24, '25, '26, '27 and '28.
>
> The true story of boozedom's past performances—its murders, vendettas, panderings, beer runnings, and briberies—is heavily

---

[10] *Chicago Tribune,* major investigative pieces by James O'Donnell Bennett that ran on five Sundays before and after the St. Valentine's Day Massacre, an

freighted with warnings of what Chicago may expect if the desperate men now lying in wait spring again from cover.

It is important to see them as they are—criminals in business and business men in crime, pimps and bawdy house keepers and safecrackers turned bootleggers—and not as cherry racketeers whom supposedly reputable officials were not ashamed to palter with and dine with and traffic for votes with.

So here begins the story which purposes the debunking of the gangsters of boozedom.

Bennett starts his gangland history with Dean O'Banion, Chicago's flashiest gangster. O'Banion openly boasted that he had either killed or seen killed twenty-five men. He was cheerful on the days of murder, referring to each upcoming victim as a "swell fellow," at the time the target's "address was in his death book," Bennett wrote.

"If a suspected colleague was booked to be killed that night, why talk rough about him during the afternoon of the fatal date," Bennett wrote.

O'Banion would shake your hand and pat you on the back, but always one hand at a time, keeping one free at all times. Tailors customized his suits, including three separate hiding places for weapons that he could reach with that free hand. In addition to all his illicit businesses, O'Banion ran a flower shop at 738 North State Street, just across from the Holy Name Cathedral where he had served as an altar boy.

At the flower shop within the morning shadows of the church, he was shot to death by three men—identity still legally undetermined after more than four years—at noon of Nov. 10, 1924.

Bennett said O'Banion's flower shop was a great front for "bullets and bouquets" because thousands of dollars were spent for funeral floral arrangements, and it was a great place to hide his less fragrant business.

---

outstanding and almost prophetic investigative series about the turf wars of Chicago's bootleggers and how it was getting worse.

On the second Sunday of the series, February 10, Bennett reports how O'Banion had crowded Capone and why Capone has been considered a murder suspect for the past four years.

As *Tribune* reporters, Burns and Bennett work in America's second largest city, surrounded by ambitious, busy, noisy, adrenaline junkies who decide what is news for more than one million readers.

The *Tribune* was rapidly outdistancing several competing newspapers in the city, seemingly printing money instead of news. Just a month before, the *Tribune* ran a full-page ad boasting of its largest circulation in history, 1,251,304 on Sunday and 824,633 readers each day.

The *Tribune* started with a single printing press in 1847 and was only four pages each day, with 400 subscribers. In 1855, Joseph Medill bought the paper, was among the founders of the Republican Party and strongly supported Abraham Lincoln for president.

Newspaper wars marked the 1900s when tabloid kingpin William Randolph Hearst opened the Chicago *American* to compete directly with the *Tribune*. By 1910 and the rest of the decade, the newspapers actually hired thugs to intimidate news vendors and try to block deliveries with fists and gunshots.

Two of Medill's grandsons, Robert R. McCormick and Joseph Patterson took over the *Tribune* in 1911. By the end of the decade, the *Tribune* had won the war with Hearst, building the largest circulation in the city.

They also started the *New York Daily News* in 1919 and then took over Chicago radio station WDAP in 1924, renaming it WGN for the acronym and slogan of the *Tribune*, "World's Greatest Newspaper."[11]

When Burns shifted from cops to Cubs, the move wasn't that big a transition as far as excitement and attention. But the hours were much better and the subjects a lot more fun.

The police beat was tough on reporters because of the *predictable* hours—you could count on having your long day shift extended by a long night.

---

[11] The *Chicago Tribune's* own published company history.

Covering baseball, Burns' final deadlines weren't so punishing since the games were all played in early afternoon. Times were changing, however, especially for the home games at Wrigley Field when a special game edition was printed. New presses could send huge rolls of newsprint flying through ink rollers pressed against lead type fast enough to get a quick early game edition of the *Tribune* to fans as they left the ballpark.

Newsboys would stand at the exits hawking Burns' stories about a game that fans had just witnessed. Burns would already have material from his pre-game interviews, mix in the first few innings of action, bang away on his typewriter as he watched the game, and then phone it to the desk.

The lead type would be set in the backshop, and presses would start cranking the first copies, pushing a well-orchestrated assembly line of papers, literally hot off the press, bundled, tossed onto trucks, with drivers ready to roll to the ballpark.

Burns boards the train with 28 people in the Cubs' two private Pullman cars, including the two rookies, Angley and Horne. On board, Burns starts typing for tomorrow's readers exactly who is riding with him: Angley; Horne; Lotshaw; Manager and Mrs. McCarthy; traveling secretary Robert Lewis; Mr. and Mrs. Fred Blake; Mr. and Mrs. Charles Leo "Gabby" Hartnett; Guy Bush; Roy Hansen; Henry Grampp; Ed Holley; Eddie Lautenbacher; Mike Gonzales; Mike Cvengros; Hal Carlson; and 10 newspaper reporters and spouses.

At each stop in Chicago and through much of western Illinois, Burns is surprised at how many fans are waiting for the Cubs, including at least 100 men and boys at one rural station.

Some casual fans make the mistake of asking for Hack Wilson or Rogers Hornsby to talk from the car platform, not realizing that they will be with the rest of the players who leave from here in eight days.

Hartnett obliges the fans, though, with brief addresses from the car platform.

"Poor, new bride, Mrs. Hartnett," Burns writes, describing how women fans come with critical eyes to see who stole the previously eligible bachelor. "A survey of the gathering revealed that the girl fans think Mrs. Hartnett wasn't flattered any by the pictures printed at the time of the wedding two weeks ago."

Burns is covering so much detail of boarding the train because he's getting very little baseball copy otherwise.

Reporters are grumbling on the train and in print that McCarthy has said nothing about the Hornsby deal or his likely batting order.

First base coach Jimmy Burke boards in Kansas City, and that's when the fun begins in earnest. "Jimmy is a genial grouch who shouts a spirited pinochle game and Trainer Andy Lotshaw, a shy fellow, finds it impossible to start any noise on a Cub train unless the radiant skinned Mr. Burke is aboard," Burns writes.

The stakes are so low that they never become an issue, largely because McCarthy tolerates the games if they don't become a distraction.

As usual, with expensive suits and ties in perfect order, the players agree they cannot beat "Pretty Boy" Guy Bush. As the most notable "clothes horse," Bush travels with two huge steamer trunks full of his three-piece suits.

The rookies stay in one of the Pullman cars and the veterans in the other. McCarthy always stays with the rookies, wanting time to know them and prepare them for what is ahead.

Each player gets both the top and bottom sleeping berth. Most spread their luggage out in one bunk and sleep in the other.

A dining area is part of the two-car special, and the players are fed very well, usually fine steaks, catered to the private car.

Other passengers on the train have no access to the two Cub cars. The slower pace of the train, with family aboard, greatly bonds the team on this trip.

For Horne, this is traveling in a style he had never experienced, with scenery rolling by that was new to him.

He is so excited about this trip that he is shooting photos of everything. This childlike excitement of a shy man actually stirs an incident that could have ruined an otherwise fun-filled trip.

In an era of powerful unions and newspaper guilds, photographers file a formal grievance with McCarthy about how many team photos Horne is taking.

The flap was big enough that Burns files his only story of the day about it, from Flagstaff, Ariz.

"Horne has been taking pictures of everything from the adobe houses to mountain peaks so this morning the cameramen demanded he show his union credentials before snapping another picture," Burns wrote.

"Horne, a quiet chap, explained that neither he nor his folks ever had been west of Danville, Ill., and that he was merely loading the family album. But the ornery photographers remained adamant and he sadly packed away his machine."

The players rally around Horne, and this embarrassing moment for him actually enhances the team's bond. From this point on, Horne is accepted as part of the team and is treated far better than most rookies.

McCarthy is so strong in his defense of Horne that he fights back, asking why the reporters and photographers allow two of their members to travel with the team when they aren't holding cards from the Baseball Writers' Association of America.

22

"Why don't you write some baseball news?" McCarthy asks. "The public is not interested in your labor disputes." [12]

New York *Post* sports editor Jack Kofoed learns of the Valentine's Day massacre the next day when another *Post* editor calls him—at Capone's Miami mansion where Kofoed and his wife spent the night.

The *Post* demands that Kofoed get a quote from Capone. Kofoed's wife, Marie, had earlier stumbled across a stash of machine guns, shotguns and revolvers while changing from her swimsuit in the dressing room.

Her husband presses Capone. "Al, I feel silly asking you this, but my boss wants me to. Al, did you have anything to do with it?"

"The only man who kills like that is Bugs Moran," Capone said.[13]

Three days after leaving Chicago, the train arrives in Los Angeles at 7:30 Sunday morning for a festive reception, Burns reports.

Dorothy and Charlie wake Della and Junior early so they can be at the station. Everything was packed the night before they left their rented Los Angeles home at 38th Place.

Joining the team are Art Nehf, Pat Malone, Ivan Green, new Cub coach Grover Land, and Charlie Root.

Burns gives the greatest detail about the pitcher everyone is concerned about, Root, who has "a comeback glint in his eyes."

"Root is in high spirits and the best of health. He did not take on weight as in the off season of a year ago, and said he had worked out a training schedule which he feels will return to him his former speed."

The California boys grumble about the coldest weather in 40 years, but Burns writes this is no comparison to how cold it was in Chicago. The players, wives and press board a bus for the Wilmington pier where the S.S. *Catalina* awaits.

---

[12] *Chicago Tribune, February* 17, 1929.
[13] Pg. 235, Kobler.

Owner William Wrigley, Jr., has arranged for a concert at the docks for Hartnett and his bride. As the musicians play a wedding march, Trainer Lotshaw directs a shower of rice and old shoes.

The twenty-seven-mile cruise to Catalina Island's Avalon harbor completes the 2,000-mile journey from Chicago.

Photo by Roger Snell

Catalina Island —
Avalon harbor, February 2009

Baseball Paradise

The only thing connected with baseball to be performed Sunday afternoon will be the assignment of lockers. Then relaxation until 10 o'clock Monday morning, when the first 1929 Cub workout will be staged under the critical eyes of Boss Joseph McCarthy.
—Edward Burns.

Berly Horne wished he could get his camera out now. The mountains around Flagstaff were amazing enough to this landlocked Ohio flatlander. He never anticipated the view from the *S.S. Catalina*, leaving Wilmington pier and heading toward Avalon harbor.

The chill didn't bother Horne as much as the others. He wasn't going to miss anything about this ride and that's why he was on the top deck, catching the strongest winds and best view.

The excitement that fans had for spring training was nothing compared to what this rookie was feeling now.

Horne's mind is racing about whether he's good enough. He has nearly two hours to think during the twenty-seven-mile voyage.

As Horne goes inside briefly to get warm, he watches Gabby Hartnett, horsing around, mugging for the *Tribune* photographer, grabbing a mop and swabbing the deck. Hartnett isn't a very convincing sailor, though, sporting his expensive three-piece suit, shiny shoes and perfectly combed hair. That's what Cub fans see when they open the sports section of the morning *Tribune*.

Charlie Root envies the stress-free life of 10-year-old Della. She stays close to his side while Junior is tucked away in the stateroom with Dorothy because he never weathers the ocean voyage very well.

Photo from Root family archives

Dorothy, Della, and Charlie Junior and Senior
at Wrigley Field

Root thinks again about their apartment in Chicago and the home they are renting in Los Angeles. So many people depend on his broken wing.

Della is surrounded by love and recognizes that life is good. For her, the best part of this experience is missing school to watch baseball on an island. She had heard her Mother explain to her protesting teacher about her long and unauthorized vacation, "Della will live with people, not just books." The teacher sniffed in disgust.

Wrigley's home, more like a mansion, is on the hilltop to the left. The valley and downtown are straight ahead from Avalon pier. The Casino, still under construction and due to be finished in May, juts out on a spit of land to the right.

26

"I hear the Casino is going to have a huge ballroom," Dorothy said. "I'll show you how to dance the Charleston the right way this time."

"Hack isn't going to like it," Root replied. "Mr. Wrigley says it won't have any gambling or booze."

Although Wrigley isn't here yet, he makes sure a band always greets the Cub arrivals. The local kids usually greet incoming tourists, too, by diving for coins thrown from the ship. They would pop the coins inside their mouths and dive again, but it was too cold for that today.

Charlie, Dorothy, Della and Junior head over to St. Catherine's Hotel with the other veterans. This grand old hotel is the highlight of the trip, especially the food. McCarthy would grumble, half-jokingly, that Wrigley fattens them up for free at the same time McCarthy is trying to get them into playing shape.

Horne and the other rookie tryouts, like catcher Tom Angley, head to the canvas cottages which are 10x10 tents over wood platforms, nestled in the valley of this small town.

Root stayed here for his first Cub spring training in 1926. Dorothy went with him, but there wasn't enough money to bring the kids, and Junior was too little anyway.

Clyde Beck and his wife, Gertrude, rented an adjoining cottage that year. The cottages had a wood frame up to the waist and then canvas the rest of the way, including the roof. They called it Tent Village.

The players got meal money only and there was no expense account for wives. Tryouts didn't get their rooms paid for at St. Catherine's Hotel so that's why they stayed in Tent Village.

Back then, the Becks and Roots didn't have enough money to eat out that first year, so they fished. Charlie and Clyde caught mackerel, "kind of snubbed like catfish in those days, but Mom said it was the finest meal they ever had," Della recalled years later.

Beck and Root made the Cubs roster after spring training in 1926, and they always stayed at St. Catherine's after that. Dorothy came with Charlie again in 1927.

After Root's landmark season of 1927, spring training in 1928 was a breeze. He had nothing to prove and knew he was tops on the roster. Della and Junior joined their parents for the first time at Catalina Island in 1928.[14]

Manager McCarthy, trainer Lotshaw and reporter Burns all head for the same destination when they get off the ship.

McCarthy wants to see the new clubhouse that Wrigley has built. He tells Burns he actually liked the old clubhouse better because it had salt baths. "It also was a better place to dry out sweat shirts, and the sweat shirts of my men are going to be plenty moist each day," McCarthy said.[15]

Burns phones in his Sunday story, noting that Lotshaw was the only man who did any work that afternoon.

"Dr. Lotshaw, though a professional, isn't too proud to smash baggage and tend to any and all big and little details having to do with the pitching of a major league training camp."

The Cubs awake to rain on Monday, but by 10 o'clock the sun is out and they line the practice field on schedule, awaiting their first orders from McCarthy.

Burns writes, "There really wasn't much baseball practice, though, on account of the swarm of cameramen who cluttered up the entire premises. As a sociologist we have been observing photographers for years, but never before have we seen half so many camera operators operating in one vicinity. It already appears that the world is more interested in the Cubs than it ever has been in any other ball club. You have no idea."

---

[14] Source for dialogue and all details about the Roots come from interviews and journal of Della Root Arnold.

[15] *Chicago Tribune,* same-day accounts.

The players were used to dealing with newspaper reporters and now radio was becoming more common. But on this first day of training, the players dealt with the newest breed of reporters—newsreel photographers. Within days, Chicago moviegoers would see the first newsreels of the team during intermission at their local theaters.

"It was the gang's first experience with the talkies," Burns wrote. "If the experience did nothing else, it again demonstrated that Gabby Hartnett is well named. Gabby could not keep from uttering baseball colloquialisms long enough for the talkies to turn out a newsreel installment until Boss Joseph ordered him locked up under the grandstand."

Actually, Charles Leo Hartnett, age 28, got his nickname for the opposite of being gabby. He hardly spoke during his 1922 rookie season with the Cubs, wisely following a tradition of keeping a low profile around veterans. He grew into his nickname over the years.

"The talkie fellows also had to make three tries to get a fine line of conversation with Owner William Wrigley and Manager McCarthy as the subjects," Burns continued.

"Mr. Wrigley spoiled the first take by letting a 'hell fire' creep into his language; the second exposure was going along all right when Hartnett escaped and came running over to tell McCarthy that he was getting too much of his back into the picture. Of course, Gabby's direction was recorded and that meant more valuable material had to be junked. The third try produced what you will be seeing and hearing at your favorite movie within a few days."

Hartnett is vigilant around the other players and knows he is especially vulnerable this spring training. Considering how many pranks Gabby has pulled on them, his teammates view his honeymoon as payback time.

Gabby's new wife, Martha, is very quiet, and she is not at ease with this boisterous group. Her excitement about the honeymoon and traveling to Catalina Island is tempered by being the center of attention—and practical jokes.

Martha is a beautiful, natural blonde, five feet four inches tall, with blue eyes and fine skin, a dignified and likeable lady.[16]

Cliff Heathcote is the ringleader. He is a loveable rogue who has endured overwhelming tragedy just three years earlier when his wife and baby girl died during childbirth.[17]

Heathcote, age 31, broke into the majors in 1918 with the St. Louis Cardinals as an outfielder and came to the Cubs during the 1922 season.

In the past two seasons, Heathcote has not been a starter, bumped by the powerful offensive outfield of Riggs Stephenson, Hack Wilson and Kiki Cuyler. Heathcote knows he will be riding the bench in 1929, no matter how good his spring training is.

Fans love him and letters to the *Tribune* occasionally question why he isn't a regular, during spells when one of the stars is slumping. Heathcote is a decent hitter, always hovering around .275, but his great speed doesn't make up for his lack of home run power.

What Heathcote excels at is practical jokes, and he strikes again on this first day of practice. When Martha and Gabby Hartnett return to their suite at St. Catherine's Hotel, they discover a mackerel sewn into one of the pillows.[18]

That is only the start. In the middle of the night, a maintenance man arrives with twin beds. Gabby explains they do not want twin beds, but as soon as he and Martha step out of the room, the twin beds are installed. Gabby gets the double bed back but the twins would arrive as soon as they step out of their room. Finally, Gabby realizes that Heathcote has recruited the whole team for these pranks.

---

[16] Della Root Arnold.

[17] ibid.

30

After this season, Martha Hartnett would rarely come to another ball game. She chose instead to devote her time to the Catholic church and later to their children.[19]

When practice finally starts, McCarthy is not pleased with what he sees. Fat shows much better in uniform than in three-piece suits that disguise the easy life the players had over the winter.

McCarthy's cure is workouts with the beefiest players—Tom Angley and Pat Malone—wearing rubber shirts.

First baseman Charlie Grimm finds humor in how Burns takes delight in their excess weight and being out of shape. Burns and Cub traveling secretary Bob Lewis are the fat men of baseball and would have been the envy of Santa Claus. "Burns was a master needler, wielding a typewriter more ferociously than most players with a baseball bat," Grimm wrote in his autobiography years later.[20]

When the players aren't picking on the Hartnetts, they are looking for other targets.

Lewis is one of the victims on a fishing trip with Root. He is not a fisherman and is feeling queasy. Lewis nods off, still holding his fishing rod.

Root takes a cigar out of his pocket and carefully sews it in the mouth of a small fish caught earlier. He quietly hooks the fish and tugs on Lewis' line, waking him up.

When Lewis takes one look at his catch, with the cigar firmly in place in the fish's mouth, he heads to the railing again in a hurry.

The players also keep getting their pictures in the paper. On the second day at Catalina, Root and the other veteran pitchers are shown in a ditch with shovels on Main Street in Avalon. They are wearing their full uniforms with heavy jackets, horsing around and acting like McCarthy is working them so hard that they also have to do street repairs.

A second photo shows Pat Malone taking a huge swing and missing as the others stand behind him laughing.

---

[18] Pg. 47, Della.
[19] Della Root Arnold
[20] *Jolly Cholly,* pg. 181.

Andy Lotshaw loves to rile up Malone, saying anyone could slug his pitches. Malone counters by calling him a busher. The exchange actually gets heated and results in a mutual challenge. At the 10 a.m. start on the second or third day of spring training, Malone warms up with Hartnett. Hartnett lets Lotshaw know when Malone is ready for the big test.

When the message comes, Lotshaw is busily working in the clubhouse, dressed for comfort in underwear, a butcher's apron and bedroom slippers. He is a wild sight rocking his bat at the plate— until he swings at Pat's first pitch, driving the ball over the right-field fence after having sweetly asked, "Are you ready, young man?"

After connecting, Andy walks back to the training room. Malone stands there on the mound with a most surprised look on his face. He can't believe it. When his victim finally shows up in the dressing room, Andy, between whacks on a rubbing-table patient, says, "Pat, never fool around with the good hitters." [21]

Chicago Daily News
Chicago History Museum s069323

Andy Lotshaw

Lotshaw is more than a trainer and is never far from the players when practical jokes are erupting. He had played in the minors but made it in the majors by taking care of the players, especially with powerful massages and lots of tape.

One reporter, not usually known for kind words, describes Lotshaw as loyal and completely devoted to the players, never hurting anyone. "No one will ever know how much money he spent helping other people," the reporter wrote.

---

[21] Ibid, pg. 125.

Lotshaw makes news on February 20, ranting to Burns about how seagulls stole his lunch. He asks if it's legal to kill the birds.

Lotshaw had stuffed a shoebox with hotel food and left the spread on a bench when the clubhouse phone rang.

"Well, to make a long story long, I came out just in time to see a seagull flying away with my lunch, and another was sitting there trying to figure how he could hoist the milk bottle."

During spring training, especially in the first days, Lotshaw is in great demand for his massages, tape and ice.

Root really needs Lotshaw now. And Hartnett realizes Root has an arm problem that Lotshaw can't solve.

Back in Miami, Capone deals with reporters by opening his Florida estate and denying Moran's accusations that Capone killed his associates.

In Chicago, the coroner reports that each body had at least twenty bullet wounds.

Suspicions about Capone are increasing, especially after police learn the night before the massacre that all illegal clubs in Cicero had closed and none of Capone's henchmen were seen.

The prosecutor's order for police to crack down on 10,000 illegal drinking establishments results in grumbling in a city that had 7,000 licensed saloons before Prohibition. Police are complaining the loudest because the police commissioner ordered them to cease work as paid guards for these establishments.

Commissioner William F. Russell said each illegal saloon amounted to "just little individual spigots on the city's big brew pot. Don't let anybody turn one of them on." [22]

---

[22] *Chicago Tribune,* all Capone details from daily accounts in February 1929.

Chicago Daily News — Chicago History Museum n087707

A crowd watches as police remove victims from the garage after the St. Valentine's Day Massacre.

William Wrigley Jr.

"Baseball is too much of a sport to be a business and too much of a business to be a sport. I'm not ashamed to confess that when the Cubs are playing in Chicago, I refuse to make any business appointments which will interfere with my attendance at the games. In fact, I follow the team all over the country through the season and attend to my other business affairs outside of baseball hours. That's how well I love baseball."
—William Wrigley Jr., Wrigleyville, p. 199-200.

Just as baseball inspired Berly Horne and Charlie Root as boys, William Wrigley Jr. loved the game. The difference was that Wrigley's goal at age fifteen was to own a team, not play for one.

Horne and Root worked hours on the mound, building their dreams pitch by pitch. Wrigley needed money for his dream.

Wrigley was born Sept. 30, 1861, in Philadelphia. As soon as he was old enough, he was stirring huge, boiling vats in his dad's soap factory.

By age twelve, he was a traveling salesman, pitching soap to housewives from western Pennsylvania to New England.

In the process, Wrigley learned about sales, advertising, hard work and how women influenced family purchases. Years later, when he let women in free to Cubs' games on Ladies' Day, he created a new fan base because they always brought paying customers, whether boyfriends, husbands or the entire family.

Chicago Daily News — Chicago History Museum s069116

William Wrigley, Jr. at the 1929
World Series in Chicago

Wrigley described his father as "a kind man, but he belonged to a generation which was work-minded. Baseball was nothing to him." Wrigley was spared no time for the fun of baseball.[23]

---

[23] Golenbock, Peter, *Wrigleyville*, pg. 199. *Wrigleyville* contains wonderful details and an oral history in separate chapters about Charles Murphy and Charles Weegh-man, pages 158-167.

Almost daily, Wrigley heard the noise of the crowd as he passed the ballpark of the first organized professional team in Philadelphia, as he trailed behind a bell-jangling, four-horse team, peddling soap.[24]

His life perfectly paralleled the history of organized baseball. When he was 8, in 1869, the Cincinnati Red Stockings formed as the first professional baseball club. Teams played around Chicago and Philadelphia at the time.

In 1865, Joe Borden of the Philadelphia Athletics pitched baseball's first recorded no-hitter against the Chicago White Stockings, forerunner to the Cubs.

Wrigley was 15 in 1866 when the National League was born. Philadelphia fielded its first team, as recorded in the bible of baseball, the *Baseball Encyclopedia*. Philadelphia finished seventh, with a record of 14-45.

Chicago won the championship, in the days before a World Series, with pitcher and manager Albert Goodwill Spalding.

Wrigley's young friends were able to skip out of work and sneak to the games, claiming the death of yet another family member. "No use to tell my employer of imaginary funerals in my family, for he was my father and had the death statistics of the family down to the minute," Wrigley said.

"One day when the cheering was particularly wild inside the park, I resolved that same day I would own a ball team and a ball park. This is really how I came to get into baseball as an owner, for my interest in the game has never relaxed an instant from that moment to this. This incident also explains why I get a greater satisfaction out of this enterprise than any other in which I am interested."[25]

Spalding opened a sporting goods store in 1868 and turned managing over to Cap Anson. Between 1869 and 1897, Anson's teams won five championships but all before Wrigley reached town.

---

[24] Ibid, pg. 174.
[25] *Saturday Evening Post*, Sept. 13, 1930.

Wrigley moved his wife and daughter to Chicago in 1891. Wanting to prove himself, he formed his own company to make the gum he had peddled as a bonus for buying soap and baking powder. He was 30.

Earlier, when his dad's company faced stiff competition for soap, Wrigley prevailed with the idea of adding freebies like baking soda and chewing gum to the line of products.

Within two years of forming his company in Chicago, in 1893, Wrigley suggested that his supplier use chicle, a sweet gum base from Central America. He introduced Spearmint and Juicy Fruit gums that year. By 1910, Wrigley's Spearmint gum was the leading brand in the United States.

He knew how to sell, once telling his dad, "I could sell pianos to the armless men of Borneo." [26]

Almost every photo of Wrigley shows him smiling, and people were drawn to this positive person. He was like a jolly bartender or a red-faced boy, amazed and delighted with everything. [27]

In the year of Wrigley's Chicago arrival, Anson had the White Stockings in the 1891 race, personally driving in 120 runs. Pitcher Wild Bill Hutchinson accounted for 43 of the Cubs' 82 wins. They finished second, 3½ games behind Boston.

In 1898, rookie Frank Chance, age twenty-one, played his first game for Chicago. Chance became manager in 1905 when Cincinnati investors Charles W. Murphy and Charles P. Taft bought the team. Mrs. Taft owned the ballpark of the Philadelphia Phillies at the same time.

They were the Cubs now, so dubbed after a *Chicago Daily News* sports editor described their "bear-like strength and playful disposition."

Murphy somehow amassed $15,000 as a Cincinnati baseball writer to buy the team. The purchase price was $105,000. Chance got shares in the team instead of his full pay. The major backer, Taft, had a half-brother, William Howard Taft, who would become president. Baseball

---

[26] Golenbock, pg. 174.
[27] Ibid.

legend has it that Taft instigated the seventh-inning stretch when he tried to relieve his 300 pounds from the discomfort of the wooden stadium seats; however, Taft's real historic claim to baseball fame is that he threw the first presidential pitch on an opening day in 1910.

Murphy started out as an owner making the right moves and spending money for players. Fans—and Wrigley was now one of them—got their first contender in fifteen years. The double play combination of Tinker to Evers to Chance sparked a poem, a pennant and an all-Chicago World Series in 1906. The White Sox beat the Cubs in six games.

In the next two seasons, the Cubs won consecutive World Series. They returned to the Series again in 1910, losing to the Philadelphia Athletics.

Wrigley built his business empire at the same time the Cubs built a true baseball dynasty. In 1911, Wrigley opened factories in Canada, Australia and Britain. Doublemint gum was introduced in 1914, gaining market share by low prices and heavy advertising.[28]

Wrigley joined the first long-suffering Cub fans to watch how one owner could dismantle a team. By 1915, Murphy did what no opposing team could ever do—bust up the combination of Tinker to Evers to Chance.

Baseball writers speculated that Murphy was running out of money because he turned cheap and was no longer making moves for the big stars.

He paraded his players in uniform by carriage and refused to build a locker room because of the costs.[29]

He didn't want to give the press the good seats that he could sell and put them in the back row of the grandstand. His actions led to the formation of the Baseball Writers Association of America.

Murphy's new enemies included players, sportswriters, and fellow National League owners.

---

[28] Corporate history of the Wrigley Co.
[29] Golenbock, pg. 158.

His cheapness and ingratitude flared when Chance asked for a four-year contract at the start of 1912.

Chance's management skills became obvious after the team suffered through the death of third baseman Jimmy Doyle from appendicitis during spring training and ace pitcher Three Finger Brown's collapse to a 5-6 record. Somehow Chance coaxed the Cubs into 91 wins

Murphy made his first move in September 1912 with his usual lack of tact, criticizing the team, denouncing the players' drinking and saying Chance would not be back for 1913. He happened to knock Chance while the beloved player and manager was in the hospital being treated for complications from yet another beanball.[30]

In that era, the Cubs and White Sox played a multi-game series after the regular season in October, while the rest of baseball was following the World Series. Considering the recent World Series championships of both teams, this was quite a matchup.

Murphy treated these games like the World Series because of the money he made from enthusiastic crowds. For the players, the games didn't count and came after a grueling regular season had ended.

During the final game of the city series between the Cubs and White Sox in 1912, Murphy went down to the bench and fired Chance because the White Sox scored six runs in the first inning.

Murphy then named Johnny Evers as the new manager and gave him the four-year contract that he refused to give to Chance. Evers lasted only a year.

An angry Chance told reporters, "No manager can be a success without competent players. Murphy has not spent one third as much for players as have other magnates. How can he expect to win championships without ballplayers?"

Murphy's trail of destruction went from Chance to Tinker to Evers. On Dec. 15, 1912, Murphy traded Joe Tinker to Cincinnati, and in July 1913 he traded pitcher Ed Reulbach to Brooklyn. Evers was gone as

---

[30] Brown, Warren, *The Chicago Cubs,* pg. 64. This 1946 book is the second important source about these years, pages 60-82

manager. One of the greatest pitchers in history, Three Finger Brown, was shipped to the minors. The Cubs finished third, at 88-65, in 1913, their worst record since 1903.

The two seasons of 1914 and 1915 posed great financial threats to the owners. The new upstart Federal League competed as a strong third league.

The new league offered a sort of free agency to horribly underpaid star players who had been totally at the mercy of owners. Murphy's cheapness helped the new league because he had dumped some of baseball's best players for salary reasons.

The Federal League triggered a brief, early scare for owners about what would happen if players could freely and openly compete for the highest salary. The owners had concocted quite a racket, creating a reserve system that allowed them to protect their best players and block other teams from paying top dollar for them. The players either stayed with the team or didn't play at all.

The Federal League momentarily busted up the monopoly and gave players a taste of freedom.

A wealthy Chicago restaurant owner named Charles Weeghman formed the Chicago Whales and dominated the new Federal League for those two years.

Weeghman acquired Tinker as manager for $10,000, landed pitchers Brown and Reulbauch, and almost lured Walter Johnson from the American League.

The top major leaguers received telegrams from Tinker inviting them to come to Chicago for negotiations, with no obligation and all expenses paid. In just two years of the league's life, eighty-one major leaguers left their teams to join the Federal League.

Murphy had dumped Chance and Tinker. Now owners feared Evers would go to the Federal League, too.

In an extraordinary deal, all the owners pitched in to pay Evers if he would sign with the Boston Braves for $25,000. Evers, as team captain, turned the lowly Braves into pennant winners in his first season in 1914. The Cubs trailed by 16½ games and, to add the final insult for Cub fans, Evers was voted the National League's equivalent to a "most valuable player" award.

Tinker led Weeghman's Whales to first- and second-place finishes in the two-year history of the Federal League.

Weeghman also spent $250,000 designing and building a new ballpark, Weeghman Park, which opened for the 1914 Federal League season and seated 16,000.[31]

The field, seeded with Kentucky bluegrass, was on land once occupied by a seminary. It would continue as sacred ground, eventually becoming today's Wrigley Field.

The success and expense of a third league led everyone to seek peace, triggered by the Federal League lawsuit against the major league owners, alleging that they were acting as a monopoly and violating anti-trust laws.

The judge on the federal bench was Chicago's Kenesaw Mountain Landis, who let the case simmer so owners could talk.

The league owners got even with Murphy, pressuring him to sell his remaining 53 percent ownership of the Cubs to Taft for $503,500.[32]

Wrigley had to be watching all of this with more than a fan's interest. He saw Murphy ignite Chicago fans with consecutive World Series and then bust it all up by failing to lure new players.

He also witnessed how a baseball nobody, a restaurant owner like Weeghman, could become an overnight success in baseball when he started with no players, no team, no league and no ballpark.

Imagine what he could do, especially with the fortune he now had.

A private taunt on a 1915 train ride stirred Wrigley to pursue his childhood dream.

Weeghman decided to go for the Cubs. He had a new ballpark that would go idle with the death of the Whales and Federal League and the end of the 1915 season.

He didn't have enough money to go alone. He focused on one partner, J. Ogden Armour, one of the richest men in America and heir to

---

[31] Golenbock, pg. 164-165.
[32] Golenbock, pg. 158-164.

the mammoth Armour meatpacking industry. Chicago was the Midwest crossroads of meat, and Armour inherited the intersection.

Armour declined Weeghman's initial proposal to kick in $500,000, but he said he would go in for $50,000 if Weeghman could find nine similar Chicago investors.

Wrigley had the cash and the desire.

According to official Cub history, the seed was planted when Wrigley was riding the train from Cincinnati to Chicago. Someone asked how a rich businessman with such a love of baseball could tolerate a Cincinnati Taft owning a Chicago team.[33]

The Cubs were clearly declining, with their first losing season in a decade, 73-80. They finished fourth in 1915. Wrigley liked reasonable gambles, especially when he thought he could fix the problem.

The deal closed Jan. 20, 1916, while Wrigley was at his winter home in Pasadena.

The new Cub partners elected Wrigley board chairman. Critics said he was involved only as an advertising ploy to promote his gum. They eventually would learn that Wrigley had the heart of a fan and a great love for the players and the game.

Seemingly unrelated, Wrigley heard news weeks earlier of a terrible fire that had virtually destroyed the sportfishing village of Avalon on Santa Catalina Island.

The fire apparently started in the kitchen of the Metropole Hotel, burned everything west of Metropole Street, and was still smoldering three days later.

Three Banning brothers, including one who was a California judge, wanted to make this a major tourist resort ever since they bought the island in 1894.

The fire changed everything.

Wrigley shared ownership of the Cubs with partners who understood how to make money while pleasing customers. Armour turned meat into dozens of new products, Weeghman spread his chain of restaurants, and William Walker was in the fish business.

---

[33] Brown, pg. 78.

Now they immediately implemented fan-friendly moves, moving to Weeghman's new park and building the first concession stands. They also allowed fans to keep foul balls and home runs. Other teams would forbid this for years.[34]

Wrigley always kept large cash reserves and never borrowed so he could leap at any investment opportunities. He paid $50,000 in cash to join the Cubs and doubled that as Weeghman got hurt by the stock market crash in 1918.

Following the team's first losing season in a decade, 1916 was worse. Tinker was back as manager, as Wrigley recommended, but the Cubs dropped to a fifth-place finish with a record of 67-86.

Wrigley influenced another change for the start of the 1917 season, convincing the owners to move spring training to California for the first time.

The Cubs were seven games better with new manager Fred Mitchell in 1917 but still finished fifth with a 74-80 record. Making matters worse, their hated cross-town rivals, the White Sox, won the World Series.

The Cubs were so weak offensively that Shufflin' Phil Douglas lost twenty games with a 2.55 ERA. No one hit over .273 and the top "power" hitter had six homers, not uncommon for the deadball era.

Hippo Vaughn was the ace with a 2.01 ERA, and a record of 23-13. Vaughn made baseball history when he lost a no-hit shutout. The problem was that Cincinnati Reds pitcher Fred Toney also pitched a no-hit shutout through nine innings—then won in the 10th when Vaughn gave up two hits and a run.

Wrigley convinced the partners to gamble on two moves before the 1918 season that promised a long-term boost to the Cubs. Before the season began, he landed one of the hottest pitchers in baseball. Grover Cleveland Alexander's salary required Wrigley to increase his ownership shares to finance the deal.

By the end of the year, Wrigley would own the most shares in the Cubs but still not have complete control. He also ended the year by

---

[34] Golenbock, pg. 167.

hiring an outspoken newspaper columnist to become today's equivalent of a general manager. In Wrigley's opinion, William Veeck printed better ideas about the Cubs than Wrigley was hearing from so-called baseball hot shots.

Alexander wanted a $10,000 bonus from the Phillies after the 1917 season ended. Philadelphia hesitated because of the uncertainty of World War I and the expense of a guaranteed salary whether he played or not. Many stars were being drafted for the war.[35]

Wrigley always proved willing to take this kind of risk when others would not. Before spring training in 1918, Wrigley and Alexander went golfing in Pasadena. Wrigley sealed the deal by promising to send the pitcher's wife $500 every two months for three years even if he was in the service longer than that.

Alexander pitched three games for the Cubs in 1918, winning two, and then was called to war. Southpaw Vaughn continued as the dominant pitcher that season, leading the league at 22-10 with an ERA of 1.74.

About the same time Wrigley was golfing, wooing and closing the deal with Alexander, the master salesman also was making his pitch to Veeck.

It happened at dinner in Wrigley's home. Veeck said his infant son could throw his bottle farther than the team could hit.

"If you're so smart, why don't you see if you can do a better job?" Wrigley said, surprising Veeck when he realized Wrigley was serious.[36]

Weeghman was getting hurt in the stock market and spreading himself thin with other investments. He kept selling more of his shares to Wrigley. Against the advice of his banker friends, Wrigley kept buying, wanting to help Weeghman and the Cubs. But his personal dream was sole ownership.

Wrigley had the most shares when the investors met in December 1918. Weeghman stepped aside as president and the directors agreed to put Cubs manager Fred Mitchell in as president and Veeck as vice president and treasurer.[37]

---

[35] Ibid, pg. 167.
[36] Ibid, Pg. 176.
[37] Brown, pg. 80; Golenbock, pg. 176.

The team improved dramatically in 1918, reaching the World Series because of the added offense of Fred Merkle and Charlie Hollocher and the pitching rotation. Vaughn, Lefty Tyler, Claude Hendrix and Phil Douglas were outstanding, with Vaughn's 1.74 ERA the best in the league. Even the worst ERA among the starters was 2.78.

The Cubs got a break when the season was dramatically shortened to end on Labor Day because of the war. The Cubs won the pennant with a record of 84-45. Just as eight years before, the Cubs lost the World Series.

The Cubs were stopped cold by twenty-three-year-old pitcher Babe Ruth, who hurled sixteen consecutive shutout innings. This added to Ruth's previous World Series streak, setting a record of 29⅔ consecutive scoreless innings by a Series pitcher. Ruth beat Vaughn in Game One, 1-0.

Ruth was proving to be an even better hitter and had played half his games as an outfielder. There was talk about changing Ruth solely into a hitter.

In only his third season as an investor, 1918, Wrigley tasted a pennant and a World Series. His beloved Cubs were building strength as he moved toward control of the team. Even with the investments in Alexander, Veeck and Weeghman, Wrigley's savings account continued to expand.

He had much more in mind for his cash.

Wrigley began 1919 with dramatic financial moves. He bought Santa Catalina Island, planned the downtown Chicago Wrigley Building, and acquired the last of Weeghman's shares in the Cubs. Advertising executive A. D. Lasker remained as the second-largest investor in the Cubs.

Veeck couldn't believe his fortunes. Having started as a lowly reporter for the Louisville *Courier-Journal*, he became president of the Cubs on July 6 on a technicality. The National League ruled that Manager Mitchell couldn't serve in the dual role as president.

Wrigley had every reason to be riding high and was excited about a new hobby, his own island. The same real estate agent who sold Wrigley his Pasadena home tipped him off about Santa Catalina Island, just twenty-six miles off the coast from Los Angeles.

The Banning brothers, including a California judge, never recovered from the fire that wiped out most of downtown Avalon in 1915, just weeks before Wrigley made his initial investment in the Cubs. Without ever seeing the island, Wrigley paid $3.5 million in cash to the Bannings. Wrigley imagined a basic, flat island, nothing fancy. He was amazed several weeks later when he stayed overnight, seeing mountains, valleys and tremendous potential. Catalina was twenty-one miles long and eight miles wide and the highest point was 2,069 feet.

Photo by Roger Snell

William Wrigley Jr.'s home atop Mount Ada (upper right),
now a bed & breakfast inn, overlooks Avalon Harbor.
Innkeeper Susan Griffin entertains guests with
stories of the Wrigleys.

Waking to their first morning sunrise on Catalina, Wrigley and his wife, Ada, weren't discouraged by an Avalon without paved streets, a sewer system or adequate electric and water. They saw an island that could be transformed into a "pleasure resort for people of modest means."

Above his $3.5 million investment, Wrigley spent another $3 million to bring fresh water to Avalon from a river sixteen miles away on the island. He rebuilt the sewer system and spent another $2.5 million for the Casino. His real extravagance was spending $250,000 for a 10-acre aviary, which wasn't just for the birds. The players would razz him about that later.[38]

He bought a steamship that had served in the Great Lakes and renamed it the *Avalon* and commissioned the building of a much larger steamship, *Catalina*.

The beautiful Hotel St. Catherine was finished a year earlier, while the Bannings still owned the island. The resort hotel was on Descanso Beach and had luxury rooms for 1,200 guests. The hotel replaced the burned Metropole Hotel.

Wrigley wanted another hotel, so the Atwater began construction. His plan was to offer tour packages that included the steamship cruise, meals and hotel. A nine-hole golf course was carved through canyon after canyon and later expanded to eighteen holes.

The Wrigleys dreamed of a mansion on the mountain peak that caught the first morning sunlight. Mount Ada, as the Wrigley home would be named, offered a spectacular view of Avalon below and the harbor where the *S.S. Catalina* docked. The twenty-two-room home was finished in 1921 with a beautiful five-acre garden and a view 350 feet above the waters of Avalon Bay.

History says Catalina Island was discovered in 1542 by a Portuguese navigator sailing a Spanish ship. But history tends to neglect that timid, friendly Indians greeted the ship from their island home when they were "discovered."

---

[38] Brown, pg. 83-85; Golenbock, pg. 175.

The island got its name on November 24, 1602, when General Sebastian Viscaino anchored in Avalon harbor to celebrate the Feast of St. Catherine. Approximately 2,500 Indians lived on the island then. The Indians had well-organized villages in the major valleys around the island. They paddled well-made canoes, lived in large circular homes covered with woven mats hung upright over forked tree limbs, and were well-fed from sea and land.

Fur traders came in the early 1800s for sea otters. The last Mexican governor of California moved here in a deal to transfer power at the close of the Mexican-American War. A cattle rancher took over in 1846, and Union troops built a barracks here in 1864.

The idea of a tourist attraction started in 1887 when George Shatto built tent spaces to rent and then a hotel, complete with channel transportation. But Shatto ran out of money. That's when the Bannings—Judge Joseph, Captain William, and Hancock—submitted the high bid at a sheriff's auction. They had big plans in 1894, but the fire in 1915 ruined everything for the Bannings and opened up major opportunities for Wrigley.

Wrigley's thoughts about attracting tourists certainly had to include the idea of bringing the Cubs and spring training here. But first he needed sole control of the team and a lot of island improvements.

The island was a nice diversion from what was happening in baseball. For just a few years, including 1919, Chicago was the baseball capital for good and bad, overshadowing New York and the Babe.

The Federal League controversies and lawsuit in Judge Kenesaw Mountain Landis' court were centered in Chicago in 1914 and 1915. The White Sox won the World Series in 1917. The Cubs made it to the Series but lost in 1918.

And now the White Sox were back in the World Series in 1919 against baseball's historic charter team, the Cincinnati Reds.

The Reds won, but reporters published immediately that something seemed obviously wrong about the games. Gamblers had all sorts of inside information and were putting down unusually huge bets, suggesting a fix.

Within one year, eight "Black Sox" would be banned from baseball for life based on evidence and confessions.

The fix nearly ruined the game. Fans strongly questioned whether to go to games if teams weren't playing to win. Many were tired of the sleaze of gamblers at the park and the number of drunks in the stands.

Veeck insisted that baseball needed to get rid of its weak three-man commission and grant absolute power to a single commissioner. Veeck's close personal friend, Judge Landis, happened to be the perfect candidate.[39]

This was Wrigley's first tangle with the second largest owner of the Cubs, Lasker, who favored the three-member commission.

Reading the headlines and watching baseball unravel were minor league prospects Root and Horne, both age twenty, and Hack Wilson, nineteen.

Babe Ruth was twenty-four and played his first full season as an out-fielder. He led the American League with 29 homers and drove in 103 runs. Nobody else in baseball had more than twelve homers.

Just when baseball looked the bleakest, Ruth would save it. The big home run swing, interrupted by equally big strikeouts, would bring an end to an era of singles, bunts, sacrifices and speed.

In 1920, Grover Cleveland Alexander had another fantastic season, winning twenty-seven games with a 1.91 ERA, both best in the league, but the Cubs had no offensive punch.

Other than their pennant-winning 1918 season, the Cubs were dis-appointments under Mitchell's leadership, and 1920 would be his last season. They finished fourth at 75-79.

The swirling criminal investigation against the Black Sox distracted all of baseball. By the end of 1920, on November 12, Landis was named as the new commissioner of baseball.

Meanwhile, Wrigley's improvements at Catalina Island were spark-ing growth and interest in Avalon. A number of people began buying the small spaces under previously leased tents.

---

[39] Veeck, Bill, *Veeck, as in Wreck: The Autobiography of Bill Veeck*, with Ed Linn, pg. 23.

Wrigley's biggest project of 1920 was the ground-breaking and start of a skyscraper, which would take four years to build. The Wrigley Building began development in the middle of a declining neighborhood on Michigan Avenue near the Chicago River.

Wrigley would spend $7.8 million for the 400-foot tower, topped with a clock on each side of the building so all eyes would look toward his building. The tower was to be coated with white terra cotta so it would stand out brilliantly at night with floodlights.

In an era when forty-eight- to sixty-hour work weeks were common, Wrigley implemented a five-day week, planned a company lunchroom, allowed stock sharing and offered life insurance to his employees.

Everything was coming together for Wrigley in 1921—except the Cubs.

The Wrigleys' new mansion, Mt. Ada, named for his wife, was finished on Catalina Island.

He bought the Pacific Coast minor league team, the Los Angeles Angels.

Most significant, he became sole owner of the Cubs, buying out financially troubled Armour first and then friend and advertising magnate Lasker.

Johnny Evers returned to the Cubs as manager.

In what should have been Wrigley's most rewarding year, the Cubs were terrible. They were so bad that Evers didn't survive the season, and Bill Killefer was brought in to manage the last fifty-five games.

That was the last straw for Lasker, who was upset about Veeck, Landis and now Killefer. It also was a convenient time to ditch a sinking ship. Lasker sold Wrigley everything except 100 shares and his box seats.[40]

Wrigley was not rewarded for his investment. The Cubs fell to sixth place, finishing 64-89, their worst record in eighteen seasons.

The Cubs' offense already was poor, and now the pitching of Alexander and Vaughn went downhill.

---

[40] Golenbock, pg. 175.

In 1922, Wrigley began exercising his control. Spring training opened for the first time at Catalina Island. The Cubs signed an outstanding rookie prospect, catcher Gabby Hartnett, 22, from Woonsocket, Rhode Island.

There was nothing else special about the season. The Cubs improved to 80-74 under Killefer but finished fifth.

Hartnett gave no indication of his future greatness, playing thirty-one games and hitting .194 with no homers.

Veeck and Wrigley were finding out how baseball was more volatile than the stock market.

Just as they began to build an offense, the pitching went away.

The Cubs had five .300 hitters in the lineup in 1923, but now the pitching was fading with Vaughn gone. Alexander was the only exception, still going strong at 22-12 with a 3.19 ERA.

Rookie Guy Bush promised to be a good pitching prospect. He was twenty-one and came from Aberdeen, Mississippi.

Outfielder Cliff Heathcote came from the Cardinals and was in his fifth season in baseball.

None of the moves seemed all that significant. Bush was not among the top starters. Heathcote hit .249 in 393 at bats.

Even the newly launched SS *Catalina* had a design flaw and had to go back for redesign of the anchor.

As the 1924 season started, the Cubs picked up another promising pitcher, John Frederick "Sheriff" Blake.

Hartnett and Heathcote started flashing what they could do, with Hartnett now a starter and hitting .299 with the most homers on the team, sixteen.

Heathcote hit .309, second on the team behind the great hitter George Grantham, who played second base.

But the pitching was poor and the Cubs were mediocre, finishing fifth, 81-72.

The Cubs made all kinds of history in 1925, involving a Rabbit, radio, and the worst record that William Wrigley Jr. would ever endure.

Rabbit Maranville and Charlie Grimm brought laughter to a team that needed it. Pittsburgh Pirates owner Barney Dreyfus didn't think they were all that funny and let them go for a song—or, more appropriately, to rid his team of their singing and banjo playing.

Maranville was also noted for his drinking. Grimm was not, but he stayed out all night with the drinkers and would become the beloved jokester on the Cubs by the 1929 season.

Grimm's brother, Bill, was just as comical. Bill joked about how often they moved and how it affected the chickens they raised. "Whenever a moving van comes to the house, the chickens flop over on their backs waiting for their feet to be tied."[41]

Spring training in 1925 could have ended the fun and games for Grimm abruptly. A photographer was posing Maranville for a golf shot with Grimm lying on his back with a golf tee in his teeth. Rabbit held the driver, as if he were about to swing.

The photographer said, "OK. Good. Hold it." Whereupon, Rabbit took a vicious swing and knocked the ball cleanly out of Charlie's teeth and over the photographer's head. Charlie arose, white as a sheet, knowing that Rabbit had only played a few rounds of golf in his life.

A few days after Maranville reported to Catalina, he disappeared to the mainland overnight and returned to the island, hung over, with a bucket of coal ashes, prepared for some Ash Wednesday pranks. As guests entered the dining room at the St. Catherine Hotel, he dabbed ashes on their foreheads, faces, elbows and all over the floor. The management had to serve more than 100 meals over again.

Maranville and Grimm were upholding their reputations, often breaking into song while waiting at the batting cage.

Maranville's colorful antics started immediately as a rookie in 1912. During one questionable call, he pulled a pair of glasses out of his pocket and handed them to the umpire.[42]

Maranville helped the Boston Braves win the pennant, World Series and a nickname in 1914. He told audiences that they won because they went to church and prayed. They became the Miracle Braves.

---

[41] References to Charlie Grimm and Rabbit Maranville come from Grimm's autobiography, *Jolly Cholly,* and from the *Chicago Tribune* of Apr. 28, 1928.

[42] Golenbock, pg. 178.

Another umpire cut himself in a fight and Maranville offered to put iodine on his face. When he was done, the umpire's face was painted with stripes.

The 1925 season was a surprising and major reversal for Veeck, Wrigley and especially Cub fans. Veeck was struggling and learning that it was easier to criticize a team as a writer than to build one. His moves were not working. The Cubs were now mediocre in pitching and hitting.

Grimm was a bright spot, hitting .306. Hartnett hit .289 and his twenty-four homers were almost double anyone else on the team.

The season got so bad that Veeck and Wrigley went through three managers, even desperately naming Maranville to lead the team.

Grimm was the most surprised with that move, knowing Maranville the best.

Maranville set the tone for his new role, waiting until all the players were asleep that first night on the train. At 2 a.m., he walked down the aisle dousing each player with ice water in their Pullman berths. "There will be no sleeping on this club under Maranville management."[43]

He had most of the team drunk, celebrating one rare win like it was a World Series victory. Losses didn't stop him from celebrating either.

Grimm and Maranville did have to look back with envy. They had joined the worst team in baseball in the same 1925 season that their old team, the Pirates, won the World Series and all that bonus money. Their former Pirate teammate, Kiki Cuyler, was the star with their old team.

The Cubs made history in 1925 when they allowed all their games to be aired on radio. The broadcasts allowed more Cub fans to follow the team, which turned out to be the worst in a long time.

Wrigley and Veeck permitted radio broadcasts by seven different Chicago stations without charge. Owners objected, but Veeck believed radio would help baseball, despite all the others' beliefs.

---

[43] Ibid., pg. 182.

54

Veeck was right. Fans started coming from out of state to see the Cubs. Attendance would double during the first seven years of game broadcasts.[44]

The 1925 season ended with the Cubs finishing dead last, with the second worst record in baseball.

Wrigley probably didn't realize that his best move came from this lowest point at the end of the 1925 season.

On Oct. 13, Wrigley announced he was going with a relatively unknown minor league manager from Louisville named Joe McCarthy.

Wrigley vowed that his Cubs would never do this poorly again.

McCarthy would help Wrigley keep that promise

---

[44] Golenbock, pg. 173-185; Brown, pg. 108-109.

Joe McCarthy

"This shows that Chicago is appreciative of what Joe McCarthy and the rest of us have been trying to do in our efforts to bring a pennant to Chicago. I'm getting a whale of a kick out of the situation, because I know the fans can't be disappointed with the gang McCarthy is going to put on the field this year."
—William Wrigley Jr., to Ed Burns, after learning Opening Day is already sold out, Chicago Tribune, 2/24/29.

Joe McCarthy had raised expectations to the highest possible level as spring training began in 1929.

McCarthy had built this team from scratch beginning the moment he arrived in 1926, wasting no time in proving he was worthy of baseball's dream assignment.

He couldn't make the Cubs worse. They were dead last before he took over. His goals were as high as the American Association pennant he had won in 1925 for Louisville.

McCarthy knew Wrigley cared more about pennants than profits and pledged the money to acquire anyone that McCarthy wanted.

McCarthy had the complete backing of William Veeck, especially since Veeck went way out on a limb to recommend his hiring. Veeck had been a Louisville *Courier-Journal* reporter when he first heard of McCarthy years earlier. McCarthy's name popped up again because of the American Association pennant.

Veeck did his homework before going with a baseball man relatively unknown in the majors. Just as in his previous days as a reporter, Veeck interviewed managers and anyone else he could think of in the minors. Everyone had kind words about McCarthy, something rarely heard among blunt, outspoken baseball men.

They raved about how McCarthy dealt with players and how he could mix firm discipline with true caring for each individual. They reported on his burning desire to win, how he motivated the most difficult players, and how he managed the intricate details on the field.[45]

McCarthy's minor league ties gave him an edge that few in baseball had discovered. He knew minor league prospects better than anyone in the game because he spent his past seven seasons bouncing around on the hot, dusty roads of the Midwest, watching his opponents pitch by pitch from the Louisville dugout.

The first moves he made dramatically reshaped the Cubs. Just like any other manager in baseball, McCarthy wanted power hitters and ace pitchers. What separated this rookie manager from the veterans was that McCarthy knew where to find talent hiding in the minors.

He went after Charlie Root, Hack Wilson and Riggs Stephenson in his first three moves. These three alone would build any franchise. They certainly added to what was to become the best Cub team ever assembled.

McCarthy's personal project was Wilson. He knew that below the surface of this tough fighter and hard drinker was a sensitive kid who never had a normal family life.

Wilson was treated so poorly by the Giants that he doubted his tremendous abilities. McCarthy saw the potential for greatness and

---

[45] Brown, Warren, *The Chicago Cubs*, pages 93-100, "Joe McCarthy Checks In."

boosted Wilson's confidence by making it clear from the start that he was the cleanup hitter.

Wilson finished the 1925 season at Toledo, batting .343, and the Cubs drafted him. McCarthy thought Wilson was the most unappreciated and overlooked phenom he had seen and knew he could deal with the kid's drinking problems. New York Giants fans would mourn the Wilson deal as one of the biggest thefts or blunders the team ever suffered.

McCarthy said it was a clerical error and that the Giants failed to put Wilson on their protected roster when the draft started. Because the Cubs had finished last in 1925, they got the first draft pick in 1926 and stole Wilson for $5,000.[46]

Root made the team convincingly after the 1926 spring training, coming from the Cubs' minor league Los Angeles Angels.

In June, McCarthy talked Veeck and Wrigley into one more move, acquiring Riggs Stephenson from Indianapolis, also in the American Association.

McCarthy also got Clyde Beck and Mike Gonzales, who would prove to be important bench players by 1929.

McCarthy didn't have to wait long for results.

Root immediately rose to the top as the ace, winning 18 games with a 2.82 ERA and pitching 271 innings in 1926.

Wilson led the league with twenty-one homers. He also hit .321 and had 109 RBI. The last Cub with that many homers played fifteen years earlier.

Stephenson hit .338 in only 281 at-bats after joining the Cubs in mid-season.

Grimm drove in 82 and Hartnett had a strong year.

What a difference McCarthy's new team made. In 1925 the Cubs were 68-86, eighth of eight teams, and 27½ games out of first. In their first year with McCarthy, the Cubs were 82-72, finished fourth, and were seven games away from a pennant.

---

[46] Golenbock, Peter, *Wrigleyville,* pages 191-199, "Marse Joe arrives."

There were doubts about McCarthy when the season started. Veterans like Grover Cleveland Alexander grumbled about a bush-league manager who had never played the game in the majors.

Alexander's contempt for McCarthy soon would establish who was firmly in control of the team.

It was rare for a manager to lack major league credentials. But McCarthy had baseball skills that many underestimated.

McCarthy had played on the semipro sandlots of Philadelphia and moved to the minors in 1906. He almost made it to the majors, signing to play for the Federal League in 1916, but the league folded before he ever suited up.

He became player-manager in Wilkes-Barre in 1913 when he was age 26. Buffalo bought his contract and won the pennant in 1915, but the Yankees didn't take him for the $3,000 asking price. He played second base and hit .300 in only two of his 15 seasons as a player. McCarthy managed in Louisville from 1919-1925.

Before baseball, McCarthy worked in the textile mills near his boyhood home of Germantown, a Philadelphia suburb, and he never knew his father. McCarthy was three years old when his dad was killed on a construction job.[47]

McCarthy never attended high school, but he won a two-year scholarship to Niagara College.

McCarthy was age 39 when he came to the Cubs. "They tell me we don't look very good on paper," McCarthy said. "Well, we don't play on paper."

McCarthy's tangles with Alexander began immediately at spring training, when Alex broke his ankle and brooded because McCarthy didn't visit the hospital.

He was angered further when McCarthy ordered him to come back to Catalina Island on crutches to be with the team. Most vocal was Alexander's wife, Aimee, who sniffed that no one had ever treated him so roughly.[48]

---

[47] Golenbock, pg. 191.
[48] Ibid, pg. 192.

Mrs. Alexander also made an impression on Dorothy Root, who accompanied Charlie to Catalina Island. Root and McCarthy would debut with the Cubs together and both were at Catalina for the first time.

"Mrs. Alexander was dressed in the type of finery and furs Dorothy had rarely seen, but had on occasion dreamed about," wrote Della Root Arnold years later.[49]

"Mrs. Alexander refused to speak to Dorothy or Gertrude Beck (Clyde Beck's wife) or any other rookie wife, explaining to someone close enough for the girls to hear, 'I never associate with rookies' wives. They're so stupid and ignorant when it comes to understanding baseball.'"

McCarthy established firm rules from the start at Catalina, insisting that players report by 10 a.m. for team meetings followed by their workouts.

If they won their exhibition game the day before, they were rewarded by having to report at 1 p.m. and team meetings were skipped.

Alexander often slept through McCarthy's meetings, once snoring loudly enough for McCarthy to hear.

Alexander came to the Cubs in 1918 when Wrigley personally wooed him to the team. He was clearly their ace for eight seasons.

But Alexander came back from World War I shattered. In France, he had fought on the front lines as an artillery sergeant, and the roar of the guns deafened him in one ear. He came home with epileptic seizures. Heavy drinking seemed to ease his suffering.[50]

McCarthy was sympathetic, compassionate and especially forgiving about hard drinkers. But he expected players to show respect to teammates, follow his rules and be prepared by game time. Alexander thought he was better than McCarthy and refused to listen to a "busher."

By June 22, McCarthy finally had enough of Alexander. McCarthy's shocking move to get rid of the Cubs' winningest pitcher showed everyone who was boss.

---

[49] Della Root Arnold, pg. 21.
[50] Golenbock, pg. 185.

60

But the move probably had just as much to do with the proven performance of obvious rising star Root, a young and eager competitor versus the aging arrogance of Alexander. He didn't know it yet, but McCarthy had just replaced the Cubs' winningest pitcher with one who would win even more, 201 games, and become the greatest right-hander ever to put on a Cubs uniform.

Rogers Hornsby and Bill Killefer were happy to sign Alexander to the St. Louis Cardinals. Hornsby then was player-manager for the Cards. Killefer, one of the three managers fired by the Cubs the season before, was now a St. Louis coach. He also used to be Alexander's catcher.[51]

The move bonded the Cubs. Alexander may have won a lot of games, but he hadn't won over his teammates. McCarthy had a way of creating team chemistry.

McCarthy immediately installed Charlie Grimm as captain, the team's top prankster and left-handed banjo player.

Grimm had been dumped by the Pirates because of his antics. Now he was rewarded by the new manager. The message was loud and clear to the players about McCarthy: Don't mess with the boss, but he'll tolerate a lot if you play hard.

"I had heard, unofficially, that when Veeck sounded out Marse Joe for the job he inquired if he approved of musicians among his players," Grimm wrote in his autobiography years later. "I prefer to think that Joe was neutral and told Veeck so. I learned later that McCarthy wasn't dead-set against a little harmony in the clubhouse—if we won—even the way we sang."

---

[51] Ibid., pg. 193.

There was one move that McCarthy didn't make as rookie manager and one of the rare times that Wrigley really pushed for a deal.

Wrigley liked Lefty O'Doul. McCarthy wasn't convinced, the deal was never made, and Wrigley never missed the chance to remind McCarthy how O'Doul was doing in the majors. Wrigley's jokes about this became more serious when O'Doul hit .396 for the Phillies in 1929.

McCarthy continued building on his successes in 1927 and, like Wilson, grabbed another minor leaguer from Toledo. The Cubs were weak at shortstop, and McCarthy knew where to turn.

Elwood "Woody" English came to Catalina as an excited rookie who had just turned twenty when spring training began. McCarthy was so sure of English's hot start that he let Jimmy Cooney go at mid-season.

English delivered with a .290 average and slick fielding.

McCarthy wanted more pitching and got Hal Carlson from the Phillies after the season started. Carlson was 12-8 in twenty-seven games for the Cubs.

Root was on fire in 1927, and the Cubs almost won the pennant because of him. He won 26 games, the most in the National League, and pitched 48 games and 309 innings.

Root began to tire and his arm faded in the midst of the pennant drive. McCarthy moved to add another arm, getting veteran lefty Art Nehf, who pitched eight games.

Root was pitching with only three days of rest and sometimes less than that. Root started May 26 and won the game, then relieved the next day for Guy Bush. Root's 309 innings pitched exceeded Blake's 224 , a distant second on the team.

Blake, Bush and now Carlson were firmly established in the rotation with Root as the ace.

Hack Wilson again led the league in homers with 30 and drove in 129 runs. Stephenson led the team in hitting at .344, and Grimm had another solid year at .311.

The Cubs were in first place in a four-way pennant race as late as August 31, but they faded and Root's tired arm wasn't the only cause.

In 20 games between mid-August and early September, the Cubs were 4-16 and weren't hitting. They finished fourth, at 85-68, 8½ games behind Pittsburgh.

Fans responded to the pennant race, and attendance topped one million for the first time in Cubs history.

The team ERA was an excellent 3.65, but the offense delivered only 74 homers, with Wilson getting 30 of them. Wilson's 129 RBIs was far ahead of Stephenson's 82.

McCarthy was getting closer to the balance he wanted between offense and pitching, but he wasn't there yet.

As the 1928 season approached, McCarthy again made balanced moves for greater offense and pitching, getting outfielder Kiki Cuyler and pitcher Pat Malone.

As with Cuyler's former Pirate teammates, Grimm and Maranville, the Cubs robbed the Pirates when they traded Sparky Adams and Pete Scott for Cuyler.

Grimm later wrote that Cuyler was the most meticulous player he had ever known. "He was the closest approach baseball ever had to a matinee idol. He wore his uniform like a tuxedo. Kiki's teammates often accused Andy Lotshaw of brushing off Cuyler's uniform between innings."

English described Cuyler as a loner who didn't hang out with the rest of the team. His teammates didn't dislike him; he just wasn't one of the boys, English said.[52]

Cuyler, like Root, Horne and Wilson, broke into baseball by playing with a tough company team. Cuyler worked in a Michigan auto

---

[52] Ibid., pg. 206.

assembly plant and moved to pro baseball in 1920 at Bay City's Michigan-Ontario league when he was laid off from the factory job.

The Pirates brought him up as a rookie in 1924 after Cuyler tore up the Southern League in Nashville and was named Most Valuable Player, hitting .340.[53]

Cuyler hit .354 in his first full major league season with the Pirates in 1924, fourth in the National League. He was even better in 1925 and the key reason why the Pirates won the pennant. Cuyler won Game 2 of the 1925 World Series with a two-run homer in the eighth inning. He drove in a team-leading six runs in the seven-game series.

He was almost as good in 1926, but wasn't even a regular starter in 1927 once the Waner brothers arrived in the Pirate outfield. Despite league-leading performances in three consecutive seasons, Cuyler didn't even bat in the 1927 World Series.

Cuyler was ripe for a trade and the Cubs really needed his power and speed for the 1928 season. Cuyler delivered by leading the National League with 37 steals. He hit .285 and drove in 79 runs. His seventeen homers made him the Cubs' second most powerful hitter.

If Cuyler was a loner and didn't hang out with the boys, Malone made up the difference.

Malone was the only drinking buddy who could keep up with Wilson, and he could match Grimm with practical jokes.[54]

Malone, age 25, was another one of McCarthy's American Association discoveries. His rookie season with the Cubs in 1928 was

---

[53] Parker, Clifton Blue, *Fouled Away: The Baseball Tragedy of Hack Wilson*, pg. 65

outstanding. He finished 18-13 with a 2.84 ERA. His 155 strikeouts in 250⅔ innings was second in the National League. Tall, heavy and menacing, he used all six feet and 235 pounds to hurl at hitters.

Malone always spoke highly of McCarthy's patience and how McCarthy stuck with him when he struggled through several games.

The Cubs finished 1928 with a 91-63 record that would have won pennants in many previous years. Their third-place finish was only four games behind the champion Cardinals who were swept by the Yankees in the World Series.

Wilson led the team and the National League again with 31 homers in 1928 and drove in 120 runs. Stephenson hit .324 and drove in ninty, and Hartnett was showing what he could do at .302.

Root's worst season and his only losing season so far was 1928 when he finished 14-18. Malone's arrival canceled out Root's slide. Root's 3.57 ERA actually had been better than that of his league-leading 26-win season of 1927, but there were real worries about whether he had worn out his arm.

The year 1928 was the best season so far for McCarthy, Veeck and Wrigley, but hopes had been raised so high for a pennant that the year was a disappointment.

McCarthy hoped for the best and still regarded Root as his ace. The weakness that really bothered McCarthy was at second base, and this needed to be fixed before the 1929 season began.

Veeck had always wanted to get Rogers Hornsby and had tried several seasons earlier. Hornsby was easily the best and most expensive

---

[54] Golenbock, pg. 205

second baseman in the game, both good enough reasons for Wrigley to go after him.

McCarthy would feel better about the upcoming 1929 season if he could just fix this last piece of the puzzle during the winter of 1928.

Chicago Daily News — Chicago History Museum s067205

Charlie Grimm (with banjo) and Cliff Heathcote,
probably on the train from Chicago en route to Catalina.

Rogers Hornsby

"Rogers Hornsby, widely heralded as a man who has been spending his life wrecking china shops and other fragile emporiums, has been on Catalina Island a full week and hasn't done a darned thing to refute the cautious notion that he's an upstanding sort of a feller."
—by Edward Burns, *Chicago Tribune*, March 6, 1929.

Joe McCarthy and William Wrigley Jr. built a lineup that balanced powerful hitting with excellent pitching, but their pennant drive of 1928 still fell short.

Every team is constantly searching for more pitching and power. Wrigley was willing to spend more than any owner to acquire what he needed.

The missing piece for the Cubs was at second base. They had three forgettable players there in three seasons. They also needed one more bat like Hack Wilson's so pitchers couldn't constantly work around him.

Rogers Hornsby was the obvious choice for average, power, and playing second. The Cubs were set with Woody English at shortstop, and Hornsby would be just the kind of veteran to help with the double play combination.

Babe Ruth was the greatest left-handed power hitter in baseball, was already playing for a champion and obviously wasn't on the trading block. Hornsby was the greatest right-hander, playing for one of the worst teams in baseball and one that could barely afford him.

The Boston Braves lost 103 games in 1928. They promoted Hornsby to player-manager during the season but didn't do any better.

As a hitter, he won his seventh batting title, at .387, with 21 homers, 94 RBIs, and 107 walks. Only Ruth had more walks.

He had hit over .400 three times, including .424 in 1924, and was player-manager when the St. Louis Cardinals won the World Series in 1926.

Hornsby's perfectionism and high expectations tortured him with such a lousy team as the Braves. He had just signed a $40,000-a-year, three-year contract with the Braves as the 1928 season ended, but nobody expected Hornsby to be there by spring. Both sides were eager to end the arrangement.

The dealing started during the 1928 season. Veeck found the Braves' owner was receptive to a deal for Hornsby as early as September. Veeck continued talks when the Cubs were in Boston for a three-game series. During pre-game practice, Hornsby walked over, shook hands with Veeck and McCarthy, and said he hoped the Cubs could make the trade.[55]

Hornsby had something to prove. He had a bad reputation of wearing out his welcome everywhere. He just wanted to show his burning desire to play for a winner. He boasted to reporters that he could personally bring the Cubs a pennant if traded to Chicago.

The deal was announced on November 7. It was the most expensive baseball deal in history, topping even what the Yankees paid to acquire the Babe. Hornsby was guaranteed his $40,000 for three years and the Braves got badly needed cash of $200,000 and five minor players.

A week later, Hornsby went to the Wrigley Building to sign his contract as Wrigley and Veeck watch. Hornsby then slipped on a Cubs uniform and posed for photos. He did something he always wanted to

---

[55] Alexander, Charles C., *Rogers Hornsby,* pg. 148-149.

do—buy a ninty-three-acre farm outside St. Louis and spend the rest of the winter getting up before eight to tend chickens, pigs and cows. He hired what he called his "darkies" from Texas to run the farm during the season.[56]

Chicago fans and most baseball writers agreed that Wrigley had just bought the 1929 pennant and maybe even the World Series. That's why McCarthy is now feeling such excitement and pressure at Catalina Island.

McCarthy gets in nine days of work for the pitchers and catchers before Hornsby and the rest of his powerful lineup board the second train from Chicago on February 23.

Hornsby knows right away that he is back with a winning team. The weather is terrible and yet at least 500 frostbitten fans are waiting on him, to get autographs, handshakes or photos. Hornsby is immediately surrounded, looks for assistance, and his new teammates drag him aboard.

Only eleven Cubs hitters leave from Union Station, including English, Cuyler, Wilson and Hornsby. Grimm boards in Kansas City and livens things up.

Once Hornsby meets Wilson and Grimm, he quickly learns about the "Hyena" car. Wilson is singing and Grimm is playing the banjo, loudly picking on Kiki Cuyler for two and a half days and 2,000 miles. Hornsby never socialized with other players anyway, so it was no surprise when he stayed to himself.[57]

Irving Vaughan goes down to the station again as the Cubs leave. In his story, he describes Wilson as "round enough to roll uphill" and knows that McCarthy will have him wearing rubber shirts to sweat off the excess beef.

Hornsby and Cuyler are in top shape and at playing weight as a result of an active winter.

Burns reports from Catalina that Wrigley joined the team to watch practice, sitting on the bench at the training field. Wrigley was bragging

---

[56] Ibid., pg. 149-150.

to Burns about how McCarthy was going to lead them to a pennant in 1929. "Look at that Charlie Root in the pink right now. Cap Malone may be weighing 202 at present but watch him throw that baseball, and what do you think of the way those two, Art Nehf and Hal Carlson, are stepping around after only five days' workout?"

Wrigley also touted Eddie Lautenbacher, now being presented as a potential phenom, and Berly Horne, the soft-voiced right hander, but it is obvious that his greatest source of gratification is in the physical condition of Root, Carlson and Nehf.

McCarthy says the schedule will favor the Cubs, who open and close at home and finish with an eastern trip when the weak clubs will falter. The club will be at home from Sept. 6 to Oct. 2.

McCarthy is pushing the pitchers harder now so that they will be ahead of the batters when they arrive next week. He gives them Sundays off to honor the Sabbath, although he is looking to schedule a Sunday game with the Navy since they have battleships near Catalina.

Bands greet the second squad of Cubs at the Wilmington docks when they board and at Avalon harbor when they get off the *S.S. Catalina*.

They arrive at noon on February 26. Hornsby and the rest of the Cub regulars pile into a wagon drawn by two aged horses for the ride to St. Catherine's Hotel.

Perhaps symbolically, Hornsby drives the team.[58]

The players are on the field in less than two hours for an intra-squad game. McCarthy and coaches Burke and Land don't meet the team or make a fuss. They make it clear that immediately after lunch, it is time to be in uniform and ready to go.

McCarthy starts this first day with all Cubs together for a practice game at 1:45 p.m., just after they have lunch. McCarthy has 15 pitchers at camp but asks the Los Angeles Angels to send over two more to assist with batting practice.

---

[57] Parker, Clifton Blue, *Fouled Away: The Baseball Tragedy of Hack Wilson*, pg. 68-69.
[58] Alexander, pg. 152.

The practice begins with Pat Malone hurling batting practice. English leads off with a base hit. Wilson is next and gets a merciless razzing from all his team when he strikes out with three lusty cuts. Hornsby socks one of three home runs off Malone and runs to his position at second base with the enthusiasm of a rookie.

The next pitcher to throw to Hornsby is Guy Bush, a pitcher that Hornsby has dominated while playing with the Cards.

Grimm and Hartnett are ready for the match-up. As Hornsby steps to the plate they shout in unison, "There's your cousin, Rogers."

McCarthy expands the practice schedule to two games a day and makes the players cut back on their golfing. Hornsby views golf as another human flaw, saying, "When I hit a ball, let someone else chase it down."[59]

During the first week on the island, the Cubs practice from 10:30 a.m. to 12:30 p.m. daily.

McCarthy tells Burns that he no longer agrees with the philosophy of gradually breaking in the hitters with exercises unrelated to swinging a bat or fielding.

Photo courtesy of Louisville Slugger Museum

Rogers Hornsby

"I used to try to toughen the fellows by letting them climb mountains and row boats before they ever picked up a ball or bat," McCarthy said. "That system is baloney for me. Those gents are working at the ball playing trade and the place for them to get toughened up is right in their own workshop."

After practice, Hornsby's first order of business is making sure the Cubs are particular about his future roommate. Considering how fussy

---

[59] Grimm, Charlie, *Jolly Cholly,* pg. 68.

Hornsby is about going to bed early, that limits the choices with this rowdy gang. The decision is a big deal, since teammates spend so much time together on the road.

"I have no preference in rooming so far as baseball talent is concerned, but I want a room with a lad who goes to bed before 10 o'clock, who doesn't stay awake reading *True Confessions*, who doesn't talk or walk in his sleep," Hornsby tells Burns.

Traveling secretary Robert Lewis jokes that there are a few crossword puzzle fiends who secretly sit up until 11 o'clock trying to figure out an Australian bird in three letters. He says the bigger problem is with snorers who claim they only snore on their back, but he has evidence they can snore from any angle.[60]

Lewis decides that Hornsby will room with Woody English because English hasn't developed any bad habits by hanging out with the drinkers and night owls on the team. English goes to bed at 8:30 p.m. and sleeps like a babe until 8 a.m. So, Burns writes, if Rogers does not bat .400 this year, he can't blame it on a prowling roommate.

The first spring training cuts are likely to come sometime around March 8, when the Cubs go to Los Angeles and then again on March 14 when they leave Catalina for the last time.

By the second day, McCarthy focuses his starting lineup of infielders on fielding practice all morning. He uses backup outfielders so Stephenson, Wilson and Cuyler can do the hitting. Grimm is at first, Hornsby at second, English at short and Beck at third. Moore, Taylor and Heathcote form the outfield. McCarthy immediately takes a look at

---

[60] *Chicago Tribune.*

his new pitching prospect—Berly Horne, Eddie Lautenbacher and Snipe Hansen pitched in the morning.

In the afternoon, aging catcher Mike Gonzales plays first, Whitey Land is at second, McMillan at short and Blair at third. The regular outfield makes its first appearance in the field together with Stephenson in left, Wilson in center and Cuyler in right. Phat (instead of Pat) Malone, Charlie Root and Art Nehf pitch, Burns writes.

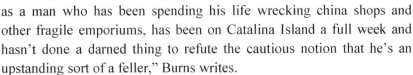

Hornsby knows the spotlight, and it's even more intense now because of what Chicago fans and reporters expect from him in 1929.

Burns keeps waiting for the angry Hornsby to flare, as previous teammates and other reporters have complained. Burns finally writes about seeing quite the opposite.

"Rogers Hornsby, widely heralded as a man who has been spending his life wrecking china shops and other fragile emporiums, has been on Catalina Island a full week and hasn't done a darned thing to refute the cautious notion that he's an upstanding sort of a feller," Burns writes.

Burns says Hornsby has been one of the first three players to arrive at all of the 14 practices so far. He listens intently when McCarthy is talking to the players. He calls the rookies by their nicknames and is nice to all. And "is the chief atta boy shouter in the pepper talk following snappy maneuvers; chums with none of the established stars, but is friendly to all."

Burns even mentions that Hornsby's reported gambling addiction, especially on the horses, seems to be a myth as well. "He didn't read the papers to find out who won the Derby at Tijuana on Sunday."

Maybe the humor of Grimm is rubbing off because Hornsby uncharacteristically leads some of the teasing.

On one play during the morning, Gonzales guns down a would-be base stealer by several feet as Hornsby runs to cover second. Hornsby surprises everyone with an uncharacteristic smile and yells, "Poor old Mike can't throw any more." Everyone is smiling, especially Gonzales.

"The flash compliment with the ball just starting on its way pleased Mike mightily, causing him to display his elaborate dentistry in his great grin for a full five minutes," Burns writes.

Burns writes that Hornsby is the most athletically fit on the team, having worked harder on his farm near St. Louis than he must have let on. "Did Rog have a gymnasium in his hay mow?" Burns asks.

McCarthy loves what he sees in Hornsby because both are dead serious about baseball. This team has its fun, but they do not loaf on defense and are expected to hustle on the base paths—even in practice. They already are playing like the team that everyone else is going to have to chase.

Photo from Catalina Island Museum Collection

Spring training at Catalina Island

Building Characters

Trader Horne and Eddie Lautenbacher are in a dead heat in the
race of pitching prospects....
    —Edward Burns, March 14, 1929.

Berly Horne is afraid that he'll wake up from this dream. He is surrounded by players that he has read about, listening to their loose
ribbing as they gather behind the plate at Catalina.

Wilson is leaning against the batting cage as Hartnett shoots home
movies with an expensive camera that is still a novelty. The camera
captures smiles and gestures of the tormenters and the effortless whip
of Hornsby's bat. There is no sound, except to the players who can
recognize the distinctive crack of Hornsby's bat hitting the ball. One
does not even have to turn to the batting cage to know that Hornsby is
getting his swings.

Hack and the others say they're studying Hornsby so they, too, can
learn to hit .400.

Horne wishes he felt as loose as the veterans. They have no worries. They're going to make the roster.

Horne is also surprised at how well he is being treated. Everyone
expected the worst from Hornsby, yet even first-time tryouts like Horne
have polite but formal conversations with Hornsby. Hornsby prefers to
be by himself, but he will always talk about baseball.

There's a special recognition, an unspoken respect, among the veterans about Horne, age 30, who has toiled 10 years to make it to this
point.

On the first day of real practice, when the team divides up to play
an exhibition game, a lot of fuss is being made about Eddie Lautenbacher. He is Horne's primary obstacle to making the roster.

Catalina Island Museum Collection

Spring training at the Catalina ball field, 1929.

Catalina Island Museum Collection

Catalina ball field, nestled in the narrow valley above Avalon.

Horne is too nice to think ill of the kid. But he knows that he must play better than Lautenbacher if he is ever to get his break.

After practice, Burns is banging away noisily at his typewriter about what he saw in Lautenbacher.

> While none of the rookies is being snubbed, it is apparent that Lautenbacher has entrenched himself in the center of the stage and probably will not be dislodged unless he gets his ears knocked off in several exhibition games, a circumstance that is considered highly improbable.
>
> His name is Edward M. Lautenbacher. He is 21 years old, six feet three inches tall, and weighs 200 pounds. Last year he won 10 games for Reading in the International League, while losing five. Although he lives in Brooklyn, Eddie apparently has an opportunity to keep working all winter, for this morning he was burning them in like it was the Fourth of July.

There's a reason why McCarthy chooses Lautenbacher as the first pitcher that he wants to see. He doesn't want to press his veteran pitchers too hard. He also doesn't need to see their stuff.

He can always use one more arm on the pitching staff, especially the arm attached to a 21-year-old who towers on the mound.

Burns always works in a lighter point in his stories, and he frets about how newspapers are going to squeeze Lautenbacher's name into the headlines and the tiny print of the box scores. He mentions how baseball and newsrooms solved the challenge of Roger Peckinpaugh, who retired from the Chicago White Sox after the 1927 season at shortstop. They just called him "Peck."

Lautenbacher pitched strongly during his years at Columbia University from 1924 to 1928. But he messed up his arm when a track coach challenged him to use his strength to see how far he could throw a javelin.

"It happened after my second year at Columbia," Lautenbacher said. "I just wasn't effective any more."

Today doctors would say he tore a rotator cuff and probably could fix it, Lautenbacher said.

But then, doctors said surgery would end his career. Lautenbacher took his chances and kept pitching. He was really only strong enough for six or seven innings, not good enough for baseball in those days where the starter was expected to finish.

Still, Lautenbacher was at Catalina with high hopes.

"This was my first chance in the majors," he said.

Lautenbacher grew up in Brooklyn and played baseball in the streets with a rubber ball. "We called it 'sewer ball.'"

"We had teams from neighborhood to neighborhood and our own championships," Lautenbacher said. He graduated from Brooklyn Tech High School in 1924, and his high school coach was instrumental in getting him a full athletic scholarship at Columbia University.

"Our freshman team did well."

In 1928, he left Columbia during his final year when the Cubs scouted him.

"I went over on a Saturday for a workout and I was throwing like a bullet," Lautenbacher said. "They told me to come back the next day and I started the game. I got through it and won."

He was signed to a professional contract with the Cubs' Reading team.

The Reading manager alerted the Cubs about Lautenbacher and he got an invitation to Catalina for 1929, and a $3,500 contract.

"Imagine what that was like," Lautenbacher said. "So many of these ballplayers I read about, and then to be standing on the same field with them. It was quite overpowering. Yet they were all so nice. They treated you as well as each other."

He remembers Charlie Root as a "fine gentleman" who was always with his family after the games. Sheriff Blake and Guy Bush spent the most time with him, showing him how he was tipping off his pitches and working on his motion.

Hack Wilson was the life of the party, surrounded by laughter, Lautenbacher remembers. "He had a love of life. I remember his big bat with the really thin handle and how very hard he was to get out."

"Charlie Grimm was so fluid, so graceful, an incredible first baseman."

The difference between the minors and majors was amazing, Lautenbacher said. He traveled in a special train car to California, stayed in the best hotels and got the best food.

Lautenbacher said the intra-squad games were tough, and he could not figure out a way to get Wilson out in spring training at Catalina.

Horne and Lautenbacher were competing for perhaps only one opening on the pitching staff. Lautenbacher already knew Horne, by his nickname of "Sonny," because they faced each other in minor league games when Horne was with Jersey City and Lautenbacher with Reading.

"Sonny Horne and I were so busy trying to make the team that we didn't mix much," Lautenbacher said.[61]

Here they are at Catalina. Horne and Lautenbacher know that only one of them will make the roster.

A similar competition is happening at third base.

The Cubs are thin at third, and there also is no real backup for Hornsby at second or Grimm at first if they get hurt or need rest.

In this era of baseball, the Cubs and every other team normally get by with four starting pitchers who go all nine innings unless they're being shelled. There are no real relievers, although it helps to have some backup starters or mop-up men.

Like most managers of the time, McCarthy prefers to fill the bench with many offensive players and keep the pitching staff to a minimum.

After one day of practice, Burns reports that the Cubs have other worries about their starting lineup, reporting for the first time that outstanding catcher Hartnett has a "sore wing."

At the ballpark, just beyond the leftfield wall, is a street and then a bluff where the golf course and country club are located. The first tee requires a drive over the road, and the hole is down by the back side of the grandstand. It is a hard course because of the steep slopes and winding fairways.

---

[61] Eddie Lautenbacher, age 97, the last surviving member of the 1929 squad at Catalina Island, described his memories in a phone interview Oct. 28, 2004, from his home in Napa, Calif. Lautenbacher was born Oct. 1, 1907.

The nine-hole course is popular with many of the players. Root and Charlie Grimm play there as often as they can. They are serious about getting into shape. Hartnett also plays frequently and "has sore feet from playing golf in dancing pumps," Burns reports.

During the winter, golfing around Los Angeles was Root's only workout routine. He often went on hunting trips. But he didn't do anything else special to keep in shape because spring training was rigorous enough, Della said.

Chicago Daily News — Chicago History Museum s067266 s067431

The Catalina baseball field overlooking the Pacific Ocean

Over the right field fence lies the downtown, ocean and harbor. There is a smaller hotel near the outfield, more like an apartment building. The players stay at the St. Catherine's Hotel, all the way at the harbor downtown, then left on the boardwalk and about a three-quarter-mile walk from there.

A number of little stores cater to the tourists, including Dorothy and Della's favorite, Catalina Pottery, where goods are made from the special clay on Catalina Island.

Down the right field foul line, Wrigley's home is on the top of the distant bluff, with a panoramic view of the harbor.

Rubber shirts and lots of running was how McCarthy thought you burned off the winter fat.

McCarthy has a strict regimen and schedule. Players report promptly to the park at 8 a.m. Pitchers get loose and warm up by running. For many of the players coming from the cold winters of Chicago and the Midwest, this morning routine is downright pleasant. Temperatures start out in the 60s, very comfortable for running, and get around 70 by afternoon.

After running, the pitchers play little games among themselves, a lot of pepper, hitting fungoes and more running. They did stretching and callisthenic exercises.

They wear their uniforms, heavy jackets, and tennis shoes, not baseball cleats. Sometimes they run from the ballpark, all the way to St. Catherine's, about a five-mile round trip on the only level ground on the island.

McCarthy spends most of his time with Root, Nehf and Malone and the other veteran pitchers. McCarthy has them pitch a few innings of batting practice against each other, getting in shape for the arrival of the hitters.

"We'll just romp around for a week to get the boys hardened up to receive our slugging infielders and outfielders," McCarthy tells Burns.

Coaches Burke and Land lecture the rookies on the elemental tricks of the trade. Lautenbacher and Horne get the most attention during the two-hour training "spasm," Burns writes.

A lot more reporters and cameras are at Catalina for spring training in 1929 than in past years. Hornsby's arrival is the biggest reason—along with the high hopes that he brings of a real Chicago pennant race.

New technology brings film crews, whose news clips and footage from Catalina reach Chicago theaters and anxious fans within days.

An advertising company sends a photographer, and Root is asked to perform for some publicity photos. Root stands on the mound, getting ready to throw at a window with four panes of glass propped up at the plate. He throws four pitches and breaks all four panes.[62]

---

[62] Della Root Arnold.

While at the hotel, players come to the dining room in suits and ties, never in sport shirts. They are even competitive about who looks the best off the field.

Telephone service is available on the island, but the telegraph is just as affordable. Reporters send their stories via the telegraph operator, who has an office at the St. Catherine's Hotel.

Woody English was one month short of his 20th birthday when his first spring training began at Catalina in 1927. The Cubs had long-term hopes for this slick-fielding rookie shortstop.

The Fredonia, Ohio, kid joined the Cubs in the same year that pitchers Art Nehf and Hal Carlson were acquired from the Reds and Philadelphia respectively.

The only concern about English in 1929 is whether he can get on base as the leadoff hitter. McCarthy's push at Catalina this spring is to keep English scrapping to get on base and not to worry about stealing because of all the power in the lineup behind him.

As English looks forward to this new season, he sees team chemistry, tremendous offense and the common attitude among players that they would score their eight runs in every game and take it easy.[63]

There are pranksters and practical jokers on virtually every baseball club because of all the idle time traveling together. The Cubs found it even easier to be loose when they keep winning and having fun.

Root has his own practical joke that he tries out on rookies any time he gets the chance back at St. Catherine's.

There is a pool table in a room extending just off the back of the hotel. Root sets up his hustle by telling the rookie how good he is at pool and that it wouldn't be fair for him to play right-handed.

"Why, I can even beat you left-handed," Root says.[64]

No rookie could avoid that bait. Few people, especially the rookies, know that Root hammers nails, eats his meals and does just about everything left-handed. He just happens to get all his attention as a right-hander on the mound.

---

[63] Parker, Clifton Blue, *Fouled Away,* pg. 70-72.
[64] Della Root Arnold

Photo from the Catalina Island Museum Collection

Selected members of the 1929 team. Highlighted, left to right, are Horne, McCarthy, Wrigley, and Charlie Root.

Root is quiet and mature, perfect disguises for an ornery streak and his humor. Root uses these jokes as ice-breakers, and he goes after rookies in friendship, not as hazing. He never forgot how miserably Grover Cleveland Alexander treated him in his first season with the Cubs.

Charlie was the highly touted kid in 1926, enough to annoy an aging and threatened veteran.

As a result, Charlie and Dorothy go out of their way to associate with the rookies and make them feel welcome. Dorothy's home is the gathering place for players to get home-cooked meals.

Catalina is such a happy place for the Cubs. Sun and warm weather, an island paradise and baseball. "Catalina was an ideal spot for training camp," Della wrote. "It was remote, the players couldn't get into much trouble, and, in those days, all players were checked to see that they were in their rooms by 10 p.m. Every night we would walk the boardwalk along the beach."

Riggs Stephenson had his own routine, as the champion checker player on the island. He would go down to the barbershop at the Atwater Arcade and challenge anyone. "He never paid for a haircut and every day he'd say, 'I gotta go now and get me a haircut,'" Charlie Grimm said.[65]

There was dancing at St. Catherine's. Dorothy and Charlie learned the Charleston at their Swanville apartment in Chicago. "They learned by standing in a doorway and each put their hands on each side of the door jamb and moved their feet. I can see them yet. They really got to be quite adept. Dad was a very good dancer and Mother was too. She loved it," Della said.

St. Catherine's hosted dancing competitions, but that was too showy for the Roots, and they never participated.

Wrigley sponsors these later dance contests, and beautiful women visitors are invited from Los Angeles and Hollywood to serve as partners in the competition. Players without wives in attendance need written permission from Wrigley to participate, however.[66]

From the very beginning, Hornsby never joined in anything that is fun or sociable. Burns even mentions in a March 2 story that Hornsby believes he is "conserving energy by not dancing, content to sit on rocks talking runs, hits, errors." Burns adds that all the Hornsby temper that everyone else has talked about remains dormant.

The Cubs are joking that they are jealous because of Mr. Wrigley's new monkey and his 7½-acre farm for rare birds.

Burns writes:

> It is the general feeling of the Cubs that anyone who owns a flock of ball players has rare birds enough and shouldn't be spending a couple of million bucks on an aviary.
>
> One of the more radical members of the squad discovered that one of Mr. Wrigley's favorite specimens is a pure white sacred monkey, a perfect beast except that he has a tail broken by an angry movie actor, to whom nothing is sacred. The monkey, a resident of Hollywood when he's working, crashed the aviary to recuperate.

---

[65] Grimm, Charlie, *Jolly Cholly.*
[66] Parker, pg. 128.

Charlie Root Jr. makes sure that all the players know his fifth birthday is approaching on February 27. The pockets of his shorts hang down with the weight of all the coins the players give him, to the supreme embarrassment of his mother.

Della's 10th birthday is February 21, and the hotel bakes little cakes for both of them.

Junior also gets in trouble for lifting polished seashells from baskets along the front walk of several stores. He thinks they are free since they are put out there so prominently in reach of his little hands.

"Mom marched him down there to apologize," Della said. "The owner wanted to give them to him, but she wouldn't allow it and made him give them back."

In a scene from some of the earliest home movies shot by Gabby Hartnett, Junior is happily turning cartwheels on the expansive lawn of the hotel. As Junior rolls head over heels, Dorothy stands smiling with the other players' wives.

William Wrigley feels like doing cartwheels himself, galloping up on his horse to tell Burns what he has just learned in a phone call from Veeck in Chicago.

Opening day is already sold out, almost two months before the season opens with Pittsburgh on April 16. This is the earliest sellout ever for Wrigley and the Cubs. Last year, the sellout came at 9 a.m. on the day of the opener.

Tickets are even sold out for the eight exhibition games the Cubs will play at Wrigley Field in Los Angeles, starting March 8. The minor league Angels would host the Cubs.

As March begins, the pressure builds for Horne and Lautenbacher. They are a month away from a lifelong dream or a return to the minors.

McCarthy doesn't waste any time testing the two pitching prospects that he's watching the closest. On the first day of official intrasquad competition, Lautenbacher starts.

On March 3, Horne starts, pitching a typical spring training outing of three innings. Against the Cub sluggers, Horne impresses by giving up only two hits, striking out four and walking none.

Burns is more confident than Horne about his future. "Trader Horne seems in a fair way to remain on the Cubs payroll for some time. Trader allowed two singles and had the pleasure of striking out Heathcote and Grimm," Burns wrote.

The Chicago *Tribune* photo from Catalina on this day shows Della, Junior, Charlie and Dorothy Root together as a well-dressed and happy family. The caption notes the family spends a few hours together every day between workouts.

Two weeks on the island and not a single practice session has been curtailed by weather. Sunshine, sunshine, nothing but sunshine, Burns writes, almost gloating, considering the weather Chicago readers were enduring. "And not a blizzard in prospect."

The Cubs play several more games among themselves, getting ready for the first of 32 exhibition games on March 9.

McCarthy announces that Horne, Eddie Holley and Lautenbacher will pitch in the first exhibition game. He also makes news by saying Hornsby will nudge Wilson from his usual cleanup spot and that Hartnett will not play because of his arm.

For the first time, rookies such as Horne and Angley get spending money to cover meals while in Los Angeles. On Catalina, meals are included with the hotel so they can't skip meals and pocket the spending money. They are not paid a penny during tryouts.

McCarthy says he's going to keep 10 pitchers and three catchers after all his cuts are made. This means that three pitchers and one catcher will have to go. Horne reads this news nervously a few days later, when the *Tribune* arrives by train.

Meanwhile, President Herbert Hoover's inauguration leads the *Tribune* in news from the other coast. The business pages rumble about stocks being over-valued and too many speculators being overcome by the excitement, from pensioners to school teachers and working stiffs.

Wrigley convinces Root to invest a healthy portion of his salary in the market because there's no way he can lose.

The game at the other Wrigley Field in Los Angeles, also owned by Wrigley, is overshadowed by an umpire's decision to halt the game because of rain.

The Cubs are winning 8-4 and it looks like the game could continue. The Angels explode to take an 11-8 lead, and that's when umpire Chet Chadbourne suspends the game.

Chadbourne officially calls off the game at the end of the fifth inning, when the Cubs are ahead, but reconsiders, on the suggestion of Manager Marty Krug of the Angels.

The game resumes and Chadbourne says, "Now we'll play 'em through, no matter what happens." But the minute the Angels get ahead, he calls off the game for the second time, this time for keeps.

"Joe told, with some merriment, how someone had kicked Chadbourne aft in his uniform as he was descending the stairs to the clubhouse runway," Burns writes. "The Cub boss would not say who gave the umps the boot caress. Joe is a modest fellow and doesn't like to talk about himself."

Burns gives little detail about how the pitchers fared in this game but notes that Horne's stock booms while Lautenbacher is shelled for four runs in the first. Hornsby homers and hits two doubles, and Riggs Stephenson has two singles and two doubles in his four times at bat.

"Trader Horne strengthened the suspicion that he is the most likely of the rookie pitchers and Rogers Hornsby, who drove in seven runs with two homers, showed he is in shape to again accept the assignment of leading the National League in batting."

Sunday's game is rained out and the team heads back to Catalina via the ferry.

Returning twenty six miles on the rough, rolling Pacific, landlubbers and sea dogs are in for a rough ride, Burns writes.

"Charlie Grimm was a victim and not up to his usual fun and games. Malone was making fun of the sick Hartnett and then Malone turned green."

Dorothy and the Root children did not join Charlie on this trip, probably because of the weather, and it is a good thing. Della said her brother frequently got seasick on these trips, "which I enjoyed thoroughly."

Horne must have suffered from the return sea voyage. He pitches terribly in the March 12 game at Catalina, allowing four hits in the seventh, two in the ninth and all three Avalon runs as Catalina wins 14-3. Horne is one for two at the plate and scores a run. He gives up eight hits in five innings and walks two.

Back in Chicago, Capone fails to appear before a federal grand jury on March 12. He claims that pneumonia and pleurisy confined him to his bed. He tells friends that he'll go, but he's taking his vacation in Florida first. Investigators will learn later that, during his supposed illness, he was at the Miami fight of Sharkey and Stribling, attending with his friend, Jack Dempsey.[67]

On the Cubs' final day at Catalina on March 15, Burns tells readers that the final cuts are coming.

"Lautenbacher, who entered training camp amidst a blare of trumpets but later caused the trumpeters to mute their horns, pumped up the pressure again by holding the winners to one hit in three innings, his performances including the striking out of Wilson and Stephenson in succession in the final batting rounds of the visitors," Burns writes.

After the last queasy, seasick voyage, the Cubs are relieved to see that the Pacific was as placid as they could hope for on their final voyage of the year back to Los Angeles.

"Manager Joe McCarthy led his troupe off the training island with the assertion that the athletes are not as far along in their conditioning as they have been the two other years he's been out here," Burns wrote.

"The situation has not annoyed Boss Joseph, however, for he has twenty-nine exhibition games ahead of him and sixteen of these will be played where heat should be sustained, in Arizona and southern Texas."

In his analysis of the rookie prospects, Burns writes, "Trader Horne and Eddie Lautenbacher are in a dead heat in the race of pitching prospects."

---

[67] Schoenberg, Robert J., *Mr. Capone,* pg. 223.

Horne, Root and Bush pitch the first game back in Los Angeles on March 15. McCarthy is closely watching Horne and trying to figure out what to do at third before the season begins.

The Cubs explode for fourteen runs on seventeen hits, including Hornsby's third homer in three consecutive games. McMillan gets three hits in three chances, fighting hard to hold his spot on the roster.

Root and Horne struggle and the Angels score ten runs on fourteen hits. Root's first exhibition start lasts five innings and includes four walks and a wild pitch. Burns writes that Root is not his usual self and didn't seem to throw very hard.

Horne pitches until Moore pinch hits for him in the ninth, yielding three hits in the seventh and four in the eighth. Horne is shaky, giving up a pair of runs in the seventh, but he settles down after Wilson makes the most spectacular catch of spring training and then tops it the next inning. Horne gives up three more runs in the eighth but gets a double play to end it.

The *Tribune* photographer shows Grimm, Cuyler and Heathcote clowning around. Grimm is singing away and playing the banjo left-handed. Even if you could play a sad song on a banjo, this group would never show a sad face. Grimm is an ironic surname for a player who is always surrounded by laughter and smiles.

Even Hornsby is enjoying himself and his teammates follow along, something rare for this loner. He convinces the others that steaks are the secret to his strength and the sure way to pump up batting averages. The Los Angeles hotel where the team stays has a great restaurant, but Hornsby leads them every day to a lunch wagon up the street where steaks are served.

Another Hornsby routine is to get a pint of ice cream every night at 9 p.m. before going to bed early. The rest of the off-time, he is usually sitting alone in the hotel lobby, just watching people come and go. He won't read or go to movies because of the strain that he thinks this would place on his eyes.[68]

---

[68] Alexander, Charles C., *Rogers Hornsby,* pg. 153-4.

Those eyes are the "blackest black" of any that Della has ever seen. New York sports writer Westbrook Pegler calls them "go-to-hell" eyes.

There is a little bit of a stir among the players when Hornsby is the first person ever invited by Wrigley to the pilot house of the S.S. *Catalina* during the trip to Los Angeles. Wrigley reports that he learned more about baseball from Hornsby than anyone before.[69]

Reporters keep waiting for Hornsby to snap and fall back to his back-biting, critical reputation. But it doesn't happen.

The next day, March 16, Wilson follows his two spectacular plays with an offensive show, knocking in 10 runs on three homers and two singles as the Cubs win 17-0. Incredibly, the first eight runs of the game are all due to Wilson. Hal Carlson and Mike Cvengros teams for the shutout and best pitching so far in spring training.

On March 17, Root's 30th birthday, the Los Angeles Angels get seven runs, including five home runs, in five innings off starting pitcher Lautenbacher. The Cubs lose 12-11 to the Angels. In six games, the Cubs have scored seventy-three runs, but their pitchers have given up fifty-two to the Angels.

On March 18, Horne shines. "Today's contest was one of the two satisfactory exhibitions played by the Cubs this year, and the feat of playing a good ball game was engineered by two gents well outside the circle of the so-called first string pitchers, said two gents being Trader Horne, fresh from the minors, and Henry Grampp, the handsome steamfitter," Burns wrote. "Horne held the enemy to three hits during the five innings he worked, no two coming in the same inning, giving up one run. Grampp's worst inning was the eighth, when a walk, triple and sacrifice added two of the three Angels' runs." The Cubs won 11-3.

On March 20, the Cubs play the Tigers, winning 13-3. Root pitches the last four innings "and was a stingy cuss, letting loose of three scattered singles."

Back in Chicago, Capone finally appears before the grand jury, eight days later than his subpoena, expecting to be questioned thor-

---

[69] Brown, Warren, *The Chicago Cubs,* pg. 106.

oughly about the St. Valentine's Day Massacre. Instead, he is surprised that all the questions focus on taxes.[70]

The Cubs win five straight games against Detroit. Horne is greeted by a homer when he comes in to relieve in one of the games.

In another, Root pitches a strong four innings, allowing no hits until the ninth when he weakens and the Tigers get a run on a double and two singles.

The season and Chicago are drawing closer now as the team packs up and begins winding home on March 25.

Capone's failure to appear before the grand jury haunts him on March 27 when he is arrested by federal agents for contempt of court. He posts $5,000 bail and walks away. The trial would come two years later.[71]

The next day, the Cubs are in San Antonio. Burns reports that Hartnett has not caught a game yet in exhibition play because of his arm. He is playing first or not at all and it looks like he won't be in the opening day lineup.

On the final day of March, Lautenbacher and Horne intensify the battle to break into the majors when they combine for a shutout against the Kansas City Blues in Beaumont, Texas.

Burns writes:

> Eddie Lautenbacher and Trader Horne, Cub rookie right handers, this afternoon advanced their prospects of getting on the McCarthy payroll by beating the Kansas City Blues, 4 to 0.
>
> Lautenbacher allowed five hits in five innings and Horne two, the second a scratch with two out in the ninth.
>
> A perfectly good triple by Michaels off Horne with one out in the eighth went to waste when Trader struck out Stahlman and Thomas to finish this inning.

---

[70] Schoenberg, pg. 224.
[71] Ibid., pg. 224.

Photo from Catalina Island Museum Collection

J.H. Patrick, Joe McCarthy, J. LeLivet, William Wrigley, Jr.

Making the Cut

With no rain or anything to interrupt the endeavors of the Chicago Cubs, about all we've been doing is writing about McCarthy's victories. We haven't been doing nearly enough baseball experting to suit us. But there it is little more than a week till the big opening at Wrigley field. And we've just got to get caught up on this experting business.

—Edward Burns, *Chicago Tribune*, April 6, 1929.

The roster cuts are coming as the train leaves Phoenix and heads to Texas for the final two weeks of exhibition baseball. As the Cubs work their way to Chicago and Opening Day, Dorothy, Della and Junior leave Charlie behind and continue on by train to Cincinnati.

They will visit family in Middletown and then rejoin Charlie in Chicago for the season opener. With summer vacation coming soon, Della will not return to school until October in Los Angeles.

Charlie's arm problems are still an issue, but Ed Burns writes only of stats and how Sheriff Blake surpasses Root's inconsistent outings. Even the inconsistencies are politely written off by noting how veterans aren't expected to be pressing that hard in exhibition games anyway.

Root flashes some hopeful signs with strong outings on April 1 in Beaumont, Texas, and April 5 in Houston.

The only reported arm problem involves Gabby Hartnett and it looks like he's out of the lineup indefinitely. Few details are given, and Hartnett keeps talking as though he'll be back any day.

Burns sends detailed daily reports of every exhibition. His enthusiasm grows with each win as he records Wilson and Hornsby on offensive streaks, spiced with hitting shows by Stephenson and Cuyler.

Any pitcher who even makes an adequate start is almost certain to get the win with this roster, Burns writes.

On April 6, exactly a week before McCarthy makes the final roster cuts, Burns sends a story back from Houston about his guess for the final roster. Burns predicts that Berly Horne will survive the cuts.

> Charlie Root. Says he never felt better in his life. Every man on the club is whooping it up for Root to duplicate his 1927 season. He is assured of the fightingest kind of support whenever he goes in there.
>
> Berlyn Horne. Little, but he has a lot of stuff. Though up for the first time, he's 29 and has had a great deal of class AA experience. He'll stick. (His 30th birthday is in a week).
>
> Eddie Lautenbacher. A great big kid who shows daily improvement.
>
> Rogers Hornsby. A million per cent Cub. We know why he had the reputation of being a loner. Most folks want to talk about something besides baseball, once in a while. Hornsby refuses to talk about anything but baseball at any time.
>
> Hack Wilson. Snorting and pawing more than ever. Secretly, the ousting of the pudgy one from the cleanup spot in the batting order has furnished a challenge that will be interesting to watch. Instead of sulking, Wilson has turned on the steam.

The Cubs play four games in Houston against the Buffs, which Burns calls "a kindergarten and boneyard for the 1928 National League Champion St. Louis Cardinals. They raid the farm every fall, but replenish the talent at the start of each season."

On April 11, McCarthy announces the nine pitchers who will make the team: Edgar Holley, Ed Lautenbacher, Guy Bush, Charlie Root, Fred Blake, Pat Malone, Hal Carlson, Art Nehf—and Berlyn "Trader" Horne.

Two days later, on April 13, Carlson and Horne combine on a shutout against the Kansas City Blues. Horne yields two hits in four innings of relief.

Burns picks the Cubs to win the 1929 pennant but notes how he has been disappointed when he predicted the same thing in the previous two seasons.

"The first reason to be given for the Cubs' improvement is the presence of Hornsby in the lineup," Burns writes. "His bat should win many ball games, but for a time the beneficial results anticipated were thought by many to be discounted by the expectation that he would upset the morale of the club. Time has shown he fits into the Cub scheme of things perfectly...

"In addition to his individual effort, Hornsby has furnished a striking inspiration for Hack Wilson. It's a friendly rivalry, but Hack is out to show the world that Rogers can't steal his fan following on the basis of slugging. Wilson has been on a rampage all spring and there is no reason to believe he won't keep right on going in the regular season."

The Cubs finish the exhibition season on April 14 with a 3-0 victory over Kansas City, improving their pre-season record to 26-5-1.

Lautenbacher is not mentioned again by Burns. His name never makes it into the *Baseball Encyclopedia*.

On the last day, Manager Joe McCarthy decides he needs one extra catcher on the roster to make up for the likely loss of Hartnett for the season. Lautenbacher learns that he is the last one cut. A coach delivers the news, not McCarthy.

"It was very disappointing to not make the team," Lautenbacher said. "McCarthy was a real manager. He didn't mix with the players and he was tough."[72]

Meanwhile, Horne gets the break that he will never forget.

---

[72] Eddie Lautenbacher, age 97, phone interview, Oct. 28, 2004.

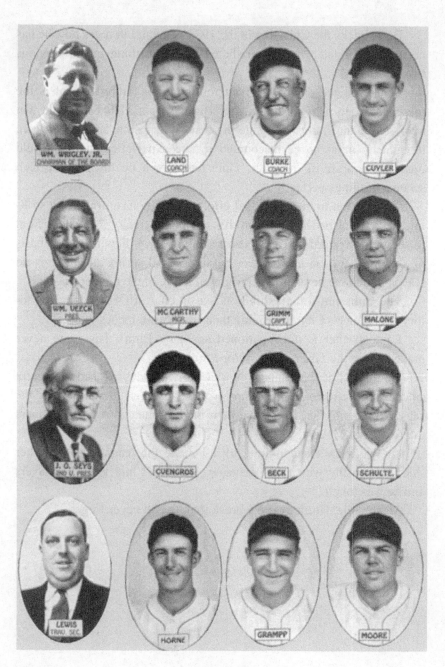

1929 Cubs

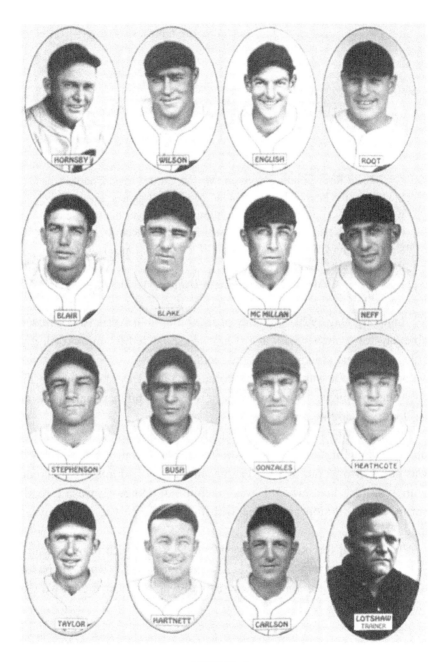

1929 Cubs

Opening Day

Charlie Root is going to pitch, Mr. McCarthy says. Charlie was the talk of the land in 1927, when he won 26 ball games. Last year he wasn't so hot. But is McCarthy a fellow to mull over the relapse of a man he knows is talented? Not Joseph. In giving Root the honor assignment, the Cub boss flashes a bit of loyalty that means more than the outcome of the day's encounter.
—Edward Burns, *Chicago Tribune*, Opening Day 1929.

Opening Day 1929 is the day of reckoning, but April 16 is a miserable day for a pitcher with a stiff arm. As expected for mid-April, it is cold, windy and cloudy at Wrigley Field.

Charlie Root wakes up early because he is always keyed up on the days that he pitches. He questions how good a pitcher really is if he isn't worked up like this on game day.

As Root told a reporter once, "Those fellows who don't get worked up about pitching are the ones who're knocked from the box. Heck, I was never thrown out of a big league game, but I had lots of arguments with umpires. See, when I was pitchin' and knew I wasn't really steamed up, I'd stop and argue with the umpire just to make myself mad." [73]

Today is different, though, for Root. There is much more pressure. A packed stadium and the crowd noise are not issues to Root. He has so much focus during a game that he actually cannot hear the crowd. He can shut off the noise. [74]

---

[73] Della Root Arnold, pg. 161.
[74] Ibid.

His nerves are about getting through this powerful Pittsburgh lineup with a wounded wing. He doesn't want to disappoint the team and fans and especially doesn't want to embarrass himself. Minor leaguers and college athletes have already tested his arm and beat him in the past eight weeks. Now he is going against the most serious National League challenger the Cubs have this season.

Baseball insiders know that St. Louis, Pittsburgh and the New York Giants are the biggest threats to a Cub pennant. Even weaker teams, like Cincinnati, are packed with .300 hitters and strong starting pitching.

Dorothy was up early as well, trying to make Charlie's routine at home smooth and free of distractions, with meals ready and Della and Junior up.

There is a new routine for this game. As Charlie sits in his favorite chair, Dorothy and Della take turns massaging his right shoulder. Charlie and Dorothy don't reveal their worries.

Dorothy and Della drop Charlie off at the stadium at 10 and will come back before game time, driving through the gate guarded by a classy black gentleman named Finnegan. They park under the stands, down the left field line.

Dorothy is one of the few wives who goes to every home game and most of the road games. And Della is always by her side at Wrigley Field. Dorothy now has a maid to help and Junior stays home.

Junior isn't here because of an incident in a previous season, on a hot summer day, when he was whining about how they were never allowed to buy snacks at the park.

Four rows in front of them, Junior spotted a woman holding an ice cream cone in her left hand. Just as an exciting play distracted the roaring crowd, Junior scampered from his aisle seat and took a big bite of ice cream.

That ended his trips to the ballpark until he was older.

Today's weather doesn't discourage the fans. This is virtually a religious holiday on the North side. They pack the park, full of anticipation and hope, the way they always feel on Opening Day. They expect the heartbreak to come later, when the reality of each day's box scores hit. But they also know this season is looking a whole lot differ-ent, especially when New York newspapers start calling the Cubs a front-runner.

William Wrigley Jr. considers himself one of the fans. He is tired of waiting since 1918 for another crack at the World Series. He has a lot riding on his investment in Hornsby, the biggest money on a base-ball trade in history during the off season.

But he also privately worries about Root. Wrigley arranged Root's visit with Doc Spenser in St. Louis about his arm. He knows just how volatile the 1929 season will be if his ace pitcher is not in top form.

This business of baseball is a lot tougher than peddling chewing gum. In that word, everything he touches turns to even more money.

But no hobby is more thoroughly interesting or challenging than baseball.

Wrigley's baseball spending for 1929 is second only to the New York Yankees.

"I've found baseball to be a whale of a business—but bigger and better as a sport," Wrigley writes after the season for the *Saturday Evening Post* in 1930. "I draw larger dividends in fun and personal satisfaction from my ownership of the Chicago Cubs than I do in money—and it's profitable now."[75]

"No man is qualified to make a genuine success of owning a big-league ball team who isn't in it because of his love for the game. He's sure to weaken in his support at some critical point of its development if his heart isn't in the sport. On the other hand, it is no undertaking for a man who hasn't practically unlimited financial resources at his com-mand, regardless of how much he loves the game. If he regards it merely as a means of making money, he'd much better invest his time and capital in an enterprise strictly commercial in character."

"Operating a successful big-league ball team is radically different from running any commercial or industrial business, because you are dealing, 100 percent, in and with human nature—and that's always a variable quantity.

---

[75] *Saturday Evening Post*, Sept. 13, 1930.

"There's a catch in this business at every turn, because you're playing with tricky, variable human nature, not inert physical commodities and mechanical methods."[76]

The fans and players are ready to shake off winter and get down to the business of winning this pennant and facing Ruth and Gehrig. Ruth made headlines in all the sports pages when he picked the Cubs as the most improved and the most likely to face his team at the end of this season. In the American League, Ruth thought the Yankees might have to fight off St. Louis or Detroit. He picked Philadelphia as a distant fourth.

Hundreds of fans are already outside the stadium at 10 a.m., when Root arrives. He always got to the park about an hour before the players officially were expected to report at 11:00.

Root isn't alone today. Among the early arrivals are three rookies, entering a major league clubhouse for the first time in their lives: Tom Angley, Earl Grace and Berly Horne. They can't believe they made it. They expected to be tossed from the locker room at any time. They are amazed when the wrought iron gate swings open for them under the bleachers, and the gatekeeper points them toward their lockers.

Even hours before game time, there is a buzz and excitement around the stadium. The rookies feel it even more than the most anticipatory fan.

Burns reports a few days earlier that Sheriff Blake has surpassed Root as the ace of the staff, based on the actual numbers from the exhibition season. Burns even thought that Blake might open the season, a real blow to Root.

But Manager McCarthy said he never had any doubt that Root would start on Opening Day. He made his decision weeks earlier and was unswayed by what he saw in two months of spring training.

The opening day starter was more than a symbolic gesture. This was a big deal, a baseball tradition, a sign of respect and honor for the ace of the team. But Root knows he hasn't earned the honor because of his inconsistent performance in spring training. His arm is an issue and

---

[76] Golenbock, Peter, *Wrigleyville*, pg. 200-201.

his teammates know it but say nothing after catching up to his fast ball like never before in those intra-squad games.

Reporters like Burns know it, too, but Burns is subtle about what he reports, noting how everyone is waiting for the old pop to come back to Root's pitches.

The Cubs missed the World Series by four games in 1928, just as Root's arm faded at the end of the season. McCarthy kept trying to pep up Charlie. "You'll be back better than ever next year," McCarthy said.[77]

"I am sure, if it had not been for the confidence that McCarthy had in Dad and the honest affection William Wrigley had for him, Dad would have been on the auction block in late 1928," Della said. "McCarthy and Wrigley sincerely liked Dad and never gave up on him."

Many years later, when McCarthy retired as manager of the Yankees, he told a reporter that his dream team would have many great pitchers, but, if he had to choose just one, he would pick Charlie Root. "He had the greatest heart I've ever seen. His determination and loyalty I'm very sure you'll never see again," McCarthy said.[78]

A few hours after dropping Charlie off at the stadium, Dorothy and Della return for the game. As they get out of the car under the stadium, the noise and the bustle of the crowd are even more pronounced. Shouts of peanut vendors and scorecard hawkers echo.

Della loves the burst of light, color and sound as she walks up the field level tunnel, opening out to a full view of the field. She immediately looks for her dad and knows just where to find him, already warming up, as best he could in swirling 47-degree winds. Root did not pitch well in cold weather, especially now with arm trouble.

He is throwing to Mike Gonzales as the Pirates finish batting practice a half hour before the game. Gabby Hartnett is in full uniform, feeling odd and disappointed about sitting on the bench without strapping on the knee pads and catching gear to get Root ready. Gonzales,

---

[77] Della Root Arnold interview.
[78] Ibid.

the aging veteran from Cuba, starts opening day. Rookie catchers Angley and Grace know they are here only because of Hartnett's injury. His misfortune is their lucky break.

Horne and the rest of the team are already in the dugout, having finished hitting and shagging flies in the outfield. Horne's eyes are taking it all in with the same kind of thrill as a boy stepping into Wrigley Field for the first time with his dad.

Horne had never been in this big of a city before and studies the skyline and all the buildings past the outfield. He is amazed at the crowd and how they have already packed the stadium. There is nothing like the smell of popcorn. He looks down the bench and sees Hack Wilson checking out all of his bats at the rack. Hornsby sits alone staring at every warm-up toss of opposing pitcher Burleigh Grimes, and McCarthy fills out the final details on his lineup card.

Della and Dorothy are already in their seats when Mr. Wrigley arrives. He walks down the steps, 10 rows in front of them, directly behind the screen and two boxes to the left of home plate. He always has a fresh white carnation in his lapel and reaches into his suit pocket for a white handkerchief.

He always rubs his handkerchief along the hand railing. Even with all the smoke and dust of industry around the park, the railing had better be clean. As usual, every seat and railing had a fresh coat of paint for the new season because Mr. Wrigley is a fanatic about the beauty and cleanliness of the park. He was the first to hire ushers to clean every seat as fans arrived. He fired all of the thugs who used to usher and hired decent young men in uniforms, without pockets, so they would not accept tips.[79]

But the fans brought more than tips. Women would come to the park with cakes for the players, and sometimes the team would have 15 or more cakes, which Wrigley asked the staff to take to nursing homes or to the poor.[80]

---

[79] Golenbock, pg. 202.
[80] Ibid., pg. 203.

103

Farmers would bring tomatoes, and a dairy farmer brought 48 bottles of this wonderful Guernsey milk for the team every day. "It was a wonderful era, the team was coming on, they were the darlings of Chicago, and every day was New Year's Eve," said Cub batboy Ed Froehlich.

During the game, Mr. Wrigley would eat a hot dog to test it out. He would eat the peanuts to make sure they were roasted correctly at the park, and he would drink lemonade, which was made fresh. He refused to skimp and wanted the fans taken care of, even as the price of fresh lemons rose. Any food left over after the home stand was taken to poorhouses and given away to charity, at Mr. Wrigley's insistence.[81]

Della and Dorothy watched as Mr. Wrigley leaned down from the stands to talk to Burns and other reporters down on the field. He was clearly a happy man today.

Della looks down to her left, near the screen behind home, and doesn't see Al Capone at his usual seat. Capone's problems will divert him from Cub games this season. Della and her mom joke that their seats are a little too close to Capone, if the lead from gunshots ever started flying.

Mr. Wrigley got Dorothy these prime seats for every season behind the screen because she worried about foul balls and the children. The other friends or families of the players sit behind the Cub dugout.

Della keeps an eye on her dad, waiting for him to walk toward center stage.

Charlie takes a deep breath and heads toward the mound. He never makes a big deal about this, but there is no way to describe how it feels to walk out there with the stadium full and everyone watching you. It is amazing how calm and confident Root can be in front of 40,000 or more fans, and yet he would truly be intimidated about having to make a brief speech in a room of less than 100.

The applause and crowd noise give goose bumps to Horne and to Della. This is the only time that Charlie would hear the crowd. During

---

[81] Ibid.

any game, he concentrates so hard that he only hears his teammates. Unless one person yelled that Root was a bum. Then he hears that.

The players joke that Hack Wilson must have the best hearing because he is ready to pile into the opposing team's dugout or into the stands if any insult is directed his way.

Charlie doesn't forget Dorothy as he reaches the third base line. He turns slightly to his right, easily spotting her in Box 59, Tier 12, and then reaches to tip his cap. If an observant fan sees this little gesture, they would think it was a polite acknowledgement to the crowd for all the applause. But Charlie does this every time he walks to the mound to start a game and the gesture is for only one person—Dorothy.

Catalina Island Museum Collection

Charlie Root delivers.

Dorothy

"We're not rich enough to be eccentric. We're just nuts."
—Dorothy Root.

Dorothy Hartman Root refused to consider that her husband's career was ending in 1929. She believed her willpower alone could carry them through the new season. Charlie might have doubts. She didn't.

Her inner strength came at an early age, thrust upon her by family tragedy and the refiner's fire. Dorothy was 8 years old when her 30-year-old mother died.

As soon as she got home from seeing her mother buried, this little girl, who could barely reach the cupboards, walked straight to the kitchen and tied on her mother's apron. As her devastated father, a dirt-poor sharecropper, and four crying siblings crowded into their home near Pricetown, Ohio, Dorothy began the care and feeding of the family that would last for nearly a decade.

Dorothy got the butcher knife and started peeling potatoes for the family meal, just as her mother had so many times before.

During the next several years, a little girl evolved into a beautiful woman, with great strength and resolve—and an equally ornery sense of humor.

Dorothy certainly wasn't looking for a boyfriend with all her responsibilities.

She finished eighth grade but abandoned any hope of going to high school after working as a maid in Cincinnati and finding the $3 a week wouldn't pay for school supplies or even gym clothes.

The family for whom she worked had a couple of boys, including one who was chasing after her. "Mother was really pretty tough and a very pretty lady," Della said. "One of the boys made a pass at her and she pinned him right to the floor and he didn't bother her anymore."

Unable to pursue high school, she moved to Middletown and went to work at the P. Lorillard Tobacco Co. At the tobacco factory, she made $11 a week and paid her cousin $6 for room and board.

Dorothy got the job because her grandfather, Jesse, worked there. She never smoked, especially after seeing how dust was swept from the floor and added right in with the tobacco.

One night, Dorothy's neighbor needed a double date for her boyfriend's friend.

At first, Dorothy resisted, saying she was not about to be seen in public with some boy in knee pants, as most young boys wore at the time.

Her blind date was 19-year-old Charlie Root, who was only two months older. He didn't dress like any other teen-ager she knew. He wore a suit and fedora. And he was quite handsome, with those steely blue eyes.

Dorothy agreed to the date only as long as they stayed home. She and Charlie hit it off from the start and three months later, on May 8, 1918, they eloped to Newport, Ky., where marriages were performed quickly and with little hassle.

They intended to keep the wedding a secret, but word reached Charlie's mother. "Two nights after the nuptials, at the dinner table, Grandma Root said, 'I hear you and Dorothy are married, Charlie. I think you'd better bring her home,'" Della wrote.

"And so the newlyweds moved to the house on Fleming Road, and occupied the large front bedroom."

Jacob built a small, one bedroom apartment as a rental that attached to the kitchen of the main house.

More than nine months later, Della was born on February 21, 1919, in the same room where her father, Charlie, was born in 1899.

By 1921, Charlie and Dorothy were 22, married three years, and had a 2-year-old daughter. Charlie already had worked nearly half his life at Armco, starting at age 12 when his dad took him out of school so he could earn money for the family. Charlie never got to seventh grade.

The only thing that made Armco tolerable was that he still was pitching, and clearly was the best on the field.

His huge break came one Sunday afternoon in the summer of 1921 when the St. Louis Browns were barnstorming through Middletown looking for players. The Browns were chasing an elusive American League pennant again, led by George Sisler, who hit over .400 the year before and was hitting .371 when the team ran into Root. The unknown steelworker shut them out on a three-hitter, with Armco beating the pros, 3-0.

On the spot, the Browns signed Root to his first professional contract.

Jacob Henry Root, Charlie's father, was unhappy about "such foolishness." He did everything he could to discourage his son, mocking him about playing a child's game while having family obligations.

When Jacob was really angry and didn't want anyone to understand, he would lapse back into German and grumble long and loud to his wife. Charlie and Dorothy couldn't understand what he was saying, but they had a really good idea.

Nobody stood up to "the Kaiser"—except Dorothy.

With admiration and humor, Charlie frequently told the story of Dorothy's first tangle with the Kaiser.

Jacob was laying down the law at a Sunday dinner that no Root woman would ever have her hair bobbed like a certain actress of the day. Della said he had probably been to church that day and was feeling especially self-righteous.

"Dorothy was awake all night thinking how early she could catch a bus to the barber," Della recalled years later about her mom. "The next evening when Mom came in with her hair cut off to the ear lobe, not a word was said.

"This tickled Dad, who would certainly never press a fight with his father or mother, but at last someone had defied the 'Ruler of the Roots' and apparently won."

Another time, little Della was at the center of the fight. Della got into the ice box and was having a splendid time dropping one egg after another on the floor to watch them break.

Dorothy set her firmly down in a chair and returned to her ironing. Jacob came out of the bedroom with a handful of jellied orange slices to try to soothe his granddaughter's crying.

"Now what's happened to Grandpa's girl?"

As Della extended her arms to be picked up, Dorothy said, "You pick her up and I'll hit you with this iron."

Photo from Root family archives

Dorothy Root

Jacob never had anyone question his authority over anything, so he didn't know what to do except retreat or surrender around Dorothy.

Over Jacob Root's objections, Dorothy pushed "Charles"—she never called him "Charlie"—to play baseball and chase his dream.

Without Dorothy, the quiet and obedient Charlie probably would have followed his father's unbending demands. His future would have been the grit and grime of the steel mills, probably scrambling for work as the Depression hit.

"Let's take a chance, Charles. You'll never know if you're good enough for the majors unless you try."

Dorothy's opinion was the one that counted.

Root reported to Louisiana for spring training in 1922 with the Browns and was farmed back to Terre Haute, Indiana, and the Three I League, named for teams from Indiana, Iowa and Illinois.

Root began his professional career in the minors with an 8-7 record, 3.57 ERA, a young wife, a toddler and another baby on the way.

He earned $200 a month and thought it was a fortune compared to the $100 a month that he was making at Armco. He didn't realize until he read the fine print of his contract that the money was good only for the six months of the minor league schedule and not for a full year.

109

The Roots rented a bedroom and had kitchen privileges in a small home shared with a widow named Rose Donahoe.

Root was much better in 1922, throwing a perfect game and a no-hitter in separate outings for Terre Haute. He won both games of a doubleheader, starting one and saving the second in relief. He finished 16-14 with an impressive 2.28 ERA. The Browns called him up for his major league debut in 1923.

Rookie Root was roughed up all season, lost all four of his decisions and had everything come crashing down when he broke his ankle sliding into third base. This was the first time that it really looked like his career was over—after only 60 innings pitched in the majors.

How hard it was for Charlie and Dorothy to return to Middletown, taking the little apartment attached to his parent's home on Fleming Road. The Kaiser was ecstatic that Charlie had learned his lesson about baseball, wrongly assuming he would return to Armco and was home for good.

"That's one thing that can be said for that old Kaiser," Della wrote years later. "He didn't nag because I guess he thought he'd won."

Dorothy never wavered and never doubted. When Charlie was traded to the Los Angeles Angels after the season ended, Dorothy was happy and excited to be California-bound.

"Who cares about the big leagues? We're headed WEST!" Dorothy said.

Della wrote about her mother, "I know she always thought on the positive side, so I know she was thinking that California would bring a better break for her Charles, and so it did."

Root knew that the Pacific Coast League was the next best thing to the majors, and the Los Angeles Angels were just one step away from the majors as the farm club for the Chicago Cubs.

He had a lot to prove to himself anyway after getting rocked in his rookie year and needing to recover from the ankle injury. The Angels allowed Root to stay in Middletown until the birth of Charles William Junior on February 27, 1924. Root left the next day for spring training. Della, her Mom and new brother joined her Dad in California three months later.

Root won 21 games for the Angels in 1924, struck out 199 in 322 innings, and posted a 3.69 ERA. They returned to Middletown for their last winter in Ohio.

Jacob became ill after Christmas and had been very quiet about Charlie's baseball career. Despite his gruffness, the Kaiser had a soft side for Della and his other grandchildren. Dressed in a Santa outfit, he scratched his legs, saying he was stiff from the long drive from the North Pole.

"I know I got a sewing basket and I also knew at age 5 that Santa Claus was really Grandpa Root because I recognized his shoes," Della wrote.

Jacob died just after the Christmas 1924 visit before Charlie made it to the Cubs and without showing any sign of a father's pride in his son.

In 1925, the Cubs called Charlie to spring training at Catalina but

Photo from Root Family archives

Dorothy Hartman (left), at age 19, the year she married Charlie Root. She is shown in her Red Cross volunteer uniform.

decided he needed more seasoning, and so he was returned to the Angels, where he led the Pacific Coast League again. But during the short stay he became friends with a third baseman named Clyde Beck, another rookie.

Rookies did not stay at the swank St. Catherine's Hotel but were housed at a small hotel downtown. They also did not receive the daily allowance given to regulars, so there was no way Gertrude Beck and Dorothy could partake of the grand life on Catalina, but the fellas managed to scrape enough money together to send boat fare to the girls and rent two cabins in Tent City in downtown Avalon.[82]

These were wood-framed cabins with canvas roofs, a wood stove and an electric light that hung from a rafter in the 12 x 14 foot space.

The girls knew there were no funds for eating out, so they carried cookies, boiled potatoes, oranges, cheese and crackers on the boat, and as soon as they had exchanged hugs and kisses and hugs again, the boys went fishing off the pier, Della wrote.

All they caught were mackerel, which are oily and generally used for bait. They are not the best eating fish, but the foursome always declared, it was one of the most fun weekends they ever had.

The Roots and the Becks remained the closest of friends until the last one was left in 1988.

Charlie and Clyde both played well in 1925. Marty Krug was the manager of the Angels and a good and caring friend to all his boys, as he called them. He wasn't a great deal older than either Clyde or Charlie and was a very popular manager with the team and the fans. Los Angeles was just a small town.

The Roots returned to Los Angeles in 1925 and rented a house on 54th Street. Charlie received a raise in salary, and so he bought a new car. It was a Hudson Brougham, brown, tan and handsome. Soon after the purchase, Charlie left for a northern road trip where the Angels would play Seattle, Spokane, Oakland and San Francisco.

Charlie's heels had barely cleared the door when Dorothy called the car salesman and asked him or probably told him to come teach her to drive.

After three short lessons, she decided to drive over to leave the children with a close friend. Dorothy zoomed out of the driveway and got to 54th Street, where there were double street car tracks. She got the car caught on the cowcatcher of a passing street car.

The conductor enlisted the help of some passengers to lift the car off. The accident held up traffic for a while, and as few women drove at that time, Della was sure the men that lifted the car off smirked and had

---

[82] All family details come from Della Root Arnold's personal journal and multiple interviews.

chauvinistic thoughts. If this bothered Dorothy even a little, it never showed. She got back in the car, waved to her rescuers and continued on her maiden drive.

After leaving the children, Dorothy drove the new car to San Francisco to meet her Charles.

The only route to San Francisco was over the infamous Ridge Route, which was little more than a cow path of curves, with steep canyons on both sides and no guard rails. The Ridge Route had the earnest respect of every driver who tried it. "I know Dorothy talked about it a lot. It was pretty scary. But not half as scary as when Charlie walked into the lobby of the San Francisco Hotel and saw Dorothy waiting for him."

Charlie soon found out the car was in one piece, his wife was in good shape, and she'd driven that Ridge Route just to be with him—or maybe just to show him—probably a little of both. Years later, Della would say her mother had the greatest resolve of anyone she ever knew and when Dorothy put her mind to something, she completed it, and usually in great style.

Whatever uncertainty Charlie Root had as he walked to the mound to open the 1929 season, Dorothy had no doubts. She saw him overcome the broken ankle the first time he made it to the majors and he would overcome this setback.

Dorothy set herself with the same determination found so many years ago, when the little girl started peeling potatoes after her mother's funeral.

Over the years, Della would buy her mother a variety of potato peelers, but Dorothy always reached for the butcher knife—because that's how her mom did it.

Horne's Debut

As for Horne, he took over the pitching task after Root had tottered for the second time in his two opening day performances. For six innings, Berlyn pitched marvelous ball, waiting for the stars to do something....

—Edward Burns, Chicago Tribune, April 24, 1929.

Charlie Root could not throw strikes on Opening Day and he gives up three runs in the first inning, loads the bases in the second and third innings and struggles through all seven innings he pitched.

From the press box, Ed Burns bangs out his prose about the loss, "Aroma from all the pretty floral pieces momentarily drugged Charlie Root..."

Burn's rival newspaper, *The Chicago Daily News,* uses Opening Day for some self-promotion about its new North Side presses. Exactly seventeen minutes after the last out, at 5:27 p.m., the complete box score and details of Root's 4-3 loss are rolling off the new presses. "The Blue Streak sets new sports-speed mark," the paper boasted in a full-page promo. Thousands of fans buy the earliest press runs as they leave the park from newsboys who hustled from the plant just blocks away.

After the game, in his usual routine, Root showers, dresses and finds the fresh cigar tucked in his suit jacket by a tobacco sponsor. Della waits for him at the walkway leading from the dressing room, where fans also congregate after games. Dorothy always avoids the crowd scene and goes directly to the car and waits.

"I loved to wait with everyone else," Della recounted years later. "When Dad would come out, the police would make such a fuss and walk Dad and me through the crowd. I loved it. That was something."

After the game, Root is his usual, quiet self. Della said he rarely talked about baseball when he was off the field. He says nothing about his arm.

Around the major leagues, Opening Day is rained out for the New York Yankees, but Babe Ruth still commands headlines. With an unexpected day off, Ruth slips away and gets married. His previous marriage ended in divorce. Only weeks earlier, he came from the funeral of his ex-wife, killed in a house fire.

After a rainout and a wedding day, Ruth opens the Yankee season in Ruthian fashion, with a home run in his first at-bat.

Over in the National League, Opening Day pitcher Jesse Haines starts his season for the St. Louis Cardinals by beating the Reds 3-1 and driving in the first run for the Cards with a single in the second inning.

Haines was born and raised less than a dozen miles from Horne's hometown, both in rural farming communities just northwest of Dayton, Ohio. Haines was 20-8 in 1928 when the Cards won the National League pennant. He is another competitor the Cubs must get past to win a pennant. (The Cards lost the 1928 World Series to the Yankees, swept away in four games by four homers from Gehrig and three from Ruth. All three of Ruth's came in the deciding Game Four.)

The Cubs bounce back from Root's loss, beating the Pirates in the next two games with strong pitching from starters Pat Malone and Sheriff Blake. Hornsby has a grand slam in one of the games and draws seven walks in three games.

Rainouts block the fourth game with the Pirates and the opener with St. Louis. Hornsby faces his former Cardinal teammates on April 21, goes four for four with two doubles and drives in the first two runs and scores the third. Guy Bush also stars, throwing a 4-0 shutout on three hits. The 51,000 fans set a Wrigley record for attendance by several hundred.

Even with two extra days off because of rain, McCarthy skips Root in the rotation, quite rare, giving him extra rest and no explanation to the writers. The Cubs win four straight after Root's loss and the rest of the pitching rotation has not given up a run in 26 innings. They are still not in first and won't be for the month of April. The big off-season move to get Hornsby has paid off immediately. Hornsby is hitting .583 in his first week in a Cub uniform.

Catcher Earl Grace makes his major league debut on April 23, but the Cubs lose 9-6 to the Cards and also lose Grace when his fingernail is torn off.

By the end of April, the Cubs start a road trip of four games each in Pittsburgh, Cincinnati and Philadelphia, followed by three each in Brooklyn, New York, and Boston.

Root struggles again in his second outing on April 24, and his problems allow Berly Horne to debut. Fourth-string catcher Tom Angley, the only able-bodied catcher at the moment, also gets his debut in this game.

Root again faces Pirates' spitballing ace Grimes, just as in Opening Day.

Manager Joe McCarthy opens with the same routine. "We'd have a meeting before every series with a new ball club, and he would have the pitcher and catcher tell how they were going to pitch to every batter on that team," Woody English said.

"The whole club was in on it. The meetings were all baseball. There wasn't any monkey business about it. So we would understand where we were to play the hitters. I soon learned things like how the Waner boys, left-handed batters, could run so you had to shorten up the distance a little bit. A guy like Ernie Lombardi, you could play left field and still throw him out."[83]

Horne, the old rookie still awaiting his debut, listens carefully as Root and Hartnett and the other catchers discuss each hitter in the Pirates' lineup.

During the game, Horne watches like everyone else as Root struggles again in the first inning and unravels in the third with Pittsburgh's four consecutive singles. Root, still lacking his usual pinpoint control, walks George Grantham and then gives up another single to first baseman Earl Sheely. By the time the third inning closes, Root has allowed the Pirates four runs on five hits.

---

[83] Golenbock, Peter, *Wrigleyville,* pg. 204.

The Cubs come up with their first run in the fourth when Grimm doubles and Angley singles to get his first major league hit and RBI in his second at bat.

Photo from Horne Family

In the seventh, the Cubs add two more runs when Angley opens the inning with a walk.

As Cliff Heathcote pinch-hits for Root, Horne hears the call from McCarthy to warm up. Horne is only minutes away from doing what he has rehearsed so many times before.

Heathcote hits into a forceout of Angley at second. English singles. Heathcote and English pull off a double steal and advance an extra base when the Pirates' catcher, Hargreaves, throws the ball into center field. Cuyler just misses a homer to center, but his sacrifice fly scores English. Horne is ready and watches the last out of the Cub half of the inning.

Berlyn Horne, playing for the Los Angeles Angels of the Pacific Coast League

Horne and Angley are about to make history as sports writers note this is believed to be the first battery to debut in the major leagues in the same game since the National League was founded in 1876.

Trailing 4-3, Horne gets pitcher Burleigh Grimes to ground out to Grimm at first base. Hornsby throws out Jones on a grounder and English gets Lloyd Waner on a grounder.

The Cubs tie the game in the eighth when Angley delivers his second single and second RBI. Horne has another leap of excitement when he sees that McCarthy is leaving him in to bat and won't go to a pinch hitter. In his first major league at-bat, Horne flies out to Lloyd Waner.

In the bottom of the eighth, Horne strikes out Paul Waner looking. Traynor flies out to Wilson. Grantham also strikes out. Horne is rolling now, fooling three of the best contact hitters in the game and six in a row.

In the ninth, Horne retires his seventh and eighth hitters in a row. He gives up his first hit, a two-out single by Hargreaves. Grimes strikes out and the game is headed to extra innings.

Wilson leads off the 10th with a walk. But Stephenson blows a bunt and Wilson is forced out. Grimm hits a smash that forces Stephenson at second. The ball is thrown wildly to first and Grimm makes the big turn, getting nailed when Hargreaves backs up first and tags him for a double play.

Horne seems unfazed and in a groove. In the bottom of the 10th, Jones flies out to Cuyler. Lloyd Waner singles up the middle, but Paul Waner pops out to Hornsby and Traynor grounds out to Horne.

In the bottom of the 11th, Pittsburgh gets a walk and nothing else off Horne.

Horne gets two groundouts and a pop fly to end the 12th with three up and three down.

In the 13th, Angley gets his third single of his debut but is thrown out trying to stretch it to a double.

The Cubs' failure to do anything since the eighth inning finally caught up to them.

From the seventh through the 12th innings, Horne had faced 21 hittlers, allowed two singles, a walk and no runs.

But Horne's second walk of the game, to Paul Waner leading off the 13th, would get him in trouble. Traynor successfully sacrifices Waner to second with a bunt. Horne pitches carefully to Grantham, knowing that a single will cost him the game and Grantham is the most likely hitter to deliver in this lineup. He ends up walking Grantham, in hopes of setting up a double play. But Sheely delivers the game-winning single to left.

In the hard-luck reality of baseball, Horne gives up only one of Pittsburgh's five runs, and it took 25 batters for the Pirates to finally get that. The box score will show that Horne lost, despite these totals: 6 ⅓ IP, 3 Hits, 1 Run, 3 BB, 2 K.

118

Chicago fans will see Horne's name in the headlines of Ed Burns' story the next morning:

Show Put on By Horne, Angley, Rookie Battery;
Root Yields 4 Runs in Third

Pittsburgh, Pa., April 24: Before you do too much sobbing about the Pirates beating the Cubs this afternoon, 5-4 in 13 innings, please fire a few salutes for Berlyn Horne and Tom Angley, who virtually took over the ball game after Mr. Wrigley's highest priced help had succeeded in making pretty much of a mess of the affair.

These two rookies formed what probably was the first freshman battery ever to work in a serious phase of a big league opening. And, fans, you should be proud of 'em, even in defeat.[84]

As Horne returns to his hotel room, the loss probably did nothing to spoil his day. Horne had reached the top of a journey that began in the minors in 1917, was interrupted by World War I in 1918, and curved through leagues ranging from the South Atlantic League, to Canada and Jersey City.

Like Root, Horne was on the mound as a young teen, pitching for money and dominating all of the adults.[85]

Horne summarized his life in baseball through 1924 in three simple pages of a personal diary:

I was born and raised in Bachman, Ohio, on old Rt. 40, about seven miles east of Lewisburg. Bachman was the beginning of baseball for me. They needed a pitcher so with the help of my Uncle Alex Hammel and his son, Howard "Dutch" Hammel, I was taught to pitch and how to throw the spitball. We had a good team of good ole farmer boys. We played all the good teams from Dayton and surrounding towns including Texters Lady Tourists who played three men on the team.

---

[84] *Chicago Tribune,* game-day account.
[85] Berly Horne interviews with the author in 1978, personal journal and records, information provided by family, and documents, clippings and other items researched by David Martin.

We beat them easily and they wanted me to join their team, but my folks put thumbs down on that deal. They insisted I join them and guaranteed me $5 a game. Much more than I made with the Bachman team, which was $2 a game, but my folks resisted as I was too young, 14 years old. I continued to pitch for teams in Dayton as we moved there. I pitched for a church team, Tri M's, and we won all games but one over all the amateur teams and I averaged 18 strike-outs a game and had two no-hit games.

I pitched for Edison Grade School and we beat Whittier School for the city championship. Edison turned out some fine athletes who entered Steele and Stivers High Schools, namely Howard Friegan, Lee Fenner, Buz Wharton, Mose Wright, Harry Whitacre and a colored boy who was signed by John Mathews for the Dayton Marcos, a fine, fine colored team. Then after the first year of High School, when the great, terrible Dayton flood came in March 25, 1913, we moved to Miamisburg where my dad's job took us.

I then joined the Dayton Wright Plant #3 team there where a lot of major league and ex-pro players were hired to play ball and work during the war years of 1917 and 1918.

I only pitched a few games for them against the weaker teams they played. It was a strong league during those two years and as I progressed I was recommended to pitch for Battle Creek in the Michigan-Ontario League in 1919 after the war, by Heine Groh of the Cincinnati club who played for Dayton Wright #3 team. That was my start in pro baseball. I went to Rochester from that league in 1924 who bought me; George Stallings was owner and manager, who had managed the Yankees and Boston Braves before. Then he sold the Rochester, NY, team; our bat boy there was Gabe Paul (future general manager of Cincinnati, president of the Yankees and part-owner of the Cleveland Indians).

Horne was 5 feet 9 inches tall and a skinny 155 pounds. He was such a good athlete for a little guy that he actually played more games as an outfielder in his early years in the minors because of his arm, speed and batting eye.

His pitching was good enough to get him into the Michigan-Ontario League, made up of four teams from Michigan and Canada. He pitched and played outfield for Battle Creek.

When Battle Creek dropped out of the league in 1920, Berly went to Port Huron, in the same league, and again played outfield and pitched. He had 10 triples in only 228 at bats in 1920 at Battle Creek and hit .276. But a home run was an accident or the result of a favorable wind. Two homers are the most he ever hit in a season, even when he was playing regularly as an outfielder.

In 1922, Horne pitched in 16 games and played the outfield in 73 games. He hit .287 and had 14 doubles and 11 triples in 296 at bats with Port Huron in 1922.

As baseball shifted from the deadball era to the home runs of the Roaring '20s, an outfielder without power had no chance of leaving the minor league roster.

"I got to hitting pretty good, so they put me in the outfield regularly in 1922," Berly said. "And one day I went back for a line drive hit over my head that hit the wall. I stopped real fast to get the rebound off the fence and tore the ligaments in my left ankle."

The injury ruined his chance to get into the majors with Pittsburgh. "They were about to close the deal with Pittsburgh when the injury occurred," Berly said. He was batting over .340 at the time.

Instead, Berly stayed with Port Huron until the team folded. He moved to Saginaw and then to Rochester, where he played from 1924 to 1926.

By 1928, he was clearly a pitcher, appearing on the mound in 44 of his 48 games. It was his best year in the minors. He won the league MVP award and capped off the season with three shutouts. He had a 3.01 ERA and a record of 16-17 on a last-place team that was remarkably incapable of producing runs for its pitching staff.

Having missed his chance at the majors in 1922, Horne pressed for what he saw as his last shot after his award-winning 1928 season.

Al Nickerson, sports editor for the *Boston Sunday Advertiser*, wrote in 1929 about how Horne made his path to the majors, based on a tip from future of Hall of Fame hitter Tris Speaker.

Speaker was managing the Cleveland Indians when they played an exhibition game with Rochester in 1926. Speaker got two doubles off Horne.

Rookie and veteran met in the showers after the game — *"Young fellow, shut off that shower for a minute,"* Tris said. *"I want to talk to you. You pitched some pretty good ball out there today. I think you can get somewhere in this game. You should aim at the big leagues.*

"I got two doubles off you this afternoon. How'd I get them? I could tell you were going to give me the change of pace. You didn't hide the ball. The pitch was an open book."

Then, for 15 minutes, Speaker shows Berly how to hide the ball before making the pitch. All this cost Speaker nothing but his time. This year it may mean $6,000 or so Series' money to Horne.

Of all his minor league experiences, Horne's favorite story was about pitching to Babe Ruth for the first time in an exhibition game when Horne was with Jersey City and Ruth was with the Yankees.

He got the Babe to pop up the first time and was pretty excited with himself. But in a later at bat, Ruth drilled a line drive up the middle so hard that Horne thought it would take his hat (and head) all the way to the center field fence, where paint chips went flying.

While in Jersey City, Horne discovered a restaurant where Ruth was a regular.

"I used to go up Hudson Boulevard to Dick's Inn, a great eating place with great steaks," Berly said. "The Babe used to come over there and he used to call me 'boy' whenever he saw me."

On one visit, Ruth called him over for a drink. "It was during Prohibition. But Dick always had a bottle for the Babe and a private room.

"A friend of mine, another ballplayer, and I were in there one night eating and we looked in there and Babe said, 'Hey, little boy, come here. You gotta have a little nip with me or you don't eat tonight.' I said, 'I'll be right there, Babe.'" [86]

He learned from a *Dayton Daily News* sports editor that Chicago had acquired him for $20,000. "He said, 'You've been sold to Chicago and I would like for you to come down and get a picture of you. I want to run a story on you.'"

---

[86] Terry Baver, sports editor of *Franklin (Ohio) Chronicle,* interviewed Berly Horne when he was age 83, published Aug. 5, 1980.

The picture that Chicago papers staged was more comical. William Wrigley Jr. hovers over a steamer trunk as his latest delivery, Horne, climbs out.

The Cubs will pay Berly $6,000 for the 1929 regular season, the best salary he will earn in his baseball career.

A rainout on April 25 gives the players more time to gripe about how they didn't pull the game out for Horne, Burns reports.

"It was the biggest collapse of prima donnas and may give them perspective since their start was a little too good to be true," Burns wrote, adding that Wilson and Hornsby had no hits in a combined nine at bats.

McCarthy and Hartnett confirm an early morning trip to Youngstown to see "Bonesetter" Reese. Burns writes, *McCarthy, as the strong man, aided the famous doc by pulling on Gabby's right elbow until something snapped. The doctor said Hartnett would be back to work immediately. Gabby kept the trip secret until tonight, thinking the improvements were too good to be true. But after dinner, Gabby could keep quiet no longer.*

Burns says Hartnett backup Gonzales has recovered from his hand injury and is ready to return.

Catcher John Schulte, acquired two days earlier, arrives April 26 from Columbus and gets in immediately, sparking a five-run rally in the third with a single and driving in the Cubs' sixth run with another single in the fifth. The Cubs win 9-6. Hornsby breaks an 0-for-14 stint with a bases-loaded triple.

On April 27, the Cubs finish their Pittsburgh visit at Forbes Field, winning ugly, 8-7, when Hornsby blows an easy double play in the ninth and the Pirates riot with three runs. Pat Malone was breezing to an apparent 8-4 win but Blake was the victim of Hornsby's misplay. Schulte caught for a second straight game and had two doubles and two RBIs. Cuyler, Stephenson, Hornsby and Wilson all had multi-hit games.

On April 28, the Cubs travel to Cincinnati's Crosley Field, and Horne gets his second chance. Footsie Blair makes his major league debut, but Horne doesn't pitch anything like his debut four days earlier. During the game, Schulte becomes the third injured catcher in the first month of the season.

The Cubs are leading 6-2 in the bottom of the third when a struggling Hal Carlson yields a leadoff triple to Chuck Dressen. McCarthy makes the rare move of immediately going to the bullpen to see if Horne can perform another long relief miracle.

"This travesty of a game was about to enter its second circus act," Burns writes. "Horne should have been out of the inning, and the infield should have gotten the loss."

With Dressen on third, Horne walks Ford to set up a possible double play. Gooch grounds to Beck and Beck sees the chance to nail Dressen as he tries to score. Beck throws to Schulte and Dressen stops and tries to get back to third. Horne cuts him off and tags him out in the rundown. Ford moves to second, Gooch is on first, but now there's one out.

Kolp taps back to the mound and Horne whirls to nail the lead runner again, but nobody covers third. Horne spins to throw to first and nobody is covering there either. Now the bases are loaded with one out.

It gets worse. Zitzmann grounds to Beck, who throws home for the force, but Schulte is off the plate and as Ford scores and spikes Schulte, who is carried from the field. Plump rookie Angley is back.

Horne should have been out of the inning with no runs. Instead, he now gives up a single that scores a run, a sacrifice that scores another run, a walk to load the bases, a walk to force in a run and a two-run double. Then Jonnard comes in to relieve and gets a groundout to English. Six runs score in the inning, when Horne should have been out undamaged. It's now 12-2 Reds.

The Cubs add a run and then try to redeem themselves in the fifth, scoring eight runs and making it 12-11.

But the Reds come back in their half of the fifth, scoring four more runs by hammering Art Nehf with six singles. The Cubs lose 17-12. Hack Wilson hits two homers and two-run single and has five RBI.

On Monday, April 29, Root finally gets his first win, 4-3, against the Reds. He spends the weekend in Middletown with Dorothy and family. The Reds make him "go through fire and brimstone" but he strikes out eight, three in major jams, hits a triple and drives in the winning run, Burns reports.

Sheriff Blake ends the month of April with a loss to the Reds, 5-4. The Reds are leading 1-0 in the eighth when Hornsby hits a towering home run into the right field stands. Wilson follows with a triple and scores on a Stephenson single to put the Cubs ahead 2-1. The Reds regain the lead in the bottom of the eighth, when an English relay throw to the catcher lands in the seats instead. The Cubs come back in the ninth when Beck walks and Wilson doubles him in. Stephenson is walked intentionally, and Grimm doubles Wilson in. The Cubs lead 4-3, but the Reds scored two to win in their half of the ninth.

The Cubs finish April, with a record of 7-5, tied for second with the Cardinals, both trailing first-place Boston.

On May 1, the final game with Cincinnati ends in a 13-inning tie, 4-4, so the Cubs can catch their train in time to reach Philadelphia. Bush pitches 11 innings. Root relieves and pitches out of bases-loaded jams without giving up a run in the 12th and 13th. Wilson hits his fourth homer of the season, tying him for first in all of baseball with Jimmie Foxx and Al Simmons of the Athletics.

The Cubs get a three-day break in Philadelphia, but Burns has a lot to write about off the field.

For the first time, he reports that Hartnett may be out for season. *Bonesetter Reese's alleged miracle straightened out one kink but others set in and are continuing with such persistence that fear grows that the great backstop may be out for the season, if not for all time.*

Team morale is low after blowing these late-inning games and with the news about Hartnett, Burns writes. Gonzales, Angley and Grace are all suffering. Schulte is also hurt.[87]

What Root will remember about Schulte this season, however, is an incident at the Commodore Hotel while waiting on a New York game.

---

[87] All game-day accounts are from the *Chicago Tribune.*

Root hears cussing and yelling in the hallway. He opens the door and sees Schulte leaning back in a chair with his feet propped on the ledge at an open window.

Schulte is yelling at construction workers to hurry up and work faster. He tells one that everyone else is working twice as fast as he is.

"What in the world are you doing?" Root asks Schulte.

"These are the same guys that yell at me all the time when I'm working," Schulte replies.[88]

There's not a lot of joking going on now, however.

Hartnett's bubbly, talkative demeanor is replaced with an "attitude of panic and discouragement hanging over the man," Burn writes. "Manager McCarthy has gone along with the star in all the experiments recommended by various specialists, but now he's obliged to watchful waiting."

Hartnett came to the Cubs in 1922 after a year with Worcester in the Eastern league. His seven years on the Cubs make him the veteran. At $18,000 a year, he is one of the highest priced catchers in the history of baseball, Burns says. His .302 average last year was one of the best among major league catchers.

The impact of losing Hartnett adds to McCarthy's concerns about sloppy defense and poor hitting by English and Beck, who are not getting on base ahead of murderers' row, Burns reports.

Unspoken, but obvious, is that Root is nothing like his previous form. All the stories focus on Hartnett's arm, but Trainer Andy Lotshaw is more troubled by Root's.

---

[88] Author's interview with Della Root Arnold.

Roots

Nearly all of the rookies lived at Swanville Apartments and they seemed to gather at the Roots with great regularity for potlucks and sing-alongs. Dorothy would play the piano and Charlie Grimm played the banjo, left-handed, which is quite a feat, I understand.
—Della Root Arnold.

On May 4, the Cubs scored 25 runs in a doubleheader. Pat Malone opens in Philadelphia with his second shutout and fourth straight win in less than a month, clearly surpassing Root as the new ace on the team. The Cubs win the first game 16-0. In the second game, Root is roughed up again but endures when the Cubs complete their offensive show, winning 9-7.

Riggs "Stevie" Stephenson finishes the day with two singles, a double, a triple, two walks, and a sacrifice. Grace's first major league hit in game two is a three-run homer. Hornsby's fourth homer of the season ties him with Hack Wilson for the major league lead.

The Cubs are batting .332, are 9-5, tied for second with the Cards and trail Boston by two games. Despite the team batting average, English and Beck are not getting the job done at the top of the lineup. Together they had only one hit in the doubleheader; pitcher Malone had three hits at the plate in his lone game.

Stephenson is hitting .465, Cuyler .375, Hornsby .372, Wilson .319 and Grimm .317.

May 5, Sunday: Philadelphia remains one of the largest cities in America that still enforces Sabbath Day laws. No baseball is played and movie theaters are closed. [89]

---

[89] All game accounts are from same-day stories in the *Chicago Tribune.*

May 6: As play resumes in Philadelphia on Monday, English throws the ball into the dugout and the Cubs lose 2-1. Blake allows the only run, on four hits, and gets his third tough loss against one win. Hornsby avoids getting thrown out in an argument with the ump about catcher's interference.

May 7: Art Nehf launches his 15th season as a pitcher with a complete game win against the Brooklyn Robins at Ebbets Field, 9-4. Grimm's two homers in the game now tie him with Wilson and Hornsby with four, at the top of baseball. English, only 1 for 27, strikes out with the bases loaded in the second inning.

May 8: The Cubs win 4-2 over Brooklyn and move into first place for the first time this season. Hartnett is back with the team after a visit to the clinic at Johns Hopkins. Doctors could find nothing wrong with his arm, but they did with his tonsils, saying they will need to be removed. Cubs President William Veeck accompanied Gabby to Brooklyn from the Baltimore hospital.

May 9: Malone wins again, his fifth, finishing a sweep in Brooklyn. Wilson hits his fifth homer. Cuyler gets on base five times with two doubles, a single, a walk, and due to an error. He also has a sacrifice RBI. Stephenson walks three times and is hit by a pitch.

William Wrigley Jr. and Veeck travel to Brooklyn to see Hartnett's workout as prescribed by Dr. Dean Lewis of Baltimore. Hartnett throws around the bases and then is checked at night to see how stiff he is.

May 10: Facing the Giants at the Polo Grounds, the Cubs win 11-4 with Root and Cvengros. Root didn't need his arm for this game, driving in four of the runs himself with a three-run homer in the fifth and an RBI single. Cuyler added an inside-the-park home run.

Wilson makes one of the most sensational catches of his career. Mel Ott hit a drive to the deepest part of center field and somehow Wilson catches up with the ball after a long run.

May 11: The Cubs lose 6-0 in a two-hitter. The loss drops them to a first-place tie with St. Louis at 13-7. Blake gives up only two runs through eight innings, but Carlson gives up four more in relief.

May 12: A Sunday rainout ends in a 6-6 tie in 11 innings with 55,000 at the Polo Grounds this afternoon. For five innings, Art Nehf holds his former teammates to one hit, Ott's homer in the second. Cuyler and Wilson homer; Wilson leads the NL with six. Gonzales catches for the first time on the road trip. Hartnett, who stays to see the game before heading back to Chicago for tonsil surgery, hits a pinch-hit, three-run homer in the seventh.

The Cubs failed to score with the bases load in the 10th. The tie puts St. Louis a half-game ahead of the Cubs.

Wilson was brought to the train station in a wheelchair after injuring his ankle sliding into second in the eighth inning when he doubled in the tying run. Wilson said he expected to be out for several days, but Lotshaw said he'd be ready tomorrow afternoon. Cuyler left the game with a pulled muscle but is expected back tomorrow.

May 13: In the opener of the last series of the long road trip, the Cubs regain first, beating the Boston Braves, 6-4, with Root to the rescue. The Cubs open with two runs, but Jonnard gives up four in the bottom of the first. Root comes in with two outs in the first and shuts the Braves down for the rest of the game. It is his first good outing of the season, but his location on pitches and not his arm makes the difference. Wilson and Cuyler are unable to play due to injuries. A whole lineup of subs plays like the stars. English loses his leadoff role for the first time this season and he answers with four hits, including a double, from the No. 2 spot. McMillan leads off. Heathcote replaces Cuyler and bats third, makes a sensational one-handed catch in the third, walks twice and scores a run. Johnny Moore replaces Wilson, bats sixth, doubles in the first inning with the bases full and singles in Hornsby in the third, for three of the six runs. Hartnett gets his tonsil operation at the Masonic Hospital in Chicago.

May 14: Malone gets his first loss, 6-5, to the Boston Braves in 12 innings. The Cubs are tied again with St. Louis for first. The team is 10-6-2 on this road trip.

May 15: The Cubs win 7-4 even though Burns writes that Bush was "as wild as a gin-drinking sophomore." Cuyler returns to the lineup with a homer, but Wilson is still out with his injury. Stephenson gets three hits, including a double. Heathcote adds another two hits, subbing for Wilson. English returns to leadoff and gets two hits. A slumping Hornsby is struggling to hit .300 after starting the month at .372.

Despite sloppy fielding, injuries, and inconsistent pitching, the Cubs have survived the long road trip and are tied for first with St. Louis at 15-8.

Root and several other players look forward to home cooking and their usual ritual after a long road trip, back at the Swanville Apartments.

The apartments are small, crowded and nothing special. But they are almost walking distance from Wrigley Field and affordable, so this was the den of several Cubs.

The Roots live on the second floor, in a small apartment where the living room and dining room double as bedrooms. A bed pulls down from the wall for Charlie and Dorothy in the living room. Junior and Della sleep on a trundle bed in the dining room, where there is a drop leaf table, four chairs and an old buffet.

In the kitchen, the stove stands on four legs with an oven on the right side. Near the stove is an ice box made of wood with a door in the top that covers a large cavity where the ice man would put a 25-pound block of ice about twice a week. As the ice melts, water leaks to a pan underneath that is emptied every day.

Despite the small space, this is the gathering place for many of the Cubs. There was even room for Dorothy's piano, an upright one that she rented for $2 a month. She received two piano lessons and learned all the rest on her own, banging out "Bye, Bye Blackbird," "Dream Train," and several hymns that she loved.

Charlie Grimm would join her on banjo, and Cliff Heathcote played the spoons.

During private, family times, Junior also loved to join his mother when she played. He couldn't resist the urge to play a note himself, and Dorothy would sweep through a song, smack his hand and go right on without missing a note.

After long road trips, this was the most popular destination. The players' wives would prepare special potluck meals and head to the Roots' apartment.

The young players, especially the rookies, gathered here because they were so warmly welcomed and probably a little homesick. Charlie and Dorothy had the maturity of parents, but they were especially sensitive to how poorly they were treated coming up through the baseball ranks.

Cliff Heathcote and Riggs Stephenson are such unlikely roommates, although both are single at the time. Heathcote was constantly pulling pranks and teasing Stephenson, a gentle, southern gentleman. Heathcote loved poking at how far Stevie's hometown of Akron, Alabama was from civilization.

"You go as far as you can by train, then as far as you can by car, then as far as you can by mule, where you grab a grapevine and swing on in," Heathcote said.

Stephenson was horrified during one meal when Heathcote blurted out, "You know, Dorothy, the other night Stevie said to me that you weren't fit to eat with the pigs, but I stuck up for you and I said, 'Of course she is.'"

"Miz Root, I nevah sayed anything of the kind evah, and Mr. Heathcote, I shall speak to you in our room," Stephenson said.

Heathcote's humor masks a tragedy only a few years earlier when he lost his wife and daughter during childbirth. His life now revolves around this closely bonded team.

Laughter, music, and great meals made the Root apartment a favorite hangout.

This apartment is where the players and their wives learned to dance. "The girls would stand in the doorway, hold onto the jamb and practice their steps while the windup portable record player boomed out the Charleston," Della said. "It was a sight to see, but, being young and confident, they soon ventured out in public."

One of those public spots for them is a North Side speakeasy owned by Al Capone, where the dance floor was covered with thick glass inlaid with silver dollars.[90]

---

[90] All personal stories about the Roots and the players off the field are from author's interviews with Della Root Arnold.

131

All the wives were good cooks, with the exception of Gertrude Beck, who made up for her lack of skill by always helping with cleanup. From these friendships, Dorothy expanded her own menu from her Ohio days of meat, potatoes and pie, and often added pasta and other new specialties.

Also within a few blocks of Wrigley Field, just north of the stadium on Sheffield Avenue, is the Carliss Hotel, where many of the other players live. Dorothy calls it the "Careless Hotel" because of what goes on among single players—and married players who act as though they're still single.

Dorothy traveled with Charlie as much as she could, enjoying the cities, the museums and especially shopping for antiques. Most players did not want their wives with them, and there was a lot of temptation as young women flocked after the players, trying to convince them to go home with them after the game.

The Roaring '20s were lose times, with hemlines getting shorter and women beginning to test their freedoms. They finally had the right to vote, and smoking seemed to be the second way to show rebellion. Drinks flowed just as freely during Prohibition as they had before.

A couple of these "liberated" women would sit behind the dugout, making sure their skirts rode up enough to make it quite obvious that they weren't wearing anything underneath. Marge Blake, wife of Sheriff Blake, had seen a lot as a former New York showgirl and offered the players' wives her own harsh observation.

"They must not be much if they have to advertise like that," she said.[91]

Dorothy traveled with the Cubs more than any of the other players' wives. She wanted to be with Charlie anyway, and he was faithful to her, but there was just so much temptation thrown in the players' paths. They made such good money and were young and athletic. Plus they were beloved celebrities in the second largest city in America.

Charlie was amused by the attention and loved to rub it in. While walking down State Street after a show, two women recognized Charlie and were giddy and giggly as they passed by on the sidewalk.

---

[91] Della's personal journal, pg. 48.

Photo from Della Root Arnold

Dorothy and Charlie Root dancing in the
Casino Ballroom at Avalon.

"I just cripple the women with my good looks," Charlie told Della.

Idle time, the players' friendship and humor were also ingredients for practical jokes.

New York was Charlie's favorite spot because it had so many novelty stores to support his pranks. Returning from one road trip, he extended a long rubber tube under the tablecloth all the way to Dorothy's plate. On his end of the tube was a bladder that pumped air through the tube, making Dorothy's plate fly up in the air.

He brought Dorothy an attractive jar of cold cream. When she unscrewed the lid, fake snakes jumped out.

But Dorothy was not always the victim. At the Commodore Hotel in New York, she convinced Guy Bush to look through a kaleidoscope that she bought at a trick shop. The inner rim was lined with ink and left two black eyes as she convinced him to look through the glass with both eyes.

She didn't say a word. Bush went to the drugstore counter for a cup of coffee and saw himself in the mirror.

Bush, at first, thought he was sick and wondered if he was dying.

Woody English was just a kid on the team, but he was like "Peck's bad boy" in the grade school books of the day. He looked innocent but wasn't. English's favorite prank was to crawl across the floor of a hotel lobby and sneak up on an unsuspecting businessman reading the newspaper. English would light the bottom of the paper and slip away as the newspaper caught fire.[92]

The time that the players and their spouses spent together created friendships that they knew could be disrupted quickly by injury or a trade.

They lived their great life to the fullest, at Catalina Island, at the Swanville Apartments, and on the road.

---

[92] Ibid., pg. 105.

Pennant Race (May-June)

"Charlie now appears to have regained his 1927 form, only more so. The athletes around the circuit have been whispering for two weeks that his fast one is jumping again. And if it keeps jumping, just have the boys polish the tarnish off those trumpets. Even the direst Cub critics admit they can hear the pennant flappings whenever they think of Root."

—Edward Burns, *Chicago Tribune*, May 18, 1929.

Cub trainer Andy Lotshaw, the big, old Swede, never made it past second grade, but he is the doctor to everyone in the clubhouse.

"Doc" Lotshaw also never made it beyond the minors as a player, but he is closer to these major leaguers than if he had been in the lineup.

He was in the middle of their stories and their pranks and he was welcomed at the pinochle table, usually relieved of his coins by Charlie Root and first base coach Jimmy Burke during the long train rides. They never played high stakes because Manager Joe McCarthy didn't want any hard feelings popping up among any of the losers.

Lotshaw fixed the mangled arms and legs of the players, but he had no cure for the way he mangled the English language.

After the Cubs were briefly knocked out of first, Lotshaw said their losing ways put them on the "brink of an abscess" (instead of abyss).[93]

During a radio interview, Lotshaw mentioned that he was a trainer for the Chicago Bears football team in the winter and the Cubs in the summer. When asked what the difference was, Lotshaw said that a Cub who gets a "strawberry" on his arm from sliding into second base is out

---

[93] Della Root Arnold journal, pg. 34-35.

for a few days. When a Bear does the same thing, you rub him, tape him and put him back in the game.

"They're back out there, fighting like they always did for their old 'alma gator,'" Lotshaw explained.

Lotshaw said a persistent ailment was a "chronicle" condition. When asked whether he believed in God, Lotshaw replied, "What do you think I am—an amethyst?" [94]

When a pitcher knew one thing and did another, Lotshaw said this was "the color of another horse" instead of "a horse of a different color." [95]

Lotshaw won special recognition for a body rub that he concocted and that was sold for a time to all of Chicago.

Charlie convinced Lotshaw to come out of the dugout and join him during a radio interview to advertise the new body rub. Lotshaw announced to listeners that his body rub was good for "women's chests and skin abortions."

The players teased Lotshaw by putting the body rub on their shoes and faking their own advertisements about how well it worked as polish.

Pitcher Hal Carlson never believed much in the patented body rub, especially since his aches and pains were so unique that no common formula would work. [96]

Carlson was one of those characters whose arm never seemed to hurt until he was called to pitch. It's almost like he was trying to lower everyone's expectations before a game so they would be pleasantly surprised when he actually performed. He had every reason to ache, though, because he was going to be 37 in May.

Warren Brown reported a Lotshaw secret that few knew until Brown published his history of the Cubs in 1946.

---

[94] Brown, Warren, *The Chicago Cubs*, pg. 129, originally published by Putnam one year after the Cubs played in the 1945 World Series. It was released again in 2001 by Southern Illinois University Press. Brown was elected to the writer's wing of the Hall of Fame in 1974 when he was 80. He died four years later.

[95] Ibid., pg. 215.

[96] Ibid., pg. 102.

Brown was a sportswriter who had played the game. He started in the Pacific Coast League as a hard-hitting first baseman in 1914 but moved to newspapers in 1916. The move assured a much longer career. He wrote for Chicago newspapers for five decades, covering the Cubs for the *Herald-Examiner* and its successor, the *American.*

Brown wrote that Carlson had one eccentricity that Lotshaw discovered as the trainer.

> Whenever it was Carlson's turn to pitch, he would begin to complain of soreness in his arm. It wasn't that he was trying to avoid duty—far from it, for he was of the work-horse type. He just craved the services of the trainer and the rubbing table.
>
> One day, the Cubs were in the midst of a double-header and Carlson hadn't figured in McCarthy's original pitching plans. In between games, McCarthy decided to switch to Carlson, who at once sought out trainer Lotshaw and asked for a quick rub to see if it would take out the soreness which had developed in his arm.
>
> Lotshaw had just started on a bottle of Coca Cola when the call came from Carlson, who had planted himself on the rubbing table, stripped to the waist. Lotshaw took a swig of the Coca Cola and approached the table carrying the bottle in his hand.
>
> "Hal," he said, "I ain't seeming to get no place with the regular rub I been giving you. Today I got some new stuff I want to try. I hear it's mighty good."
>
> "Try anything," said Carlson, "but hurry. I have to pitch the next game."
>
> So, dousing the pitcher's arm and shoulder generously with the rest of the Coca Cola, Lotshaw proceeded to give Carlson a regulation rub, and sent him on his way. Carlson pitched and won his game. He was never better.
>
> For the rest of his stay with the Cubs, until his untimely death in 1930, Carlson would have no other rub save that new stuff "Doc" Lotshaw had tried on him—but he never did find out that it was Coca Cola, that being one of the few secrets Doc Lotshaw ever kept for long.[97]

---

[97] Ibid., pg. 102-103.

Chicago Daily News — Chicago History Museum s069663

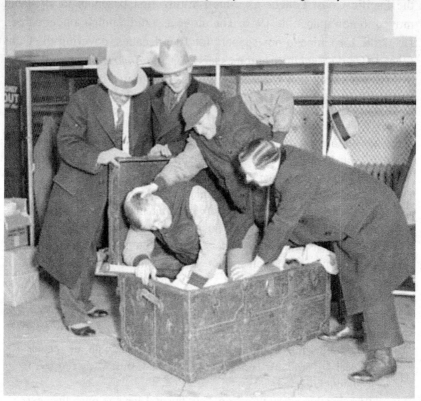

Blake, Bush, Heathcote, and Cubs secretary Bob Lewis
pack trainer Andy Lotshaw for travel.

Although the 1929 season was just under way, Lotshaw was facing all kinds of challenges in the clubhouse. Every one of the catchers had suffered some sort of injury, with Hartnett's being the most severe. Wilson had sprained his ankle.

And Charlie's arm just wasn't right.

Coming out of spring training in 1929, "Dad's arm was crooked and he couldn't straighten it," Della wrote.

Lotshaw kept rubbing and massaging and working on it before and after games. The problems continued and Della, Dorothy and Junior were helping with the arm massages as the 1929 season approached.

Sportswriters were hinting about problems through spring training, Opening Day and his few starts after that, noting that Root didn't have the old zip on his fastball.

Before his start on May 18, Root is getting a rough massage from the powerful Lotshaw, who had never been pinned in many friendly wrestling challenges that came from these younger, well-conditioned players.

As Lotshaw pushes and rubs, harder and harder, he notices something very odd at the elbow of Charlie's pitching arm. A tendon or muscle, or something, seems completely out of place, rolled over on the wrong part of the elbow. Lotshaw firmly works it until the entire strand rolls back where Lotshaw thought it should be.

He isn't sure what he has done.[98]

But Ed Burns spots the big change and writes about it in the hours after Root walks off the mound on May 18.

On the same day that Clyde Van Dusen wins the Kentucky Derby and dominates the Sunday *Tribune* in photos and stories, the bold headline stripped across the top of the sports section is about Root's 7-0 shutout of the Cincinnati Reds at Wrigley.

Burns' excitement is obvious. After leading his story with the score, his next words are that Root is back to his 1927 form: "Polish the tarnish off those trumpets" and prepare for a pennant race because "the fast one is jumping again."

Root wins without any offensive support from the heart of the lineup when Hornsby, Wilson and Stephenson go hitless. Cuyler's four singles and McMillan's double and two singles make up for the sleeping bats of the Cubs' "murderers' row."

The Cubs scored four runs in the fourth, including Root who got on base with a walk. That was more than enough cushion.

---

[98] Della Root Arnold, author's interview.

Somehow Root has won five games since the Opening Day pounding, even when he didn't have his arm or his stuff, and he is tied with Pat Malone at 5-1 for tops on the Cubs.

Root's shutout puts the Cubs firmly in first place as two consecutive wins trump the two consecutive losses of the St. Louis Cardinals. The Cubs are 1½ games ahead now.

Even better, the Cubs make their move by victimizing the Reds, a team that rivals them for bench jockeying, heckling and fights.

Before the season even started, Reds manager Jack Hendricks mocked the Cubs, calling "the Wrigley athletes an awkward coterie of overrated clowns." The Cubs kept talking about this during their travels and wanted to get even. Root's shutout really fueled that.

The celebration doesn't last long, however. Pittsburgh comes to town and the dreaded Burleigh Grimes beats the Cubs 4-1—his third straight win over the Cubs in three matchups. The Cubs have lost only nine games for the season, and Grimes is personally responsible for three of them.

Bush comes back with a five-hitter on May 20 and the Cubs beat Pittsburgh 6-1. Stephenson hit a bases-loaded triple in the game and Bush is now 4-0.

On May 21, Berly Horne pitches in his third game, this time relieving during the fifth when the Cubs are losing to the Pirates 6-2. Cvengros is having such a rough time that he balks in a run when his cap slips over his eyes during his windup and he wavers with his delivery. When Cvengros follows with a single, Horne comes in.

Horne gets things going with a single in the bottom of the fifth and hustles to third when McMillan singles to right. Horne scores when English is forced out and then Hornsby hits a two-run homer, making it 6-5 with the Cubs still trailing.

Horne gets the win when the Cubs score two more runs in the sixth, including an RBI for Beck when he pinch-hit for Horne.

Who seals Horne's first major league win? Root, on two days rest, throws the final three innings of shutout ball.

On May 23, the pennant race moves to St. Louis, where the three games will decide a leader. St. Louis, the defending National League champions, trail the Cubs by a half-game.

Hornsby always gears up for battles against his former teammates, and Joe McCarthy had his best rotation ready with Blake, Malone and Root.

The Cards win on Thursday, May 23, when Wilson blows a play in center field that turns into a two-base error and rattles Blake. Wilson immediately redeems himself with a brilliant throw to third to nail the runner, but the Cards regain first by a half-game with their 6-3 win.

On Friday, the Cubs pull the game out in the eighth when Hornsby, Wilson and Grimm hit consecutive doubles for three runs sealing a 5-4 victory.

On Saturday, St. Louis takes the series and the National League lead 7-6 by scoring in the bottom of the ninth and the 12th innings. Root is winning the game in the ninth, but McCarthy lifts him after he opens the ninth by walking Frisch. Cvengros loads the bases and Horne comes in with nobody out. Horne gets out of the jam with only one run scoring, charged to Cvengros, and the game heads to extra innings. Nehf finishes the game and loses in the 12th.

The Cubs beat the Reds 5-1 on May 26 as Bush remains perfect, at 5-0. Hornsby homers and singles, Stephenson doubles and triples, and Wilson doubles and triples. The win puts the Cubs back in first.

On May 27, the Cubs blow a 4-2 lead in the eighth inning when Sheriff Blake unravels by allowing a single, two doubles and another single before McCarthy can get Root warm to come in as a reliever. The Reds win 8-5, and now Pittsburgh is chasing the Cubs and pulls to within a half-game. Blake has now lost six of the Cubs' 12 games this season.

On the same day, headlines and photos proclaim Charles A. Lindbergh marries Anne Morrow, daughter of the American ambassador to Mexico.

A disastrous road trip to Pittsburgh tumbles the Cubs out of first and all the way down to third place. Once again, Burleigh Grimes wins, with a shutout. Root matches him with a shutout until the ninth, when he runs out of gas and is hurt by errors behind him. All four runs score for the Pirates in their 4-0 win and Pittsburgh moves to first, ahead of the Cards and Cubs.

June continues with a three-way pennant race between these historic rivals and each team has the balance of hitting and pitching to win it all. The Cubs don't return to first until June 19, when their record stands at 32-20. Horne relieves in six games, but gets no decisions. He is inconsistent, allowing no hits or runs in four of his appearances and getting shelled in the other two.

As July 4 approaches, Hack Wilson will ignite the Cubs with fireworks of his own against the hated Reds.

Zee-nut candy baseball card

Charlie Root,
(1924) pitching for the
Los Angeles Angels of
the Pacific Coast League.

Zee-nut baseball card. [99]

---

[99] Zee-nut was produced by the Collins-McCarthy Candy Company of San Francisco and consisted of a mixture of popcorn, coconut, peanuts, and honey—similar to a large granola bar. Zee-nut baseball cards featured only the players of the Pacific Coast League.

Hacking (July-August)

He didn't talk much, but he liked to laugh. No matter if a joke didn't have a point to it, Hack would respond and his face would glow as red as a tomato. He slicked back his blond hair. He was short and chubby, and he perspired even in the clubhouse before a game. He was real good with kids...He never pushed away a lad who wanted an autograph.

—Charlie Grimm, in his autobiography, *Jolly Cholly*,
about center fielder Hack Wilson.

Hack Wilson was built like a whiskey barrel and often contained the same ingredients.

His stout build and drinking habits started early and were directly connected to a rough start in life.

From the very beginning, nobody wanted Wilson. His first jobs were the most hellish of their time.

Drinking destroyed him and shortened his baseball career, but briefly with the Cubs, he was the right-handed version of Babe Ruth in raw home run power.

Yet players marveled more at his deceiving speed, spectacular plays and ability as a center fielder for such a bulky and muscular little guy.

Wilson's biggest break in baseball came because minor league manager Joe McCarthy saw something in this troubled kid that others had ignored. More importantly, McCarthy would depend on Wilson and put his faith in him as no one before. That connection enabled both of them to make baseball history.

Lewis Robert (Hack) Wilson was born in Elwood City, Pa., on April 26, 1900, to 16-year-old, unmarried Jennie Kauhn. His father,

Robert Wilson, abandoned both of them, thinking Jennie was trash that he could just discard.[100]

Hack's mom and dad didn't want him, and both were heavy drinkers. He was an illegitimate baby, the worst stigma of that day.

Photo courtesy of Louisville Slugger Museum Archives

Hack Wilson selects his Louisville Slugger, "Big Bertha"

His mom died when Hack was 7, of a burst appendix. His father wasn't going to raise a 7-year-old boy. Instead, Hack was watched over by a grandmother and then, as a teen, by the landlady of a boardinghouse.

---

[100] Parker, Clifton Blue, *Fouled Away: The Baseball Tragedy of Hack Wilson*, pg. 7-12. This powerful biography captures the heart and soul of the tragically troubled star. It is the most important source for this chapter.

Elwood City was a factory town of steel and textile mills. The dust, noise, and inferno of molten steel made the work hellish, and Wilson and most of the other workers eased their daily grind with booze.

Wilson's other jobs were just as punishing, but that's where he built his incredible upper body strength for his future in baseball.

He carried lead type at a print shop—the official job title was "devil" because of how punishing the work was. Then he worked at a locomotive foundry, swinging a sledgehammer and driving hot rivets into metal over and over again.

His first "pro" baseball was played at the Viscose Silk Mill where he assembled boxes. But he really was hired because of his baseball ability, back when companies fielded the best teams in communities and were serious about their competition.

Others at the mill earned $60 a week. Hack made $120 a week during the baseball season. Witnesses of his early baseball described in awe his line drives that looked playable in the infield and somehow continued over the fence. No one ever saw a ball hit that hard.

In the spring of 1921, Hack reported to his first professional baseball tryout with the Martinsburg, West. Virginia., Blue Sox, a team in the Blue Ridge League.

They were looking for a catcher, Hack's position. Only a year earlier, the team had an obvious star pitcher, Robert Moses "Lefty" Grove. Grove was with the minor league Baltimore Orioles in the International League when Wilson arrived. Connie Mack was part owner of Hack's team.

Nothing in Hack's life was going to be easy. In his debut, he tagged up from third on a flyout and broke his right leg sliding into home. He was out eight weeks, but he fought his way back too quickly and he couldn't catch because of continuing problems with his leg.

Hack only played 30 games because of the injury but hit .356, 5 home runs and 17 RBI in 101 at bats.

He really wanted to play for the Pirates, but they passed because of his injury. That winter, Hack put labels on socks for 20 cents an hour at the mill.

In 1922, Hack played center field for Martinsburg. His 21st home run at mid-season broke all the league records. He finished with 30, hit .366 and carried his team to the pennant and championship.

In 1923, Hack married the hospital nurse who cared for him and his broken leg. Virginia knew the softness under his rough exterior. Hack was hitting .388 with 19 homers and 101 RBIs when John McGraw of the New York Giants brought him to the majors.

McGraw used him in only three games and really wanted the pitcher who came in the deal. McGraw dismissed Wilson, saying, "He ain't got no neck." [101]

Hack played so little that he wasn't eligible for the World Series when the Yankees beat the Giants. But Hack got to meet Babe Ruth for the first time.

In March 1924, Hack went to the Giants' spring training camp at Sarasota, Florida. Baseball writers noticed Hack for his hard-charging play, remarkable ability to cover center field with such stumpy legs and for always having the dirtiest uniform.

He finally got to play more than 100 games in 1924, finishing at .295 with 10 homers and 57 RBIs.

His defense made headlines, including one dive where he caught the ball with his bare hand and incredible hustle on a towering, wind-swept popup—on the pitcher's mound.

Hack played his first World Series in 1924, when the Giants faced Walter Johnson and the Washington Senators. Hack had seven hits in the seven games, including three RBIs.

In the fourth inning of Game 7, he made full contact with the wall, falling head first into the stands, failing to make an amazing catch. Reporter Grantland Rice said the impact sounded like "a barrel of crockery being pushed down the cellar stairs."

Hack was dazed by the crash, and bleacher fans actually helped him to his feet. Just as soon as he recovered and play resumed, Sam Rice smashed a ball to left and Hack made a headlong dive for the

---

[101] Ibid., pg. 23.

sinking liner, catching the ball just inches from the turf and sliding six feet on his stomach.[102]

The 1924 pennant was McGraw's last as a manager and the last for the Giants in the 1920s. Hack and Virginia went home to Martinsburg that winter.

In 1925, Virginia was pregnant and Hack started hot in spring training and early in the season. Then he couldn't hit the curve. His temper flared during a card game in the Giants clubhouse when a pitcher, described as a large bully, provoked Hack. Wilson spun him completely around with a punch. The pitcher got up from the floor without a word. The players rallied around Hack.

Hack was harassed repeatedly by other teams because of his size and looks and especially because he was an illegitimate child. He was riled into a fight during the first game of a doubleheader and then became the first player in National League history to homer twice in the same inning in game two. Incredibly, McGraw benched him for several weeks and then sent him to Toledo in the minor leagues to cure him of his "strikeout habit." [103]

McGraw called every single pitch from the dugout for his hitters and didn't like this new world of power baseball that Hack represented. Hack once ignored McGraw's sign to take a pitch, slammed a home run and was fined $500.

Wilson fumed that his career would end in the minors, with the Toledo Mudhens.

For once, fate was on Wilson's side. Toledo was in the same American Association as Joe McCarthy's Louisville team.

Free of McGraw, Hack's free swinging for Toledo resulted in a batting average of .343, four homers and 36 RBIs in 55 games.

During this trip to the minors in the last half of the 1925 season, McCarthy got to see Wilson for the first time.

McCarthy won the American Association pennant in his seventh and final year managing at Louisville. An ex-Louisville sports writer,

---

[102] Ibid., pg. 36.
[103] Ibid., pg. 38.

William Veeck, talked William Wrigley Jr. into hiring McCarthy, 39, as the Cubs' manager for the 1926 season.

On the last day of the 1925 season, Cub catcher Gabby Hartnett dropped a foul pop up that led to the Cubs' loss, a loss that put them in last place by a half-game and unwittingly gave them the first pick in the minor league draft.

Without hesitation, McCarthy used his draft pick to pluck Hack away from Toledo and bring him to the Cubs.

Whether McGraw didn't want Hack or the Giants made a clerical error by failing to exercise their option on Wilson at the end of the 1925 minor league season, the Giants had just made one of the biggest blunders in the history of player trades. The Cubs got Wilson for $5,000.[104]

McCarthy guarded Hack like a son, keeping him with the other young players so he wouldn't feel pressure in his first spring training at Catalina Island.

The veterans treated him like a rookie but welcomed him in with good-natured hazing that came with the territory. They sent him to the lower deck of the S.S. *Catalina* looking for the non-existent bowling alley and hid fish in his pockets, a Gabby Hartnett specialty.[105]

Hack's life was looking up. He had a new son, Bobbie, who remained at home in Martinsburg with Virginia. Hack's strong spring training performance was rewarded when McCarthy said he would be his cleanup hitter every day in 1926.

McCarthy was the first father figure in Hack's life to show total confidence in his abilities. Hack would reward McCarthy for his trust, and National League pitchers suffered the consequences.

McCarthy had a sympathy and understanding about Hack's roots— because his own childhood was similar. McCarthy grew up in a tough neighborhood near Philadelphia and his father died at a young age. McCarthy dropped out of high school to work and to help his mother and siblings with the bills.

---

[104] Ibid., pg. 43.
[105] Ibid., pg. 47-48.

Like Hack, McCarthy also worked in a textile mill. He played in the minors for 15 years and never made it to the majors—until the Cubs brought him up as a manager.[106]

Hack arrived the same time as Riggs Stephenson, Guy Bush and Charlie Root, when McCarthy wasted no time making the big moves in his first season.

Hack's 1926 season ended when Hal Carlson, then with Philadelphia, hit him in the temple with a pitch on Sept. 14, knocking him unconscious. Minutes later, Hack tried to stand and collapsed again as the ballpark groaned. He was out for the rest of the season, except for the final game. He finished at .321, led the National League with 21 homers, and had 36 doubles, 8 triples, 109 RBIs and an on-base average of .406, leading the league with 69 walks.

The right-handed Hack had unusual power to the opposite field because he waited to see whether a pitch was a breaking ball or fastball. His plate discipline was better in the majors than in the minors, and he now walked more than he struck out—in between all the homers.

When Ed Burns interviewed Hack for a detailed profile in the *Tribune,* it was obvious that Hack was full of humor and hid any childhood pain.

Burns noted that Hack weighed 200 pounds but his shoes were a tiny 6½ C.

Wilson said he once thought of being a soldier and football player. But as soon as he learned about the strict curfew at Pennsylvania Military Academy, "I told him to hell with the education noise."

His schooling ended around seventh or eighth grade at Eddystone, Burns wrote, quoting Wilson, "I liked the readin' and writin', but the 'rithmetic was the bunk so I left the joint flat."

Wilson once thought about delivering mail in the morning and playing ball in the afternoon when he was a "busher," in the minor leagues. "I was about to achieve my purpose when, at a dress rehearsal, an inspector noticed my bag of mail was dragging. He disqualified me, saying my shoulders were built too close to the ground for a mail carrying career."

---

[106] Ibid., pg. 41-42.

Photo from Root family archives

Charlie Root and Charlie Jr. in Hack Wilson's arms.

Pat Malone arrived in 1928 and was an instant drinking buddy of Hack's.

One legend is that McCarthy, Veeck or Wrigley showed Hack a glass of liquor and dropped in a worm that immediately died. "What does that tell you, Hack?" Hack gave an unexpected answer. "If I keep drinking, I won't get worms." [107]

Wilson said he never played drunk, but did play hung over, and never took a drink "after 11 a.m." on the day of a game.

Teammates like Root and Grimm didn't hang out with Hack and weren't wild about his habits. But they were adamant that Hack's drinking never interfered with his hustle or his play on the field. Grimm

---

[107] *Fouled Away*, pg 49-57

said Hack may have played with headaches and hangovers, but never under the influence. Hack would have considered that disloyal to McCarthy.

His first year with the Cubs led to his first police station bailout.

This was McCarthy's favorite Hack Wilson story, told to reporters and recounted in Grimm's autobiography, "I had a call from a friend who told me a beer joint had been raided and that my boy, Hack, was one of the 10 or 12 who had been hauled off to a police station."

"I phoned William Veeck, who had some good connections with you newspaper fellows, and by the time the photographers arrived at the station the next morning, Hack had been sprung.

"I called him in and asked what had happened, and in a nice way. Hack said he and his wife had gone to a movie and that he suggested they buy a couple of sandwiches and a couple of bottles of beer, then go home and listen to the radio. He just pushed the button to get into the speakeasy when, he said, all of a sudden a lot of cops converged and pushed him into the place.

"The other version, told at police headquarters, varied slightly. During the raid, Joe recounted, a policeman inspected the lavatory, looking for more customers. There was a little window in the rest room and Hack, trying to escape, had become wedged in it."

Wrigley was very uneasy about Hack's drinking and his after-hours dealings with police. McCarthy was very tolerant, especially compared to McGraw, when players said they never saw Hack take a drink.

"Hack's only trouble was that he was overgenerous," said Bill Veeck, son of William Veeck, and author of *Veeck as in Wreck.*

"He gave everything away he had," Veeck wrote. "Always. His money, the shirt off his back—little things like that.

"Chicago was the toddling town in those days. Hack's drinking buddies, a rollicking crew of about two dozen Chicagoans, would wait for him after the game and they'd toddle over to the joints on the North Side and the West Side.

"Hack picked up every check. When he longed for the companionship of his teammates, there were always a dozen or so heading out on the town. The players' favorite joint was the Hole in the Wall over in

Cicero, a speakeasy which could easily be defined as the fallout shelter of the Prohibition era; it was the gangster hangout, and that made it the safest place in town.

"At the core of the rollickers, in addition to Hack, was Pat Malone—a name to inspire any old Cub fan to hoist a mug of beer himself. Pat Malone was another of the perennial minor-leaguers. My father bought him cheap, and he pitched us to the pennant." [108]

The Sporting News called Hack "the Babe Ruth of the Cubs" as he continued slugging in 1928, plagued by an ankle injury.

Pitchers started throwing at Hack's head in 1928 and he fought back, once throwing a bat all the way into center field after a knock-down. Some pitchers starting backing off because Hack was intimidating.

Hack even went after an especially abusive fan during a June 1928 doubleheader against the Cardinals at Wrigley Field. A milk wagon driver named Edward Young wouldn't stop harassing Wilson, thinking of the loudest, most obscene things to say about Hack. He finally went into the stands and beat the heckler.

Young was charged with disorderly conduct and showed up in court the next morning with welts covering his face. Hack was fined $100 by the National League but Young sued him for $50,000.

The matter was settled out of court for $20,000 on Oct. 31, 1929. The players speculated that Wrigley paid the bill. [109]

Hack went into an unusually long slump and his batting average dropped below .300 by early August 1928. He heard his first boos from Cub fans. Wilson, then 28, was surprisingly sensitive to public rejection. He disappeared for nights on end, began drinking much more heavily and didn't come home as usual.

The increased boozing did not stop his on-the-field performance. In the last series of the season against his old New York Giants, Hack almost single-handedly knocked the Giants out of the pennant race with

---

[108] Veeck, Bill, *Veeck—As In Wreck,* pg. 32.
[109] Parker, pg. 63.

eight hits in three games, including his 31st home run, tying him with that year's MVP, Jim Bottomley.

With 91 wins, the Cubs finished four games behind the Cardinals, who beat the Giants by just one game.

Players respected McCarthy's firm rules and discipline, but they also recognized that he was easier on Hack.

"Hack was a much misunderstood man," McCarthy explained. "He needed someone to hold him by the hand. His background was meager. I'm afraid the public jumps at conclusions and decisions too fast and pays too little attention to the handicaps which some of our players have to overcome as youngsters. If you come out of a coal mine into the sunlight, your psychology is not likely to match, at once, that of the youngsters who went from a good home to college and then into the major leagues." [110]

Even though his father had little to do with him, Hack brought him to the locker room after games in nearby Philadelphia, Stephenson said. Old man Wilson beamed like a proud father.[111]

Hack tried to be a good father, once photographed smiling in a Cubs sweater as he pushed the baby stroller with Bobbie inside.

Hack always had trouble with his leg injury from that first minor league game. Trainer Andy Lotshaw would tape him up extensively every game, using up to 10 yards of two-inch adhesive tape around his ankles.

Wilson's uniform was always dirty and he would mutter frequently at the plate, swinging his arms like clubs. He was intimidating. He would step out of the box between pitches, bathe his sweaty hands and arms with dirt and then wipe them dry all over his uniform.

Off the field, Hack was a dapper dresser like the other players but was always sweating even when it was 30 degrees.

Woody English said Hack always had a red neck, sunburned from all those day games in center field or reddened by booze. If called out on strikes, he'd bounce the bat off the plate, usually breaking the long

---

[110] Ibid., pg. 54.
[111] Ibid., pg. 12.

bat and skinny handle that he used, delighting the crowd. The bat was a huge 40 ounces, similar to the Babe's. He named his bats "Big Bertha" and liked them blackened.

Hack loved his towering home runs and could barely hide his glee, lowering his head to hide his exultation. Hack could move to joy as quickly as rage, depending on the circumstances.

His rage during a July 3 doubleheader in 1929 spilled off the field and got him suspended.

He was the target of Reds pitcher Ray Kolp, who yelled from the dugout that Wilson was a "no-good bastard" after yet another single in the doubleheader. Wilson flew from first to the dugout but was stopped and ejected before reaching Kolp, nicknamed "Jockey" for his ability to badger opponents with a salty tongue and loud mouth.[112]

The Cubs won 10-5, but the battle resumed at Chicago's Union Station when both teams were awaiting trains near the baggage area.

"Where's Kolp?" Wilson asked. "I'm going to make him apologize."

Reds pitcher Pete Donohue popped off, "No, you're not."

Wilson shut him up with one punch that knocked him unconscious, tumbling over suitcases on the station floor.

"The fight was on," Della recalled, as a witness to the whole thing with her mom and dad. "It ended just before the police came.

"Hack was a boozer and would fight at the drop of a hat," Della said. "I used to love it when they would fight. It was just swell. I always liked it when the police came."[113]

Hack got a light suspension of only a few days since he didn't start the fight and the punishment was only for what happened on the field.

The incident fired up Hack, who went on a 27-game hitting streak that extended through July 27. Just past the midway mark, he had 27 homers, 98 RBIs and a .341 batting average.

---

[112] *Baseballlibrary.com.*
[113] Della Root Arnold, author's interview; her account matches reports in Parker's *Fouled Away*, Charlie Grimm's *Jolly Cholly,* Peter Golenbock's *Wrigleyville,* and the *Chicago Tribune.*

McCarthy moved Hack back to cleanup since Hornsby was not hitting as expected. That would change, and when Hornsby started rolling, the Cubs never looked back.

The two stars were quite a contrast. Hornsby was the perfectionist who wouldn't go to a movie or a dance to protect his eyes and feet. There wasn't anything that Hack hadn't tried.

Hornsby was absolutely obsessive at the plate, refusing to swing at a bad pitch, forcing himself to wait until the third pitch or two strikes before offering to swing.

In his autobiography, *Jolly Cholly,* Grimm gave the best detail of what Hack was like at the plate.

> Was he a good judge of a pitch? Actually, I don't think he knew the strike zone too well. He'd take the inside pitch and seldom pulled to left. "Any ball I can reach, I'm going to swing at," he'd say.
>
> For all his roisterings, he was a gentle man.
>
> He was a slugger in the Babe Ruth manner. Oddly, both had thick ankles. He could knock a ball over the left field wall and just as easily, swinging late, had the power to put it away in right field. I'd say that his power was to right center. He frequently struck out, but he always gave it a good riffle. Hack stood far back and outside in the batter's box. He wielded a long, thin-handled bat that weighed 40 to 41 ounces.
>
> I think that Hack was tipped—that's our word for being dusted off—more than any hitter in the National League when he was having his good years. But he always came back after that warning pitch. He never fell away from the plate and because of his great strength he could swat that outside pitch from here to there.
>
> Wilson never blamed lack of rest or overindulgence for the fact he was feeling poorly. "I guess I'll have to get my appendix out one of these days," was his stock saying to Andy Lotshaw.
>
> "How can you abuse yourself so much and still hit the ball?" a fellow once asked him.
>
> "That's easy," Hack replied. "I see three balls coming at me and always swing at the one in the middle. It's usually the real one."
>
> Wilson always beefed when he was called out on a third strike, even if it was a perfect pitch. One afternoon he was called out by Bill

Klem and tossed his bat in the air in disgust. "I'm sorry, Hack," said Klem, "but if that bat comes down you're out of the game."

Hack calmly walked to the dugout and made no move to go out on the field when the Cubs were retired in the inning. McCarthy told him to get moving, but Hack said he had been chased, though Klem had not gone into his usual flourish indicating banishment. McCarthy checked with the umpire, who told him that he had indeed chased the slugger.

I will say that Hack Wilson was the Cubs' most exciting player—both on and off the field—in my times. I realize he didn't have the wearability of many of the other greats, but while he lasted he was socko all the way.

Wilson got his nickname from the dumpy German strong man, Hackenschmidt, whom he resembled physically.

1929 would be his best career year to that date, with 39 homers and 159 RBIs.

Some of my younger pals in baseball have asked me why Wilson played center field over Kiki Cuyler, who had dazzling speed and great defensive ability, including a strong throwing arm. Kiki played right and Riggs Stephenson left.

The least of Stevie's skills was throwing, and so it had to be left field or nothing for him. He had suffered an arm injury playing football for the University of Alabama. Right field in Wrigley Field is the sun field, and the man playing out there also must have a strong throwing arm to keep the runners from going from first to third. Actually, Cuyler helped Wilson cover the center field area. Hack was only adequate in the throwing department. I'm sure that 20 Major League managers today would gladly play a guy in center field, overlooking his deficiencies in exchange for 50 homers and 150 or more runs batted in. [114]

Grimm said Pat Malone had his two best years at the same time Wilson peaked and they did a lot of celebrating together.

Pat and Hack were nightclub companions during Chicago's so-called Prohibition days. "McCarthy never took a bed check or em-

_____

[114] Grimm, pg. 51-64.

156

ployed snoopers to follow his athletes, but he usually found out where his wandering boys had been the preceding night," Grimm wrote.

"He'd casually ask Hack for a match, quickly note its origin, and later tell him, and Pat, where they had been on the previous evening. Hack, tipped off by Pat, once handed McCarthy a pack of matches carrying no identification and challenged, 'Now tell me where I was last night.'"

The split lips of the Cubs as they split the July 3 doubleheader with the Reds, and Hack's competitiveness, demonstrated what the Cubs needed in this tough pennant race.

The win in the first game, the Cubs' seventh consecutive victory, puts them in first. The loss in the second game drops them to second place, and they wouldn't return to the top until the end of the month.

Root is clearly back to his old form, winning seven of the nine games he starts in July. Root's 2-0 shutout against the Giants' Carl Hubbell on July 23 begins a nine-game winning streak that firmly puts the Cubs on top with a 62-30 record on July 30. From this point, they will never look back.

They open August with another winning streak of five games, and Hornsby is pounding the ball, getting as hot as the weather.

Root throws a seven-hit shutout against rookie Benny Frey of the Cincinnati Reds on Aug. 8. The only run in the game comes from a Hornsby homer in the fourth, one of his four hits.

Bush wins his 11th straight game in Philadelphia on Aug. 9. When he pitches again on Aug. 12 against the Boston Braves, he gets only his second loss of the season and now stands at 16-2, making him the National League's best pitcher. The Cubs now have an eight-game lead over the Pirates.

Grimm Ending for Horne

> With this introduction, we will now tell a little of how pleasant things are with the present pace-setters of the National League or rather how pleasant the veterans of the Cubs have made it for a newcomer like Horne. He informs me that Hornsby has been great to him, that Charlie Root has been great to him, that Joe McCarthy has been wonderful to him and that he has gone out of his way to give him a pat on the back or to praise him for some little thing in which he was showing improvement.
>
> —Ernest J. Lanigan, Aug. 15, 1929,
> in his column, "Fanning with Lanigan."

Something as simple as a foul pop to first baseman Charlie Grimm on Aug. 21 would dramatically change Berly Horne's future.

Charlie Root starts the game against the New York Giants at the Polo Grounds. The Cubs are so far ahead and the pitching so sound by now that Berly Horne hasn't appeared in a game since the second game of a doubleheader on July 11 when the game was out of reach. The Cubs lose 16-12, but Horne accounts for only one of the runs in his 2⅓ innings pitched. He gives up a hit, two walks and a wild pitch.

The long gap between appearances and his spotty outings did not diminish what Horne writes about his rookie season.

Just a week earlier, Horne sent a letter to Ernest J. Lanigan, a columnist who had followed his minor league play on the East Coast.

Lanigan dutifully recorded Horne's letter in his Aug. 15 column, "Fanning with Lanigan."

> This heading should be changed a bit this week, the writer having heard from a young man who is a member of the Chicago Cubs, who apparently are going to win the National League flag. The young

man's name is Berlyn Dale Horne and he is a most esteemed corre-spondent as well as friend. The column might be labeled Fanning with Horne, Berlyn kicking in with a lot of information about how pleasant things are in the McCarthy family.

Horne is always a favorite with the managers he works for, the reason being that he is a worker and not a moaner. He was tickled pink when he was purchased from Jersey City last fall. He had been kicking round the minor leagues for quite a few seasons and scouts were passing him up because of his size.

Hornsby has a reputation of not being any too kind to young players or he had such a rep the year he managed the Cardinals. Horne says the ex-Card, ex-Giant and ex-Brave has treated him mag-nificently.

Also Horne retails the information that the Cubs' Boosters' Asso-ciation has made things very pleasant for the boys. "We are deluged with invitations to this and that function and our meals cost us almost less than nothing," Horne said. "I certainly have been in luck getting with the Cubs and now I will have to stay with them. I never saw such a ball club in my life, though there may be others like it. For the good of the pastime, I hope there are. This club has spirit, teamwork, everybody pulling for the other fellow and everybody making it pleasant for rookies like myself. I had to wait a long time to get in fast company and when I did get in I got with one of the most re-markable baseball organizations."

Just six days after Lanigan publishes Horne's letter, Berly's major league days are over for good. But Horne had made it, no matter how briefly.

The end of the dream happens in the eighth inning, when Giant out-fielder Edd Roush hits a towering popup over by the stands near first base. As Grimm races toward the concrete wall, his spikes slip, and both knees hit squarely when he tries to stop.

Grimm goes back to first, only then noticing the pain in both knees. It isn't until after the last play of the game, when he flips the ball to the dugout as a souvenir, that he feels a sharp pain in his hand.

Root wins the game, 9-2, with eight strikeouts, including all three batters in the ninth. The victory starts a five-game team winning streak.

Grimm's pain continues that night, so Andy Lotshaw wraps hot towels around his hand, but there is no relief. An X-ray the following morning shows a broken bone in his hand. Grimm is going to miss the rest of the regular season.

Charley "Slug" Tolson gets the call to replace the injured Grimm. Slug" was hitting .365 for the Los Angeles Angels.

Tolson subbed for Grimm in 1927 and fans remember his pinch-hit, grand slam homer in 1928.

Zee-nut candy baseball card

Horne edged Tolson off the 1929 roster when manager Joe McCarthy decided to go with an extra pitcher after spring training ended at Catalina.

McCarthy tells the *Chicago Tribune* that he "really didn't want the lad to get away," referring to Horne.

"We had to have a first baseman," Horne said. "We had Cliff Heathcote, a utility man and outfielder who played first base. But he didn't satisfy McCarthy.

Berly Horne, 1930, playing for the Los Angeles Angels of the Pacific Coast League

"So [McCarthy] looked around and made a deal to get Slug Tolson from LA," Berly continued. "They wanted him to report right away."

"After the game, McCarthy and Bill Veeck called me up to their room," Berly said. "As soon as I heard that, I said, 'Uh, oh, there's some kind of deal now.'"

They told him that Los Angeles wouldn't send Tolson unless they could have Horne. McCarthy and Veeck said they talked about sending another pitcher from the staff, but Los Angeles wanted Horne.[115]

Horne leaves with a 1-1 won-loss record in 11 appearances and 23 innings pitched. He never makes it back to the major leagues, but he can tell everyone that he had a career batting average of .400, with two hits in five at-bats.

Root wins his next appearance on Aug. 26 at Wrigley when 3B Norm McMillan hits an inside-the-park, grand slam home run, a line drive down the left field line that bounces wildly in the corner. This is the eighth grand slam of the season for the Cubs, and perhaps the most exciting one.

MC MILLAN

When Blake beats the Reds 4-1 on August 27, the Cubs lead the National League by 14 ½ games, the largest margin on this date since the 1906 Cubs.

When the Cubs clinch the pennant, the players carry Guy Bush in full uniform and spikes into the shower and soak him good.

For several days leading up to the pennant-clinching game, Bush had worn the same underwear and uniform so that he didn't jinx the Cubs big lead and the pennant drive. The players grumbled that he was getting very "ripe" in the locker room and dugout.

Bush was their obvious target when the celebrating began.[116]

In Root's final appearance of the regular season on September 29 at Wrigley, he beats the Reds' Benny Frey by the same score by which he bested the rookie in August, 1-0.

---

[115] Berly Horne, 83, in interview with sports editor Terry Baver of the *Franklin (Ohio) Chronicle,* published Aug. 5, 1980.
[116] Della Root

Even with his arm struggles and slow start, Root finishes the season with the best winning percentage in the National League, .760, with a 19-6 record. Only one pitcher in the American League had a better winning percentage at .769, Lefty Grove, the Philadelphia starter the Cubs would soon see in the World Series.

Root started 31 games, relieved in 12, tied his career high of four shutouts and had a 3.47 ERA, third best in the National League.

Pat Malone led the National League with his 22 wins and 166 strikeouts.

Guy Bush was just as tough as Malone and Root, with his 18-7 record and 3.66 ERA. Bush pitched in a league-leading 50 games.

Hornsby was as great as everyone expected, scoring 156 runs, hitting .380 with 229 hits and 149 RBI. His 409 total bases were the best in baseball in 1929. This season would be the Rajah's last great hurrah. He would never play over 100 games in any of his remaining eight seasons.

At age 29, Wilson had turned in the best season of his career to date. Wilson broke a National League single season record with 159 RBI, topping the mark of 152 set by Hornsby in 1922. Wilson had 198 hits and a .345 average.

On Oct. 5, two other National League season records of Hornsby's fell, most hits (250) and most home runs (42). Phillie Lefty O'Doul got 254 hits for the season, after collecting six hits in a doubleheader against the Giants. Teammate Chuck Klein hit his 43rd homer.

Hornsby and Wilson tied with 39 homers each, chasing Klein's 43 and Mel Ott's 42. Ruth hit 46 in the American League, followed by Gehrig's 35.

Grimm missed .300 by two points but knocked in 91 runs.

Kiki Cuyler led the National League with 43 stolen bases. He hit .360 with 15 homers and 102 RBI. Riggs Stephenson hit .362 with 17 homers and 110 RBI.

The Cubs hit .302 as a team and led the league with 982 runs.

The Cubs ended the season on Oct. 6, at 98-54. Attendance reached 1.6 million, a figure they would not top until 1969. [117] No other team in

---

[117] *Baseballlibrary.com.*

baseball in 1929 drew even a million fans. The team with the second-highest attendance was the New York Yankees, trailing far behind the Cubs at 960,148, with Ruth and Gehrig as their obvious draws.

The Cubs had won their 12th pennant, finishing 10½ games ahead of the Pirates. They took the lead for good on July 24 with the start of a nine-game winning streak.

To prepare for the World Series, Wrigley ordered 10,000 more seats, temporary bleachers, to be installed behind the outfield fences.

The Cubs had every ingredient—batting power and average, speed, defense, and solid pitching. They would face a Philadelphia Athletics team that was just as tough in every category, with starting pitching even a notch better.

Chicago fans had waited 11 years for another pennant after losing the 1918 World Series to Babe Ruth and his Red Sox.

It had been 21 years since their 1908 World Series championship. And that had come on the heels of a 1907 World Series win.

The Cubs had lost the World Series to the Philadelphia Athletics in the 1910 World Series. They planned on getting even in the 1929 rematch.

The Philadelphia Story

> All my life I've waited for this hour. I've schemed and dreamed
> of the day when I would lead a major league team into the world's
> series against Connie Mack. And here it is, all come true.
> —Manager Joe McCarthy, *Chicago Tribune*, Oct. 8, 1929.

World Series tickets went on sale Tuesday, Oct. 1, as William
Wrigley Jr. celebrated his 68th birthday. He called it the biggest and
best of them all.

Wrigley finally made his 1916 investment in the Cubs pay off. No
business deal ever compared to the excitement stirring around him as
Chicago prepared for the 1929 World Series.

Wrigley got to make up for a childhood that kept him away from
baseball and the roaring crowd. His 91-year-old mother still lived in
Philadelphia and now his Cubs were going against legendary Philadelphia manager Connie Mack.

Wrigley would have the best seat at his first World Series in the
owner's box. It was quite a contrast for the kid who envied the other
boys going into the ballpark during those summers in Philadelphia
while he trailed behind a bell-jangling, four-horse team peddling soap
for his dad's factory.

William Veeck finally achieved what he had preached as a sportswriter and found his baseball philosophy worked in actual practice
from inside Wrigley's front office.

Veeck started out as a reporter. He had gone to school for only four
years, but his ability to write got him a job with the Louisville *Courier-
Journal.*

At age twenty-five, he moved to Chicago to work for the *Inter Ocean,* a paper that folded within a year. Newspaper magnate William Randolph Hearst owned the *Chicago American,* and Veeck eventually got on the sports desk, where he befriended the paper's greatest sportswriter of all time, Ring Lardner.

Chicago Daily News — Chicago History Museum s067251

William Veeck

Veeck took over the Bill Bailey column and that got him to Wrigley's dinner table, where his newspaper career would end. Wrigley wanted this kind of unvarnished truth on his payroll.

"If you're so smart, why don't you see if you can do a better job?" Wrigley asked, surprising Veeck when he realized Wrigley was serious and was offering him a job as the main executive of the Cubs.

Years later, his son, Bill Veeck, wrote in his autobiography, *Veeck as in Wreck:*

One of the great differences between my father and me is that he was always "Mr. Veeck" to everyone who knew him and I am always "Bill." Not even the members of the Cubs' operating staff, all of whom remained with him throughout his entire 16-year tenure, would have dreamed of calling him by his first name.

I went to school with the Lardner boys. In Chicago, our families lived in the same apartment house, and when we moved to Hinsdale, a suburb, the Lardners moved to nearby Western Springs.

It was as Bill Bailey that my daddy wrote the series that brought him to the attention of William Wrigley, who had only recently bought control of the club.

He did not blast the Cubs; he wrote a sane and thoughtful series telling, in a sane and thoughtful way, what changes he would make if he were running the club. I can remember seeing that series a long time ago, and it was what you so often hear about and so seldom see: constructive criticism without any attempt to be either colorful or clever. My father was not one of the great sportswriters of his time, he had little facility with words. But he was a good, solid reporter.

If you asked anybody who knew my daddy to describe him in a word, that word would undoubtedly be "dignified." And then they would be constrained to add, "dignified without being stuffy." He had a good sense of humor and he was always scrupulously fair. I can say, without any fear that I might be a little prejudiced, that he was the most popular fellow in baseball.

The elder Veeck always dressed formally, tie perfectly in place, outfitted with a vest and jacket, usually topped with a wide-brimmed hat.[118]

Bill Veeck said his father never cussed, believing curses showed a weakness for the English language. "If you want to show people that you're stupid, that's up to you," he would say.

William Veeck worked tirelessly to improve the Cubs at every position.

---

[118] Eskenazi, Gerald, *Bill Veeck, A Baseball Legend*, , McGraw-Hill Book Co., New York, 1988, pg. 3.

Nineteen of the twenty-five Cubs on the 1929 World Series roster were selected by McCarthy, with Veeck working in the wings to make them happen in the previous three seasons.

The Hornsby deal was the final, headline move before the 1929 season. All of these players, especially Hack Wilson and Charlie Root, had reached their prime.

They should have had one more player in his prime in this lineup. Gabby Hartnett had the best season of his career to date in 1928, but he was only available as a pinch hitter in 1929 and for the World Series because his throwing arm was dead.

The truth never came out in print. Woody English said years later that Hartnett hurt his arm from the recoil of a hunting gun while he was shooting clay pigeons at Lincoln Park in Chicago during the off-season prior to spring training at Catalina Island.[119]

Losing Hartnett's arm and his bat on a regular basis made the catcher's position the only striking weakness as the Cubs headed into the World Series against another great catcher, Mickey Cochrane.

Not having his favorite target also had to make things tougher for Root. Root had pitched more than 800 innings for the Cubs during his previous three years with Hartnett behind the plate.

After throwing thousands of pitches to Hartnett since coming up with the Cubs in 1926, Root had one less thing to think about when Hartnett was in the lineup.

In 1929, Root threw to four different catchers: Mike Gonzales and Zach Taylor and two rookies, Tom Angley and Earl Grace.

Away from the game, Root was never really close to Gabby, but they really knew what they were doing in a game. They knew what each other was going to do, almost without signals.

Sometimes, just to throw the hitter off and just for the humor of it, Dad would shake Gabby off and Gabby would come out to the mound, Della said that Gabby would look real serious and come out and tell a joke. Dad would shake his head and look like they were arguing over the sign, and they weren't even talking about baseball.[120]

---

[119] Golenbock, Peter, *Wrigleyville,* pg. 206.
[120] Della Root Arnold, author's interview.

Chicago Daily News — Chicago History Museum s069153

Root confers with catcher Hartnett in front of the dugout.

In his autobiography, Grimm described Hartnett:

If any catcher had a greater arm than Gabby, I must have been looking the other way. He threw it hard, he threw it accurately—and it came in like a feather. When Gabby was catching, there were two umpires back of the plate. He could give the man in blue a pretty good going over when he thought he had booted one. But he'd do it without turning around, and the fans never suspected it. Gabby was uncanny on high popups along the line and back of the plate. I believe he dropped only one popper in his nineteen years of wearing the harness for the Cubs. This was all the more remarkable because Gabby has small hands.[121]

---

[121] Grimm, Charlie, *Jolly Cholly,* pg. 134.

Reporters and fans flocked around Root, who never acted as though he was a star. He tipped his hat to the crowd's applause and signed autographs, but he never really understood what all the fuss was about.

Dorothy and Della certainly felt like movie stars, however, as they bought new outfits to look sharp for the photographers and for the World Series.

"I can tell you we were no longer in the rookie class," Della said.

"Dorothy got a most beautiful ermine coat with large rolled collar, as well as several very spiffy outfits to wear with it," Della said. "She looked as wonderful as any movie star because she was a very pretty lady.

"I also got overhauled," Della said, "and had a lovely plaid coat with a real beaver collar, a toque hat, and a very fine navy blue suit to wear to the first game of our first World Series.

"My coat and hat cost $75, which was quite a price in those days," Della said.[122]

Monday was supposed to be the only day of rest between the end of the regular season and the start of the World Series in Chicago. But the city's excitement was spilling over to the players.

Charlie Root had never seen so many reporters, coming in from all over the country. Root picked up some extra money from the *Chicago Herald and Examiner,* which contracted with him for his preview.

"I'm not much of a talker or a writer," Charlie said, according to the reporter who interviewed him and converted his words into a first-person column from Root.

The paper described Root as the steadiest and stoutest-hearted hurler on the team.

"Well, I know that I would rather be pitching against Cochrane, Simmons and Foxx than against Hornsby, Cuyler and Stephenson," Root said. "I may think differently after the series, but we'll see. I have a lot of respect for them."

---

[122] Della, journal, pg. 35.

"This season has been incredible. It seems like any player in our regular lineup—except our pitchers—broke up any ball game. We're loaded with dynamite. There isn't a weak spot in our lineup. I honestly believe they have two weaknesses in Bishop and Boley.

"Good pitching will not win these games unless we get runs behind us. The Rajah is our key and I look for him to devastate whatever Mack's pitchers have to offer. I consider him to be more valuable than Al Simmons, the big gun of the Mackmen, and a more dangerous hitter.

"Hack Wilson, who has lost more baseballs into the seats than anyone on their team, is at his best when it counts. It seems like he always homers when the game is on the line.

"After Hornsby and Wilson, you've got Cuyler, Stephenson and Grimm, and I don't think any team has sluggers like that. In fact, I think we have the best sluggers that ever entered a World Series. The National League pitchers couldn't stop them so I see no reason why Philadelphia should.

"Kiki is the best base-stealer in baseball and he turns a lot of singles into doubles. In close games, a stolen base is often the turning point.

"I wish Gabby could play every game for us, but we can still use his bat so that means we'll have the best pinch hitter to bring in from the bench. The Macks don't have anybody to compare to him on the bench.

"In the field, English and Hornsby have turned far more double plays than the Athletics. We've had some trouble at third, but McMillan has ended up strong for us and will lead off for us in the series. Grimm may not hit as hard as Foxx, but he's got the kind of experience that will really count.

"I think it really helps us that we're opening at home because the team that wins the first game will be a big favorite to capture the series and everything seems to be in our favor.

"Today's the big day. Give me a few runs, that's all. I'll win if the fellows can do that for me. I'm in great shape. I never felt better. I'll give everything I've got; you can bet on that."

The newspaper asked Jimmie Foxx to give the enemy's point of view. "I don't want to appear boastful, but it seems we'll out-hit the Cubs by a big margin. Bishop may not be the slugger that Hornsby is, but there's a reason why we call him 'camera eye.'

"Mule Haas is greatly improved over last year and he keeps saving games for us with sensational catches. Cochrane is a mighty hard man to fool, batting third for us all year.

"Al Simmons is one of the greatest hitters of all time.

"I don't like to compare myself to Charlie Grimm, who, I'm glad to hear is in good shape and will probably play through the series. I was in a slump toward the end of the season.

"Bing Miller has just enjoyed his best season and I rate him above Kiki Cuyler, and Jimmy Dykes is one of our most popular, playing every position of the infield in tip-top manner this year."

Both of their columns appeared side by side on Oct. 8, below the lead story. Reporter Wayne K. Otto built the drama around four men: McCarthy ("who waited a lifetime to lead a championship baseball club"); Connie Mack ("who waited 10 years to erase the blot from his World Series escutcheon") and Root and presumed Athletics starter George Earnshaw ("two who find themselves on the threshold of every pitcher's ambition, that of opening a World Series.")

"We're ready. Charlie Root is at his best under the strain of a big game and there's none bigger than the opening game of a World Series," McCarthy said. He expected the Cubs to face Philadelphia pitchers Earnshaw, Grove and Walberg in the first three games.

At the Edgewater Beach Hotel on the shores of the North Side, Connie Mack prepared with his two coaches, Kid Gleason and Eddie Collins.

The Athletics arrived in Chicago at 2:30 p.m. after a 17 1/2-hour train ride. The team saw Wrigley on game day and made no advance trip to check out the field or get acquainted with the park.

"It has taken 10 painstaking, persevering years to bring Philadelphia back to baseball's crest," Connie told a reporter. "Ten years of disappointments, broken hopes, but finally we have succeeded. Chicago will see a great Philadelphia team in action. The Cubs are practically as great, yet I'm confident my boys will win."

Collins had been a key part to Mack's World Series wins as a player in an earlier decade and now had the chance to serve beside Mack as a coach.

For Gleason, this was a return to the top for him. He was managing the 1919 White Sox when the players sold him out, fixing the games and scarring that team as the Black Sox for the rest of baseball history.

New York sports columnist Westbrook Pegler profiled Gleason on Oct. 3 about how disgusted Gleason became with baseball because of the scandal.

Gleason was the first to question what was going on when pitcher Eddie Cicotte cut off a ball thrown to the plate that would have easily caught the scoring run.

Gleason appreciated the new life that Mack gave him as a coach, with a legitimate World Series contender.

Mack was 66 and still had something to prove, despite winning three of five World Series that Philadelphia reached in 1905, 1910, 1911, 1913 and 1914.

He had to bust up his earlier championship team for financial reasons. Mack was old enough to be questioned about whether his managerial skills were slipping. The team had nothing to show for itself since the 1914 pennant.

The drought and anticipation for fans in Chicago and Philadelphia was equally intense. Both teams had waited a long time for this kind of blend of power and pitching.

Mack was born Dec. 22, 1862, as Cornelius Alexander McGillicuddy while his dad was fighting for Lincoln's Army, as he described it. He was the son of Irish immigrants who had settled in East Brookfield, Massachusetts.

Baseball was his life. He started as a catcher in the minors for four years and then reached the majors for 11, hitting a career .245. In his last two seasons as a player with Pittsburgh, 1894-1896, Mack was also the manager. In 1901, he became the manager of the Philadelphia Athletics, the only manager they would have for half a century.

His history as an owner matched the history of the American League.

"I was awarded the Philadelphia franchise and hurried to the City of Brotherly Love in 1900 to dig up local capital," Mack wrote years later. "Benjamin F. Shibe, one of the owners of the A. J. Reach Co., manufacturers of baseball equipment, organized a corporation with Mack, and Shibe was made president. Charles Somers, a Cleveland friend, joined them.

"We now had our franchise, but we had no team and no park."

"According to the custom of the times and considering the National League good game, I looked over our rivals, the Phillies, and began negotiations with four of their players. I signed up Napoleon Lajoie."

"I found a boy wonder at Gettysburg College who looked like a comer to me. His name was Eddie Plank.

"Our rivals, the Phillies, were not happy over our invasion of Philadelphia."

A court battle forced Mack to give up Lajoie and two other players. He still had Eddie Plank, Monte Cross, Lave Cross, Mike Powers, Harry Davis and Socks Siebold.[123]

Mack rarely displayed anger or profanity and dressed in a three-piece business suit as manager.

Mack's devout Catholic faith was displayed in quiet service. Several of his younger players enjoyed a college education because of his generosity. He never forgot his former ballplayers, either. Collins once said that he "didn't know of any needy old ballplayer who was ever turned down by Mr. Mack for a loan." Instead Mack helped those in need without any fanfare or publicity.

One day, a frail, hunchback man showed up as Mack's new bat boy.

The Philadelphia Record described Mack's daily baseball ritual:

---

[123] Mack, Connie, *My 66 Years in the Big Leagues: The Great Story of America's National Game,* The John C. Winston Co., Phila and Toronto, 1950. Most of the bio and other details about Mack are from his autobiography.

Mack awakens at 7 a.m. and dresses in a dark business suit with a fresh, tall white collar. Breakfast is at 8 a.m. sharp. He has grapefruit or sometimes baked apple or prunes, followed by oatmeal or cream of wheat and coffee. He reads the Philadelphia Record as he eats, of course.

Then it's off to Shibe Park and his tower office where he spends 30 minutes reading about the other American League teams in out-of-state papers, opens mail, receives visitors, and dictates for about an hour. He keeps his office door locked.

Lunch is taken at 1 p.m. promptly. He spreads a towel across a chair to serve as a table cloth. His house servant James packs him sandwiches and vegetable soup and Mack brings it to the ballpark in a wicker basket and thermos bottle.

After lunch he takes a one-hour nap, reclining on his office sofa. At 2:45 p.m., Mack leaves for the clubhouse where he makes out the batting order and talks with the players. At 3:10 p.m. he leaves the clubhouse, picks up his scorecard and takes his place on the steps of the dugout. For the next two hours, he manages the game. Mack admits that those two hours are the toughest and that he is physically and mentally drained after a game.

After the game, he returns home and has dinner at 6 p.m. He then retires to the living room where he turns on the radio and listens to boxing. Later in the evening, he joins Mrs. Mack to play bridge or to go to the theater. He is always in bed by 11 p.m.

Mack said he quit wearing a uniform and dressing with the players after witnessing the usual arguments after losing tough games, hearing the hot words of players trying to fix blame and finding himself getting so mad that he couldn't talk calmly.

He would remain hot at home and even the next morning.

From that time on, I never again dressed with my players, either in Milwaukee or afterward in Philadelphia. My coaches are in the clubhouse, but I do not go near the players unless I have something I especially want to take up with them. I save my own feelings as well as theirs that way. If we are on the road, I see the player who may have made a mistake in the hotel lobby or call him to my room. If we are home, I let it go until the next day. By then we both are calm and can discuss the matter with no bitterness. Often I am able to point out to the player his mistakes, show him how the play should have been made; and, if the player has the natural ability, he may learn from his mistake.

Mack did not fine his players. He never argued with an umpire during a game, but did give them a piece of his mind as they made their way to the clubhouse after a game. He held his players accountable, did not want to hear excuses. "If you've made a mistake or a misplay, take the blame for it good-naturedly. You will only gain stature in the eyes of your teammates if you do so."

He said, "The greatest ball teams in history have always been those where the friendliest relationships prevailed between the individual players and where there was present that most essential element called 'team spirit.'" [124]

While knocked for cutting players and costs, he still would pay top dollar for a top prospect that he estimated was worth it. And he knew how to spot them.

The Athletics were in the World Series because of the foundation that Mack started rebuilding in 1925, about the same time Wrigley made his moves.

Mack always had his eye on pitchers, telling everyone that pitching was 80 percent of the reason why successful teams won. He spotted Rube Waddell, Jack Coombs, Plank, and Chief Bender.

Mack's ownership of the team moved to 50 percent by 1914, the same year he busted up his winning combination when the newly established Federal League pushed salaries too high.

Charlie Grimm was a 19-year rookie playing for Mack when they really hit bottom. Grimm could still see Mack waving that scorecard in the dugout.

"In 1916, the Athletics lost 117 games and won 36, their all-time worst record," Grimm said. "Mack was signing players wholesale. There was a saying that he had one team on the field, one leaving by train, and a third one on the way." Grimm remembers getting something like $125 a month, but "it was better than grabbing the handle of a paint pot."

"Mom ironed a blue shirt for me and I put on my jazz-bow tie, stuffed a few things in a straw suitcase, and was on my way," Grimm said. "Mom made some sandwiches for me. It was a long train ride to Philadelphia, and it wasn't in a Pullman."[125]

Mack also found second baseman Eddie Collins at Columbia University.

Shoeless Joe Jackson played his first two seasons with Mack in 1908 and 1909, and picked up his nickname when he played a game in stocking feet because his new spikes didn't fit.

During his first week in Philadelphia, Jackson missed his family so much that he hopped a train to Greenville, S.C., without Mack's permission.

Mack ordered a coach to bring him back with all of his family if necessary. Mack patiently stayed with the difficult Jackson, even offering to pay for a tutor to help him learn to read and write. Jackson refused.

One day a heckler yelled, "Hey, Joe, can you spell 'cat?'" Jackson replied, "Can you spell 'shit?'"

Jackson went to Cleveland in 1910 and was among the eight Chicago White Sox accused of throwing the 1919 World Series.

Waddell was another eccentric, problem ball player that Mack took a chance on. Waddell agreed to sign if Mack would pay his debts and recover some belongings from a pawn shop. Mack agreed, only if Waddell reported daily to a guardian hired by Mack who would assure that the young pitcher's wife received half of his $2,400 salary.

Mack built his first 1910-1914 championship dynasty with the "$100,000 infield" of Collins, Home Run Baker, Stuffy McInnis and Jack Barry. It helped that the pitchers included Plank and Bender.

---

[124] Kashatus, William C., *Connie Mack's '29 Triumph: The Rise and Fall of the Philadelphia Athletics Dynasty*, McFarland & Co., Jefferson, NC, and London, 1999.
[125] Grimm, Charlie, *Jolly Cholly*.

Mack won the American League pennant four times in five seasons and the World Series in 1910, 1911 and 1913.

Unlike Wrigley, Mack derived his only fortune from baseball, and he had to bust up the team after the 1914 season when he lost $60,000 despite winning the pennant. Mack had to waive Bender, Plank and Coombs. He sold Collins before the 1915 season.[126]

Fifteen years later, Collins and Mack are reviewing the game plan at their Chicago hotel, looking over a 1929 roster that delivered the best record in baseball, 104-46, and ranked as Mack's greatest masterpiece.

George Earnshaw's 24 wins and Lefty Grove's 2.81 ERA were the best in the American League in 1929. Another tall lefty, Rube Walberg, was 18-11 with a 3.60 ERA.

Jimmie Foxx was at first (.354, 33 HR, 117 RBI), Max Bishop at second (.232), Joe Boley at shortstop (.251), Sammy Hale at third (.277), with Al Simmons in left (.365, 34 HR, 157 RBI), Mule Haas in center (.313, 16 HR, 82 RBI) and Bing Miller in right (.335, 8 HR, 93 RBI). Mickey Cochrane was the catcher (.331, 7 HR, 95 RBI), and Jimmy Dykes was the outstanding pinch-hitter and utility infielder (.327, 13 HR, 79 RBI).

Mack got Walberg in 1923. In 1924, Mack acquired Bishop and Al Simmons. Simmons hit .308 that rookie season and would turn out to be the most significant find of all, pushing near .400 twice, getting 253 hits in 1925, and flashing home run power leading up to 1929.

In 1925, Lefty Grove joined the team, immediately becoming a dominant pitcher. Jimmie Foxx made his major league debut on the 1925 roster at age 17. Catcher Mickey Cochrane also was acquired for the start of that season, costing $50,000, five players, and one other bonus that made this one of the most unusual deals to acquire a single player. Mack bought the entire Portland minor league franchise so he could get Cochrane.[127]

Cochrane, a Massachusetts farm boy, spent only one year in the Pacific Coast League, where he hit .338 for Portland. An outstanding athlete, he also played football at Boston University.

---

[126] Kashatus.

By 1929, Cochrane and Hartnett were the best offensive catchers in baseball, in an era where hitting was not a job requirement for a catcher. Bill Dickey of the Yankees was the only other catcher in their class.

Several players rented rooms within half a mile of Shibe Park in North Philly, near Lehigh Avenue, a main drag slicing through a neighborhood of churches, businesses, offices and mostly Irish residents. Grove rented a house, Dykes and Boley stayed at a dance hall, Bishop lived with a dentist and his family, and Simmons usually was oversleeping at Mrs. Cromwell's, just behind the right field stands.

"Upon her signal, a local kid would wake the great star with the words, 'Hey, Al ... you got to get your batting practice if you're gonna win the batting title,'" wrote Jim Kaplan.[128]

Mack could usually find his players just by driving up Lehigh Avenue, with the rookies drinking cherry Cokes at Don Hoffman's restaurant or Grove sneaking out of a speakeasy with a bottle in hand.

Just a season ago, in 1928, Philadelphia pushed the Yankees all the way to the last week of the pennant race, falling back by 2 1/2 games. It was a remarkable finish, considering they were 13 1/2 games behind the Yankees near the halfway point on July 4. They pulled to within a half-game during a series against the Yankees in mid-September, but Ruth and Gehrig were too much.

Ty Cobb, 40, and Tris Speaker, 41, played their final seasons with the Athletics in 1928. Cochrane was the 1928 MVP in the American League, and Foxx was about to make up for the losses of the veterans. Grove and Jack Quinn won 42 of the Athletics 98 games.

The Athletics ran away with the 1929 season, besting the Yankees by 18 games.

Babe Ruth was disappointed about 1929, missing 19 games for a suspected slight heart attack and then another injury. Reporters began speculating that he was nearing the end of his career, at age 34. Ruth

---

[127] Ibid.

[128] Kaplan , Jim, *Lefty Grove: American Original,* The Society of American Baseball Research (SABR), 2000.

dismissed that nonsense by hitting a blistering .345, leading the American League with 46 homers and a .697 slugging average.

The problem with the 1929 Yankees wasn't the absence of Ruth. It was the horrendous downfall of the pitching staff, with each star allowing almost a full run more per outing.

Everyone knew Ruth could play baseball. But he was turning out to be a popular columnist and a great forecaster. He accurately went out on a limb in spring training when he said he thought the Cubs would win their first pennant in a decade. Now he predicted a World Series win for them.

"I like the Athletics and I want them to win because they were my friendly enemies all season. But, in giving my opinion to the public as a baseball writer, I think the Cubs have a slight edge.

"I say that because they seem to have some advantage in pitching and a considerable advantage in World Series' experience. I've played in a lot of World Series since I broke into baseball and have seen a lot of others, but I'll be durned if I ever saw one where there was quite so much excitement as this one. Or one where there were so many people trying to get into the games."

With Groves' league-leading ERA and Earnshaw's 24-8 record, it was a pretty good guess that one of them would open the World Series. But Mack would not tell reporters.

While most of Chicago was reading the sports pages in anticipation of the World Series, the finance section of the papers reported the volatile stock market.

In one day, stocks would boom and sell at twice the amount that dividends would provide by hanging on to investments. One story reported how U.S. Steel now has more than 110,000 stockholders, the most in the nation.

At the start of the season, Wall Street stories questioned why stock prices were soaring so far beyond the financial performance of the companies.

Stories in the *Tribune* on February 4 and 5 said stock speculation was getting out of control, with banks experimenting with the idea of loaning huge amounts of money to invest in stock that kept generating even larger returns.

"If half a billion dollars of credit is to be poured into the Wall Street market every month, if it is to be supplemented by the activities of companies into whose lap the public thrusts such prodigious sums of money, to be used for no other purpose than buying stocks on a rising market, what is to stop the indefinite further rise?"

A story headlined "Speculation is National Game; Borrow to Play," warned about the increasing amounts of stock market loans.

But nobody seemed to be paying attention. Chicago was a spectacular boomtown in 1929, adding hundreds to its 3 million in population every day, second only to New York City.

Office towers were changing the skyscape. The new Palmolive Building opened in April at 919 N. Michigan Ave., opposite the famed Drake Hotel.

The Chicago Board of Trade building was nearly finished on Lasalle Street.

Everybody was getting into the stock market, not just big investors. U.S. Steel was organized on the stock exchange in 1917, only 12 years earlier, with 40,000 stockholders.

Hornsby had salted away a lot of his extra earnings in the stock market, and even Root was talked into a significant investment in stock earlier in 1929—by Wrigley. Wrigley told Root that he needed to build up investments that would support him after his career was over and said there was no way he could lose.

The volatile stock market dropped the most since 1896 on the Monday before the World Series started. But stocks always seemed to rebound, and everything seemed temporary.

Union efforts by the American Federation of Labor meant that the five-day, 40-hour week was starting to become the norm and catch on at America's factories.

But baseball fans were following another business, tracking the stats of the Cubs and Athletics and speculating on which team was better.

As the *Tribune* reported in an unbylined story on October 7:

180

Captains of big business are pigeonholing financial statements and poring over batting averages. Gentlemen of leisure are packing bags on country estates and thumbing time tables. Farmers are leaving harvest fields and factory hands the punch press. Even the bookkeeper shoves a pen behind his ear, looks dreamily out the window, and wishes he had two tickets. From north, south, east and west, they're coming—the lucky ones who have tickets and the courageous ones who believe they'll get some."

Irving Vaughan of the *Chicago Tribune* said the Athletics were better on paper, with the edge in pitching and catching because Hartnett could only pinch hit.

Vaughan figured Grove would start the opener even though he would be facing a Cub lineup of righties. Grove's fastball was not as threatening to this lineup as some of the other lefties the Cubs had faced, Vaughan wrote.

The southpaw pitching that beat the Cubs during the regular season was the slow, slower and slowest kind.

Unlike Grove, Walberg, the other left-handed notable on Mack's staff, can mix 'em up in dazzling fashion.

Earnshaw is the man the Cubs fear more than any one member of the Mack corps. He has the same stuff as Walberg except that he belongs to the right handed breed. It is his curve ball, if anything, that will do the damage.

Ehmke needs be reckoned only as a relief man. About the only chance for (Ehmke) to start a game would be for the Big Three to be slaughtered by the Cub batters and that's not likely.

In Root, the Cubs have a hurler of strange attainments. Root apparently has only average speed. He seldom attempts to slow up. His curve hooks just enough to deserve its name. Yet he ranks with the most effective in the league. The reason is excellent control and a peculiar quick delivery that puts the ball on top of the hitter before he knows it has been thrown. He's also side armed which adds to his effectiveness in his own park because of the background. This is especially true against a right handed batter.

Malone, who with Root, will have to share the big portion of the burden, is an opposite type. There are days when he is faster than Vance in his prime. There are days when he is a bit slower, but still goes well because of control. And there are days when inability to keep the ball over or inside the corners makes him almost helpless.

McCarthy said he is relieved the season is over and says the Athletics' edge in pitching will be matched by the Cubs' hitting.

Keystone View Company Stereograph – Library of Congress

Cubs in the dugout — 1929 World Series at Chicago

Game One

If we hated all the other Cubs, we'd be pulling for them to win today on account of Charlie Root being the pitcher. As fine and quiet a gentleman as ever pitched a World Series opener or a Sunday semi-pro game for the Armco's of Middletown, Ohio. Charlie ought to win today, if smart, calm pitching means anything. If he does conquer, there'll be no tooting of the Root trumpet—he hasn't got a trumpet. If he loses, he won't cuss his supporting cast. Root hates to lose just as much as any pitcher that ever lived, but he dislikes, "Tough luck, Charlie," consolations. Let's hope there won't be any opportunity for this form of consolation."

—Edward Burns, *Chicago Tribune*, on the morning
of opening day of the 1929 World Series.

It was a breezy spring day in St. Louis in April 1923 when the manager of the St. Louis Browns motioned to the bullpen to send in the rookie from Middletown, Ohio.

Charlie Root strode to the mound trying to show a confidence he certainly didn't feel.

This was Root's first day in the major leagues, and the first batter facing him was Detroit's Ty Cobb, a tough way to debut. The game was already lost, and the manager just wanted to see what this new kid would do against the best hitter in baseball.

Della's own words add great detail and match the essentials of what Root told sports columnist David Condon of the *Chicago Tribune*:[129]

When he reached the mound, he glanced to the stands where he knew
Dorothy was sitting and touched the brim of his cap, raising it just a

---

[129] Della Root Arnold, journal, pg. 161

fraction in a small salute. A gesture he would use every time he pitched, for more than 30 years, when she was in the stands.

He took the customary warm-up throws to the catcher, Hank Severeid, who had met him at the mound and said, "Don't let Cobb scare you; just throw what I call for."

Charlie took a long look at Cobb, one of his great baseball heroes, and heard him snarl, "OK, busher, let me see what ya' got."

Cobb had been raking the batter's box with his spikes and then set them deep.

So, thought Charlie, this is the great Ty Cobb! His first pitch came in under Cobb's chin knocking him back from the plate.

"You bush son of a bitch, don't you throw at me."

It was obvious that Severeid was trying to placate Cobb, to just give the rookie a chance. Cobb re-raked the batter's box with his spikes, then set them firmly in place. The next pitch knocked him down.

Cobb got up, grabbed his bat and started for the mound.

"You fresh, bush bastard, I'm gonna kill you with this bat."

Cobb started for the mound where Charlie stood motionless.

Severeid followed Cobb to the mound, yelling, "You lay a hand on that kid and I'll beat the shit out of you with this mask."

The first baseman said, "Go back to the plate, Ty, for God's sake this is the kid's first game in the majors."

"I know that," yelled, Ty, who was managing Detroit, "and he throws one more at me and it's gonna be his last."

The next three pitches were strikes.

Root started his career with a strikeout against the most feared player in the game and even had the guts to knock him down twice.

Cobb retired from baseball in 1928, at age 41, finishing on this same Philadelphia Athletics team that would now face Root in the World Series.

As Root prepared for his first World Series, the biggest game of his career, he must have been thinking about all of his highlights. In addition to his debut against Cobb, there had been the day in 1926 when Manager Joe McCarthy asked him to start his first Cub game.

"He was seated on the steps of the dugout chewing tobacco and watching the warm-ups and pepper games, when Joe McCarthy walked

184

up to him and said, 'Why are you lookin' so scared, Charlie?'" Della said.

"Charlie stood up and said, 'I'm not scared.'"

"'Well, you'd better be,' said Joe, 'You're pitching today.'"

"Then McCarthy turned and walked away."

"Charlie won that day and continued to win 18 for the season."

While the players honor early curfew and sleep, some probably restlessly, fans begin gathering throughout the night outside Wrigley Field.

At 6 a.m. a *Tribune* reporter counts 3,000 men, women and children in a line that extends from the ticket windows on Sheffield and Waveland avenues completely around the walls of the park and for another four blocks.

Several fans are playing cards and games. "At one point a checker match is in progress with watchers hanging over the shoulders of the contestants," the reporter wrote.

One man sleeps on a full-sized spring mattress that he somehow has wrestled to the park.

The morning *Tribune* reports that Root is today's starter based on how steady he is "even when the fire is hottest." They are still reporting that Connie Mack has not named the Athletics starter, but it probably will be Grove or Earnshaw.

Temperatures are expected to be in the 60s for Tuesday and Wednesday with moderate westerly winds by the 1:30 p.m. game time.

Gamblers favor the Athletics, the newspaper reports.

The *Tribune* has just finished erecting a huge scoreboard on the south side of the fifth floor in the rear of the *Tribune* Tower to show the inning-by-inning scores.

Quin Ryan and Pat Barnes are going to do the play by play of each game through WGN, the *Tribune* radio station.

Microphones have been installed in the new glass broadcasting booth at Wrigley Field, which will be used for the first time as the series opens.

Ryan has been broadcasting baseball games constantly since the Cubs and White Sox city series of 1924. He and Graham McNamee had been selected as the radio reporters on the national chain broadcasts to announce the Pittsburgh-Washington World Series in 1925 by Baseball Commissioner Judge K.M. Landis.

Ryan and WGN have broadcast more baseball games than any other announcer and station on the air.

For the last three seasons there has been a baseball broadcast from WGN every day during the season. During the last season every play by play was broadcast from the Chicago parks. Minute-by-minute telegraphic reports also were broadcast as if they were dispatched from out-of-town parks.

A competing newspaper, Hearst's *Herald and Examiner*, has announced that its radio station, KYW, will begin broadcasting with McNamee at 1 p.m., just thirty minutes before Root is scheduled to throw his first pitch.

The newspaper has also provided another choice. Fans press into Hearst Square, at Madison Street and Wacker Drive, ready to watch the big "Playograph" mechanically reproduce every play as fast as it comes in over the direct telegraph wire from Wrigley Field.

Several radio stations have covered the Cubs throughout the season, thanks to how open Wrigley was to the idea. Other owners frowned on what Wrigley had started, believing radio would be the death of ticket sales. They couldn't understand why an owner would give away anything for free.

Instead, attendance began to soar in every city where radio started to follow baseball. Wrigley correctly understood that hearing the game would build loyalty, and fans would want to see the games for themselves. It also didn't hurt that he put one of the best teams on the field for them to follow at the same time radio was on the rise.

Owning a radio was a luxury because the best sets cost more than $100, but it was second in popularity to having a car. Families who got their first radio would invite the neighbors over to sit around this piece of furniture that looked like a wardrobe perched on four spindles to put the radio dial at eye level. Edison Radio and phonograph combinations were the most heavily advertised. It was possible to get small, less powerful sets for a lower price.

The first World Series broadcast on radio was in 1921, when *New York Tribune* sports editor Grantland Rice phoned in an inning-by-inning summary to an announcer who did the broadcast.[130]

The Cubs have sold approximately 51,000 tickets for Game One, the most ever to attend Wrigley Field because 8,000 bleacher seats have been added behind the left-and right-field fences.

Fans are allowed to come into the ballpark and start filling the bleacher seats at 8:30 a.m. Even with the extra seats, the Cubs refunded more than $1 million to fans who could not be accommodated.

By 11 a.m., fans are getting impatient and the first of about a half dozen fights breaks out in the stands.

The whole Cuyler family is on hand by 11:00. They occupy a box just back of the Cub dugout that Wrigley has provided for them.

Della and Dorothy are in their seats a little later, several rows behind Wrigley, the screen and home plate, in Box 58, Tier 12.

From the number of five-gallon hats in the audience, it looks like most of Texas has moved into Chicago for the series. The Texans all claim to be boyhood friends of Rogers Hornsby, a reporter writes.

Photographers are all over the field, catching Wrigley as he shakes hands with Connie Mack and others. Sure enough, photographers are shooting Della and her Dad.

Politicians, like the Illinois and Wisconsin governors, make their way to the Cubs' dugout to shake hands with McCarthy and then visit Wrigley's box.

Babe Ruth is first spotted in the Philadelphia dugout, attired in a natty brown suit. It is a rather novel experience for the Babe to watch a World Series. He has played in six of the last eight.

At 12:30, the Athletics come up the tunnel and are tossing about a dozen baseballs back and forth, pausing now and again to autograph envelopes, old laundry lists and scorecards or to pose for the photographers, generally in company with Ruth.

---

[130] *World Series: A complete pictorial history*, pg. 94.

By 1 p.m., the Cubs trot out for fielding practice, getting the crowd stirred to their feet.

Mike Cvengros and Hank Grampp pitch batting practice and the crowd roars when Wilson arches a towering shot out of the park.

The game was delayed 15 minutes, until 1:45, because of the crush of fans trying to pack into their seats.

There is another baseball World Series going on in Chicago, and the Chicago American Giants win for the second year in a row behind player-manager Rube Foster.

The Cubs and Athletics had played these Negro League teams in exhibition. Hitters who knew the heat of Lefty Grove had learned that Satchel Paige was just as tough.

Catcher Josh Gibson hit home runs as far as only one other player that anybody ever saw—the Babe.

The shame was that fans never got to see how great these players would have matched up in the same major league baseball world.

> Every now and then there was a chance to compare the talents of these two baseball worlds. While blacks were banned from major league ball, sometimes white players played their Negro League counterparts in off-season barnstorming tours or for charity events.
>
> One day in such a game Hack batted against Leroy "Satchel" Paige, perhaps the greatest Negro League pitcher. The Cubs' slugger, the terror of National League pitchers, was none too successful against Paige.
>
> In one of his more memorable quotes, Wilson said of Paige's pitching, "The ball starts out like a baseball and, when it gets to the plate, looks like a marble."[131]

Connie Mack waits until game time to announce his starter, driving sportswriters crazy. Some report that Mack can't decide because he has three top choices—Grove, Walberg and Earnshaw.

Since Grove and Walberg are lefties and every pitcher in the Cub lineup except Grimm is a righty, Earnshaw is widely reported as the

---

[131] Parker, Clifton Blue, *Fouled Away,* pg. 60-61.

188

obvious choice. Earnshaw also has the league-leading 24-8 record and one of the team's best ERAs at 3.29.

But most of the writers don't know that Grove is having problems with his pitching hand and in four straight starts has had to come out early because of blisters.[132]

Mack decides that he has the luxury of using Grove in every pinch they get into in the Series, rather than wasting him in an entire start. Mack is ahead of his time to think of using his power pitcher as a closer in as many games as possible.

Not even Mack's players know who will start.

"Hey, Jim, look who's warming up," Al Simmons says to Jimmy Dykes.[133]

Howard Ehmke, 35, has only pitched 54⅔ innings all season, hasn't started in seven weeks, and has been told this is his last year with the Athletics.

More than 50,000 fans at Wrigley Field start to buzz in disbelief when they see Ehmke warming up.

"Everyone on the Cub bench grabbed a bat and asked to be put in the lineup," Grimm said. "Even the bat boy wanted to play."[134]

Earlier in the year, Mack had been so loaded with pitching that he'd considered dropping the aging veteran from the roster. But Mack reconsidered, and later he relates his strategy in his conversation with Ehmke —

> Ehmke was a veteran for whom I had deep regard. This was a hard decision for me to make. It was a sort of professional death sentence.
>
> "Mr. Mack," Ehmke replied, "I've always wanted to be on a pennant winner and in a World Series, and this is as close as I ever got to it."
>
> "Do you believe you could win a game in the World Series, Howard?" I asked.
>
> "Mr. Mack," he replied, shoving his pitching arm forward, "I've got one more good game in me, and I'd like to give it to you in October."
>
> "Howard," I said, "I've changed my mind. You're going to pitch that game in the series. You stay home and work out here in Phila-

---

[132] Kaplan, Jim, *Lefty Grove: American Original.*
[133] Ibid.

delphia. When the Cubs come here in their final games with the Phillies, go to every game and study their hitters carefully."[135]

Ehmke, a submarine pitcher, had started with the Federal League in 1915. Mack acquired him in 1926 even though he was 9-20 in 1925 with Boston. Ehmke completed 22 of the 31 games that he started and was a strong workhorse.

He is 7-2 in 1929 but hasn't pitched for weeks.

The shock carries as far as Philadelphia, where hundreds of Athletics fans gather on the streets outside the *Bulletin* newspaper building to watch the game's progress on a scoreboard and listen to an announcer with a direct wire to Wrigley.[136]

George Nikolas home movie

Submariner Howard Ehmke warms up before Game One of the 1929 World Series. The George Nikolas home movie from which these frames were taken shows only two warm-up pitches by Ehmke, one delivered from about 8 o'clock, and this one above from 6 o'clock. The middle frame captures the ball leaving Ehmke's hand.

---

[134] Grimm, Charlie, *Jolly Cholly*.

[135] Mack, Connie, *My 66 Years in the Big Leagues: The Great Story of America's National Game*, The John C. Winston Co., Philadelphia and Toronto, 1950.

[136] Kashatus, William C., *Connie Mack's '29 Triumph: The Rise and Fall of the Philadelphia Athletics Dynasty*, McFarland & Co., Jefferson, NC, and London, 1999.

As the game begins, fans have every reason to expect a high-scoring game. The Cubs have scored 982 runs during the season and the Athletics 901.

But pitching is just as strong, with the Athletics having the edge, having allowed only 615 runs during the season, compared to the Cubs' 758. In addition to the National League's greatest number of shutouts, the Cubs' defense has allowed the fewest errors in the league.[137]

As Root prepares to make the first pitch, Eddie Lautenbacher is in the stands watching. He had been on the field with the Cubs at Catalina but would never make it into a major league game. He is at Wrigley with his free lifetime pass, a gold card given him by the Cubs.[138]

George Nikolas home movie

Root, warming up before Game One —
Note his side-arm delivery

[137] Gilbert, Warren N., *A Cunning Kind of Play: The Cubs-Giants Rivalry, 1876-1932,* 2002, McFarland & Co., Inc., Jefferson, NC, pg. 187.
[138] Eddie Lautenbacher, phone interview with author, Oct. 28, 2004.

George Nikolas home movie

Root delivers during Game One of the 1929 World Series.

Root and Ehmke breeze through the first inning, with Root striking out Haas and Simmons.

Ehmke goes after the Cubs with two pitches—slow and slower.

Reporter Irving Vaughan of the *Tribune* wrote:

> Sometimes he throws one a bit overhand. Sometimes it is turned loose with a sidearm motion. Frequently he dangles one in front of the batter with an underhand delivery. The Cubs hadn't seen a man like this all season. They were swinging as if speed balls, instead of slow foolers, were coming up to them.

In the second, Root gets into trouble when he allows a couple of hits, but a double play bails him out.

Ehmke gets his first two strikeouts in the bottom of the second when he fans Cuyler and Stephenson.

Root retires the next 12 batters, rolling through the sixth inning.

Ehmke is putting on a record-setting performance. When he drops down for his submarine delivery, his hand looks like it will scrape the mound. The ball is delivered from below Ehmke's left knee, appearing to come out of the white shirts of the fans crowded into the new bleachers in the outfield.

Universal Newspaper Newsreel – National Archives

Root delivers during Game One
of the 1929 World Series.

Ehmke strikes out Root to open the third. McMillan singles and English follows with a double. With only one out, McMillan holds at third. But Hornsby and Wilson both strike out to end the threat.

Cuyler strikes out again when he faces Ehmke in the fourth. Root and McMillan strike out in the fifth.

English, Hornsby and Wilson strike out in the sixth.

Jimmie Foxx spoils Root's two-hit shutout with a solo home run in the seventh, the only mistake Root makes.

Foxx is only 21 and already in his fifth season in 1929, ending a sensational year with a .354 average, 33 homers, and 123 RBI.

The only home run hitters better than this kid in the American League are Ruth, Gehrig and Foxx's teammate Simmons.

Home Run Baker had retired from the Athletics and was coaching in a Class D league when he discovered Foxx at age sixteen and signed him in 1924. Baker turned to his former manager who had discovered him—Connie Mack— and launched Foxx's career.

Mack signed Foxx on December 1, 1924. Foxx bulked up doing chores on his father's dairy farm in Sudlersville, Maryland.

"He even has muscles in his hair," a pitcher once said of his appearance and strength.

Foxx dropped out of high school, despite his mom's objections, and two months later was on a train to Fort Myers, Florida, for spring training. The trip would launch 21 seasons in professional baseball by one of the greatest power hitters of all time.[139]

The Cubs try to rally behind Root in their half of the seventh with hits from Cuyler and Stephenson.

Grimm advances both with a sacrifice. But Heathcote flies out as a pinch-hitter and doesn't hit it deeply enough to score the run. McCarthy has no choice but to lift Root for a pinch hitter and try one last time to get the run.

The move fails when Hartnett becomes Ehmke's 12th strikeout victim, tying the World Series record.

The Athletics score two more runs in the ninth when Cochrane bloops a single past Hornsby, and English boots the first of two sure double play balls that follow.

The Cubs go down fighting. Wilson slashes a nasty line shot back at Ehmke and is out. Dykes hustles on a grounder from Cuyler but throws the ball into the dugout, and Cuyler reaches second with only one out.

Stephenson drives a single to center and Cuyler scores. Grimm singles to right but is forced out at second when Blair bats for Gonzales.

Tolson, in the roster spot vacated by Berly Horne, gets his first and only career at-bat in a World Series.

With two strikes on Tolson, Ehmke calls time and motions for catcher Cochrane to come to the mound.

---

[139] Ibid.

"When you get back there, delay as much as you can," he orders his backstop. "The longer he stands in the box, the more nervous he's going to get."

Umpire Bill Klem gets tired of waiting and orders an end to the conference. Cochrane returns behind the plate and gives his pitcher a sign. Ehmke shakes him off. Cochrane gives another sign, and again Ehmke shakes it off.

They continue the ritual in an attempt to frazzle Tolson. It works. Ehmke takes the sign for one last time, shakes it off, and quick-pitches a strike right down the middle of the plate. As he releases the ball, Cochrane yells at the top of his lungs, "Hit it!"[140]

Tolson takes the cue and whiffs. The game is over. The Athletics win their first World Series game in 16 years.

"It was one of the greatest thrills of my life to see Ehmke pitch that game and break a world's record," Mack wrote years later. "He smashed the record that Big Ed Walsh had held for 23 years when Ed struck out 12 men in a World Series. Ehmke raised the ante to 13." [141]

> After Ehmke had fanned Wilson a second time, someone on the bench asked [Wilson] what he was throwing. "Looks to me like a bean bag," said Hack.
>
> "Well, why don't one of you guys knock the beans out of it," suggested Malone.
>
> When we did make contact, it sounded like we had hit a wet sponge.
>
> Ehmke killed us with amazing control, only walking one. [142]

Grantland Rice writes, "The long right arm of Howard Ehmke, the Philadelphia veteran, sounded the drum beat of woe to 51,000 Chicago rooters this afternoon as it fell across the back of the Cubs like a whip."

Cochrane gets in trouble for how loudly and profanely he harassed the Cubs during the game.

"Hello, sweethearts," Cochrane repeatedly said as he greeted the Cubs who stepped to the plate. "We're gonna serve tea this afternoon."

---

[140] Ibid.
[141] Mack, Connie, his autobiography.
[142] Grimm, Charlie, *Jolly Cholly.*

Commissioner Kenesaw Mountain Landis, a Cub fan second and powerful baseball arbiter first, threatened to suspend any player who continued such harassment.

After the game, Cochrane raves about how great Root was. "The dope we had on Root didn't do him justice," Mickey said. "It was indeed unfortunate for him that he had to be pitted against a pitcher who was hurling such brilliant baseball."

In the *Tribune* coverage was this one-paragraph brief: *Ralph A. Wertheim, 45, a Cubs fan, died of a heart attack after hearing Foxx hit the home run off Root. His home was at 5455 Greenwood Ave.*

Game Two — Lefty Grove

Our poor Cubs! Sick at heart and sore of mind and body are they.
And extensively disillusioned about their own prowess.
        —Edward Burns, *Chicago Tribune*, Oct. 10, 1929.

There is no mystery about the starter in Game Two. Reporters joke, however, that Connie Mack may go after one more surprise and start spitballer Jack Quinn.

But Mack goes with his most reliable starter of the season, George Earnshaw.

Cubs manager Joe McCarthy goes with an equally reliable starter, Pat Malone.

Wrigley Field feels more like Soldier Field during a fall football game and fans cover up with wool blankets.

Malone starts strong by striking out the side in the first. Woody English tries to get something started with a one-out double, but Hornsby strikes out yet again. Wilson walks and then Cuyler strikes out.

For the first time all season at Wrigley, Cub fans are booing Hornsby.

Earnshaw and Malone are matching each other, and it looks like Malone is going to breeze through the third after he gets the first two outs. But then Cochrane singles and Simmons walks.

Up comes Jimmie Foxx, whose wife, Helen, is listening on the radio from Kent General Hospital in Dover, Deleware.

Malone delivers and Foxx blasts a three-run homer into the temporary stands over Waveland Avenue. Mrs. Foxx is cheering while their six-day-old son, Jimmie Junior, is crying.

Earnshaw lets up with the lead, walking McMillan. English strikes out and, yet again, Hornsby does the same. Earnshaw walks Wilson and Cuyler and then runs the count to 3-0 on Stephenson with the bases loaded. Stephenson pops out after a 3-2 count.

In the fourth, Dykes singles to right and moves to second on Boley's sacrifice. English boots a grounder from the pitcher and Dykes moves to third. Malone walks Bishop to load the bases. Dykes scores when Haas hits into a force, but Simmons drives in two more after Malone loads the bases with another walk.

At the end of four, the Athletics are leading 6-0.

Hornsby and Wilson finally break out of their funks and hit singles to open the fifth. Earnshaw fans Cuyler and gets two outs before Stephenson scores Hornsby with a single. Wilson scores on a Grimm single. Then Stephenson scores on Taylor's single.

At 6-3, Mack was taking no chances and lifts Earnshaw to bring in Lefty Grove for the rest of the game.

Robert Moses "Lefty" Grove is similar to Root in many ways, working up from the minors and into the majors on almost the same career path. They started as teens on industrial teams, and hit their prime at this moment in 1929, both appearing in their first World Series.

They were born in March, although a year apart. Root was 30 and Grove was 29, the typical best years of a major league pitcher.

As kids, both were deadly to rabbits and squirrels with rocks and could throw hard with either arm.

Root got his first shot in the majors in 1923 and came up with Chicago in 1926. Grove was a 25-year-old rookie in 1925, held back longer than he should have been because he was so valuable to his minor league team, already having won 100 games before he came to the majors.

Mack paid an unprecedented $100,600 to get Grove after his eye-popping 1924 minor league season of 26-6 and 3.01 ERA. Grove joked that he was traded previously in the minors so the owner could improve his ballpark, saying he was the only player traded for a fence. By 1929, Grove was making between $20,000 and $30,000, less than the Cubs were paying Root.

Wrigley actually was in the final running to acquire Grove from the minors, offering $100,000 and being bested by only $600—and by a strong friendship between the seller and Mack. Brooklyn also had offered $100,000, in a bidding war that made Grove's the most expensive baseball transaction in history by that date, topping the Babe Ruth deal of 1919 at $100,000.

Grove and Root really had only one pitch, a fast ball. They would change speeds and locations to baffle hitters, although Grove easily had the most blazing heater when he needed it and was the dominant pitcher in the American League, having led every year of his career so far in strikeouts, including this season. At 20-6, Grove had the best winning percentage in the American League (.769) and the best ERA (2.81). Root also had the best winning percentage in his league, at 19-6, (.760).

Both could throw a curve but rarely did. Neither could stand to lose and could not tolerate less than perfection in himself. The difference was that Root seethed quietly. Grove would tear up the locker room.

Athletics teammate Jimmy Dykes said, "You never talked to him on the mound. No matter if he was ahead by 10 runs or behind by one, he was just plain fierce during a game. Not even Mr. Mack would go near him. If he lost a close game, he'd come in and tear the clubhouse apart. I mean literally—stools and equipment would be flying and lockers kicked in."

Grove was so intense that on the day he was scheduled to start, he reported to the clubhouse with a scowl. He ignored his own teammates and snarled at the sportswriters. It was suicide for a photographer to try to take his picture because the pitcher would pick up a ball and throw it through the lens. His behavior was worse if he lost, including tearing off his uniform and destroying everything in sight, from water coolers to teammates.[143]

Despite these exhibitions, Grove's teammates found him a "lovable character" and knew that he was giving everything he had to win. He

---

[143] Kashatus, William C., *Connie Mack's '29 Triumph: The Rise and Fall of the Philadelphia Athletics Dynasty*, pg. 99.

actually was shy, uneasy with strangers, and uncomfortable in big cities. He would rather be alone, fishing.

Like Hornsby, he was most likely to be found sitting alone in the hotel lobby, watching everyone pass by. He also enjoyed a steak dinner the night before his big games. After a cigar in the hotel lobby, Grove headed to his room at 9 p.m. and read a detective or western magazine until 10 p.m. He was up by 6 a.m., except on days he pitched, when he slept later.

McCarthy knew Grove well. McCarthy's Louisville Colonels won the minor league World Series in 1921 against Grove and the Orioles, five games to three. Grove was wild and nervous, losing three times and walking 15 batters in 13⅓ innings.

Root and Grove had the confidence of aces, fearless because they believed they could get any batter out in baseball if the game was on the line. They were remarkably similar in their control and ability to keep runners off the bases in 1929, averaging about a hit per inning and walking one batter in more than three innings. In 272 innings of 1929, Root walked 83 and gave up 286 hits. Grove pitched 275 ⅓ innings, walked 81 and gave up 278 hits.

They caused more fear at the plate because of their willingness to plunk hitters, especially those who dug in or tried to crowd the plate. Both adamantly avoided being headhunters, however.

At 6 feet 3 inches, Grove towered over everyone in baseball except his boss. The Tall Tactician, Connie Mack, was 6 feet 1 inch. Grove's height and arm were even more threatening on the Shibe Park mound, raised five inches higher than other ballparks because the rule wasn't really enforced. He wound up like a windmill, throwing his arms over his head two or three times and kicking his right leg so high to distract the hitters. He would reach back so far that it looked like the knuckles of his left hand were scraping the mound and then he launched with a huge stride coming right at the hitter. [144]

The Athletics now had a roster of one of the most fiercely competitive teams ever, with several players who obsessively hated to lose.

---

[144] Kaplan, Jim. *Lefty Grove: American Original.*

Grove and Cochrane would go into rages, and Simmons would get himself as riled as possible before facing enemy pitchers.

Cochrane was the undisputed team leader and was just as serious about losing. One player said that if the team lost 1-0, Cochrane would have stools, gloves, and bats flying in all directions in the clubhouse. [145]

Grove does exactly as Mack had hoped in Game Two. He slams the door on the Cubs, allowing no runs in 4⅓ innings.

The Athletics add three more runs on an RBI single by Foxx in the seventh, and a two-run homer by Simmons in the eighth.

The Cubs lose 9-3, blowing both games at home, and now head to Philadelphia.

Earnshaw and Grove have combined for 13 strikeouts, matching the record just set by Ehmke. Twelve strikeouts in a World Series had stood as a 23-year-old record, and now the Cubs have topped it twice as the victims.

Cuyler has struck out five times, Hornsby four. Four of six pinch-hitters have struck out. Hartnett has pinch hit in both games and struck out both times.

The *Tribune* contrasts how tough this game is. Root loses Game One when he gives up only three hits in seven innings. Earnshaw wins Game Two after getting pounded for three runs and nine hits in just 4 ⅔ innings.

---

[145] Kashatus, pg. 100.

Game Three — Train & Travel

When the Cubs arrived at the Benjamin Franklin Hotel in Philadelphia, a string orchestra on the balcony played the "funeral march" as
the Cubs walked into the lobby.
—Della Root Arnold, p. 37 of her personal journal.

Irving Vaughan was on the train to Philadelphia with the Cubs,
along with Ed Burns. "It wasn't exactly a funeral train that conveyed
the Cubs eastward tonight for a change in scenery in the world strikeout
series," Vaughan wrote.

"Here and there in compartments or common, everyday Pullman
sections, you could locate a gentleman with a long face," Vaughan
wrote. "He was a stockholder, an official or a favored fan and, occasionally, a player.

"In the main, however, the athletes, who should be depressed over
their miserable display, were laughing out loud and remarking that a
winning streak might start any moment."

Manager Joe McCarthy was so stressed by the two games that his
first bites to eat since the Series began were on the train because his
stomach had been so upset, Vaughan wrote.

"McCarthy is a worried man. He could have put on a false front
and laughed it off, but he was only a few miles away from Chicago
tonight when he pointed out that even a good team is gone when its
hitters have fallen down."

Hornsby was having an uncharacteristic, awful slump. "I struck out
on pitched balls that in the season I would kill nine times in ten attempts," Hornsby said.

"They were right down the middle. When I missed them I actually thought they must have gone through my bat."

English was down in the dumps about his three errors and two other throws that blew double plays. The other players were patting him on the back and trying to reassure him.

All the hitters had tightened up and were not swinging with confidence, Vaughan wrote.

Root is mentioned as the Cubs' most important chance to come back because of how well he did in Game One. McCarthy said he's holding Root for Game Four but will use him in the next game if he needs relief for Guy Bush.

Normally two special cars were on the train. But five Cub cars were on this World Series Special because of the number of wives, reporters and others accompanying the team.

During the regular season, there was a special Pullman for sleeping and dining. The other car was where the cards were played and the team gathered.[146]

"They particularly liked pinochle, two- or three-handed, and that can be a very cutthroat game," Della wrote. "Dad knew bridge and poker but liked pinochle. When we traveled with the team, Dad didn't play cards.

"He didn't know one rule about bridge and he could whip you. He had a very mathematical mind."

"Riggs Stephenson and Cliff Heathcote are reputed to be the best bridge players on the club, but their supremacy is challenged by Hal Carlson and Root, Burns wrote.

"Coach Jimmy Burke claims to be the best pinochle player on the club, and one of the best in the world. There are several who question this, notably Dr. Lotshaw.

"Gabby Hartnett, Pat Malone and Guy Bush are the best rummy players because of their great persistence. Bush particularly will withstand all number of torture to emerge triumphant in the end.

---

[146] Della Root Arnold, journal, pg. 47-48.

"Hack Wilson, perhaps, is the best all round card player on the club, though he never plays. His passion is kibbitzing. He likes to kibbitz a heart-game best."

"Peeking wasn't considered cheating, and Hartnett was the champion," Grimm wrote. "As if this weren't bad enough, he'd brag about it. He could innocently lean forward and photograph with his eye the 13 cards in an opponent's hands. And he picked up information, too, from the reflection of enemy cards from the Pullman window. Ed Burns was just as bad at peeking." [147]

Grimm wrote that railroad travel was his favorite thing about his early years in baseball, where players spent so much time together and developed "a community spirit." [148]

Dorothy, Charlie, and the other players were not amused by the "funeral march" greeting they received from the orchestra when they entered the hotel lobby in Philadelphia.

According to the *Tribune*, the Cubs occupied one whole floor of the hotel and had a private dining room downstairs with a special chef and two assistants to cook for them.

Also greeting them in the lobby was a flashy, 40-year-old woman with a dazzling smile, hanging out with the gamblers. Her dress and the way she walked made all the men turn to watch, Della wrote.

Root found a note in his hotel door key slot asking him to call Room 316.

Puzzled, Charlie told Dorothy, "We don't have any players on the third floor."

"Well," Dorothy replied. "If you gave me a hundred guesses, I'd say it was the shill every time."

As Dorothy and Charlie went downstairs for dinner, Charlie checked the front desk and confirmed that Room 316 did belong to the flashy woman.

"He didn't think much about it, as he wasn't the least interested in molls, dolls or falls, so he promptly forgot it," Della wrote.

---

[147] Grimm, Charlie, *Jolly Cholly,* pg. 96.

But Dorothy didn't.

After dinner, the woman walked by, and Dorothy confronted her about trying to lure her husband.

"You don't think that Charlie Root would look at an old hen like you, do you?" Dorothy said. "Why don't you go back and cover the Army camps you missed in World War I."

"That did it," Della wrote. "The next day, neither gamblers nor the shill were in sight."[149]

McCarthy thought about having a grueling practice and getting the players familiar with Shibe Park Instead, he decided to give them a day entirely away from baseball to get their minds off what everybody thinks must be trouble. The only thing he did was to ask them to get plenty of rest.

Burns wrote that the team was still confident but quieter. He said McCarthy's orders were no church suppers, no radio spiels and no autographs, so they would get away from baseball.

Shibe Park was one of the early stadiums to take advantage of the new way of mixing concrete and steel to have large columns and open spans. Shibe opened in 1909, and an upper deck was added in 1925 to all parts of the park except right field.

The dimensions were massive with center field a mammoth 468 feet from home plate. Left was more like the norm at 334 feet, but right was deep at 380 feet.

The 12-foot wall in right, with no other obstructions, was perfect for enterprising residents in the neighborhood.

Streetcars delivered many of the fans to the game, and often they would see the players coming the same way. Nearing the stadium, the sounds of vendors, police whistles, ooh-gahs of automobile horns and the clanging bells of the streetcars.

Just for the World Series, the right field neighbors constructed portable bleachers on their rooftops but also removed all four windows

---

[148] Ibid., pg. 94.
[149] Della, pg. 37-38.

from their front bedroom and packed another dozen spectators there as well.

Mothers made lemonade and sent their children to buy hot dogs from the corner store. The kids would purchase a dozen for a nickel, return home and sell them for a dime each.

Tax collectors didn't miss a beat, taxing each house that added bleachers. One family still made a killing. They made up the $20 tax with one individual alone, charging the cameraman for Pathe Newsreel Service that amount to shoot from the roof. The same money rolled in when Fox Movietone News and Universal News also wanted the same prime spot.[150]

Connie Mack was making plans on the Athletics train ride back home. He decided to go with Earnshaw again, since he went only half of Game Two and would have a day's rest.

"You were working too fast yesterday when they knocked you out of the box," Mack said. " I want you to take more time between pitches tomorrow. Step off the mound, look around at your outfielders, rub the ball, pick up some dirt. Just slow down your rhythm and you'll beat those Cubs."

Coming off two losses, 26 strikeouts and overwhelming pitching from Ehmke and Grove, the Cubs hear Athletics fans yelling about a sweep as they arrive at Shibe Park.

Just before the first ball is pitched, the crowd stands for a minute of silent prayer for Miller Huggins, late manager of the Yanks.

In the first, Earnshaw seems to be chasing the strikeout records, getting McMillan and Hornsby to fan.

In the second, Wilson triples, hitting the ball over Haas in center. Cuyler bounces deep to short and McCarthy doesn't send Wilson. Then Stephenson grounds to Bishop playing in on the grass and Wilson is an easy victim at the plate. A separate story questions McCarthy's judgment and his stress increases.

---

[150] Philadelphia details come from Kashatus book about Connie Mack.

In Philadelphia's second, Bush fans Foxx on curves. Miller flies to Cuyler. Dykes and Boley single with Dykes sliding into third. McMillan loses the ball and Boley moves to second. As Dykes starts to steal home, Earnshaw strikes out.

Bush gets into trouble in the third when Haas singles over Grimm's head with one out. Cochrane hits straight back at Bush, and the ball rolls into center. Bush runs the count to 3-0 with Simmons. He gets a strike and then Simmons pops out to McMillan. The dangerous Foxx hits an easy roller to English, who makes yet another error, loading the bases. Miller flies to Stephenson to end the inning.

The Cubs go down in order in the fifth. Philadelphia gets a run on two hits. Cochrane bounces to deep short, but beats English's throw to first. Miller singles to drive in Cochrane after Simmons and Foxx were retired.

In the sixth, Bush leads off with a surprising walk. McMillan fouls out on a bunt, caught by Cochrane. English bounces to Dykes who charges but can't pick up the ball. Hornsby singles past Boley and Bush scores to tie the game, 1-1. Wilson grounds out, moving English to third and Hornsby to second.

Cuyler fouls off several pitches and then bounces a single over the pitcher's head, scoring English and Hornsby, for a 3-1 Cubs lead. That stands up as the final score, and the Cubs have finally won a World Series game.

Bundled in blankets and celebrating the win was Manager Joe McCarthy's mother.

Mrs. Guy Bush said her husband's World Series win was "one of the happiest days in my life."

Grimm had left his banjo in Chicago and didn't feel like playing until the win. As soon as Grimm made the final putout of the game, Grimm, Cuyler and Heathcote went searching for a banjo.

"Grimm's exuberance was typical of the entire outfit. Pandemonium prevailed in the clubhouse after the game," Burns wrote.

Instead of talking baseball, Grimm, Cuyler and Heathcote talked about their upcoming vaudeville debut on Oct. 18 at a Chicago loop theater, including the prospect of sawing a lady in half and a slide for life from the third balcony to the stage.

The shouting and celebrating had turned Grimm's voice into something too husky to be sweet, Cuyler lost control of his vocal chords completely, and the team had confiscated Heathcote's ukulele.

Many of the players had bylined articles about the World Series, but the *Tribune* reported that none was spotted with a typewriter or even chewing a pencil except to figure out their winners' share of the series money.

A player complimented Foxx for his great column. "Thank you very much," Foxx replied. "What does it say?"

1929 World Series 12-page Program and
Scorecard with photos of Cubs and Athletics

Game Four — Debacle

We've looked at our scorebook glassy eyed for an hour now, thinking there must be some mistake, but 10 she is, folks.
—Edward Burns, *Chicago Tribune*.

After Charlie Root shut the Athletics down in his seven innings of work in Game One, the Cubs felt Root gave them the best shot at tying up this Series in Game Four.

Much better than Game One, however, the Cubs decide to help Root with a lot-of-runs support.

Root mows through the first six hitters in two innings, almost effortlessly, and has a three-hit shutout going as he enters the seventh.

Root has repeated his phenomenal start of Game One. Typical of his control, Root issues no walks. The only hits are a single by Dykes in the third, a double by Cochrane in the fourth and a scratch infield single by Miller in the fourth.

None of these hits amounts to anything because of spectacular, solid defense by the Cubs for the first time in the Series.

With the center field wall 468 feet from home plate, Wilson has a huge area to patrol and the sun glares just over the upper deck in perfect line with home plate, adding to the difficulty.

In the fifth, Wilson loses a Dykes fly in the sun and is charged with an error. Even with dark sunglasses, Wilson struggles to see any fly rising over the upper deck.

On the very next play, Wilson makes the most spectacular play of the World Series. Wilson robs Boley of a sure triple with an incredible, running, one-handed catch of a drive hit deep to right center. Wilson saves at least one run, maybe two, and preserves Root's shutout as players slap him on the back upon his return to the dugout.

Just as his first appearance, Root allows no runs through six.

This time he is sitting on an 8-0 lead as he starts the seventh.

The Cubs take a while, but jump all over the spitball and slow ball garbage of John Quinn. Mack was hoping for a repeat of what Ehmke did, fooling the power hitters on junk.

Grimm's two-run homer in the fourth gets it started. The Cubs add five more runs in the sixth, starting with four singles in a row by Hornsby, Wilson, Cuyler and Stephenson, and Quinn is gone. Walberg comes in to relieve. Grimm bunts back to Walberg, who throws the ball into the stands, with Cuyler and Stephenson scoring and Grimm going all the way to third.

Root family archives

Charlie Grimm — photo autographed to Charlie Root. They remained friends until death.

Taylor's sacrifice fly was the first out, and Grimm scores to make it 7-0. Root and McMillan strike out to end the Cub explosion.

The Cubs add a run off Rommell in the seventh when Hornsby triples and then scores on a Cuyler single.

Guy Bush is getting even for all of the bench jockeying and harassment the Athletics threw his way during his previous start. Every time Chicago scores, Bush places a blanket over his head and does a mock Indian war dance.

Root has never relinquished this kind of lead.

Simmons blows Root's shutout by opening the bottom half of the seventh with a home run all the way up on the roof of the second deck in left field. Foxx follows with a single to right. Wilson blows an easy fly ball from Miller, losing it in the sun, moving Foxx to second.

210

George Nikolas home movie

The *Herald and Examiner* "Playograph" scoreboard outside Wrigley Field (1929). Note pedestrians, horse-drawn vehicles, and streetcar tracks below. During Game One of the Series a crowd blocked the street to monitor the game's progress on the mechanical scoreboard.

Dykes singles to left, scoring Foxx and moving Miller to second. Boley singles to right center, Miller scores, and Dykes stops at second.

Burns pinch-hits for Rommel and pops up for the first out. Bishop singles to center, scoring Dykes and sending Boley to second.

McCarthy lifts Root and is getting nervous about an eight-run lead now shaved down to 8-4.

Art Nehf comes in to pitch and it looks like he is going to get the second out easily when Haas flies to center. But Wilson again loses it in the sun. It rolls all the way to the wall for a three-run, inside-the-park home run.

Still leading 8-7, Nehf walks Cochrane and he is gone. McCarthy brings in Sheriff Blake. Simmons singles for his second hit of the inning. Foxx drives in Cochrane with a single, his second hit of the inning, too.

McCarthy goes to Malone, his fourth pitcher of the inning. On his first pitch, Malone hits Miller, loading the bases.

Dykes doubles for his second hit of the inning, scoring Cochrane and Simmons, with Miller going to third. Boley and Burns mercifully end the inning with strikeouts.

The Athletics score 10 runs in the seventh and win 10-8 when Lefty Grove comes in and slams the door again.

Several World Series records for one inning are set in the disastrous seventh: Most hits (10); most men at bat (15); most batters up twice (6); most times for same pinch-hitter to appear (2); most home runs (2); most base hits by one player (2 each by Simmons, Foxx and Dykes); most total bases by one player (5 with Simmons' home run and single); most runs scored by one player (2 each by Simmons and Foxx.)

Eighteen runs in the game tie 1921 records set by the Giants and Yankees.

Edward Burns captures the pain and suffering as he types out his game account from the press box:

> It remained for our beloved Cubs to furnish the greatest debacle, the most terrific flop, in the history of the world series and one of the worst in the history of major league baseball games of all kinds.
>
> It doesn't seem possible, fellow mourners, but the Athletics scored 10 runs—10, count 'em if you've the heart—10 in one inning to gulp up a handsome 8 to 0 lead which our boys boasted going into the seventh inning.
>
> No other team ever has scored 10 runs in one inning of a world series.
>
> We've looked at our score book glassy eyed for an hour now, thinking there must have been some horrible mistake....
>
> Until that all destroying seventh, Hack Wilson was the old reliable of the Chicago forces but tonight he has the assurance that he will take his place at the head of the list of World Series' goats. Snodgrass and Peckinpaugh now have solace. But for Hack's blindness, the Athletics couldn't have made more than three runs, if that many.

The Cubs beat one World Series record by allowing 10 runs in one inning and they tied another by striking out eight times. Their four-game record of 44 strikeouts ties marks that were set in a six-game and an eight-game post-season series. If just one man strikes out Monday, they will have the undisputed and dubious title. [151]

Hack Plaque – Baseball Hall of Fame

---

[151] All game details draw on five key sources as follows: *Baseball's 10 Greatest Games,* pg. 61, including detailed box score. Charles Alexander's book, *Rogers Hornsby,* p. 157. *Chicago Tribune.* William C. Kashatus' book, *Connie Mack's '29 Triumph: The Rise and Fall of the Philadelphia Athletics Dynasty,* McFarland & Co., Jefferson, NC, and London, 1999. Clifton Blue Parker's book, *Fouled Away,* pg. 80-87.

Champs, not Chumps

I have caught other balls in the sun and I should have caught
those yesterday. I'm a big chump for missing them, and nobody
is going to tell me different.
—Hack Wilson, *Chicago Tribune*, Sunday, Oct. 13, 1929.

Charlie Root didn't believe in good losers, bluntly calling that kind
of talk "horse shit."

He was brilliant until the seventh inning in his first two World
Series games. Deep into both games, Philadelphia didn't score or get
more than three hits. That still did not make him a good loser.

Root was so competitive that he even had to beat young Della and
Junior at cards or other games.

Dorothy once asked, "Why don't you let them win?"

Charlie bristled, "When they're good enough, they'll win."

Her dad's focus on winning rubbed off on Della. She kept a scrapbook of her dad's games—but only clipped the stories about his wins.

Based on her scrapbook, Charlie joked, people would say, "Charlie
Root was the greatest pitcher who ever lived. He never lost a game."

"Well, who in the world would save clippings of losses?" Della explained.

Her scrapbook contained nothing about the 1929 World Series, except
for the pre-Series stories about her dad.

Hack Wilson was an equally fierce competitor. Losing two flies in
the seventh inning sun had opened the floodgates for the 10-run deluge
and Wilson showed an emotional side in the dugout that his teammates
had never seen.

Coming off the field after the worst inning in baseball history, Wilson ran straight to Root, in tears, to apologize.

214

Root replied, without hesitation, "There will be other games. We wouldn't be here without you." [152]

Woody English gave the same account. "Bet you could kill Hack," English said as he came off the field.

"We wouldn't be in the World Series if it wasn't for Hack." [153]

Reporters surrounded Root after the game, egging him on to blame Wilson. As Irving Vaughan reported for the *Tribune,* "Charlie Root, who had more reason than any man on the club to feel bitter about what happened to his pitching because of the sun blindness suffered by Wilson, took the trouble to tell the stocky outfielder that, after all, it was just a ball game."

Wilson could not be consoled. "That's a swell speech, but it's a lot of baloney," Hack told Vaughan.

Vaughan reported that Root was not putting on a false front, calmly picking up a bag of golf clubs to go out with his Chicago banker friend Murray MacLeod. Vaughan added, "... to play a game in which catching the ball doesn't count."

Wilson tried to mask how deeply hurt he was, but his suffering was clear during private moments with his teammates.

In public, Wilson acted as though he was taking the disaster in stride. That night after the game, Wilson entered a Philadelphia restaurant, pulled down the window shades near his table, and sardonically asked the maitre d' to dim the lights so he wouldn't misjudge the soup. [154]

Manager Joe McCarthy also defended Wilson.

As Vaughan reported:

> "They may want to blame Wilson. You can't fasten it on him," McCarthy said. "The poor kid simply lost the ball in the sun, and he didn't put the sun there....
>
> The fancy writers of the future may paint him as the goat as Fred Snodgrass was painted when he dropped a fly ball that gave Boston a

---

[152] Della Root Arnold, author's interviews and her journal.

[153] Ibid, as told to her by Woody English.

[154] Kashatus, William C*., Connie Mack's '29 Triumph: The Rise and Fall of the Philadelphia Athletics Dynasty.*

world title over the Giants in 1912. Hack knew that the game went away because the sun blinded him, but he wasn't moaning and putting on a false face of lengthy vertical dimensions. He didn't hide in the clubhouse after the game. Neither did he dash to his room the minute the two police escorted buses unloaded the unhappy party in front of the club's hotel.

Hack walked into the lobby with a smile on his face. There were hundreds on the sidewalk and other hundreds inside the hotel. Hack stopped and talked to anybody who hailed him.

"Couldn't see the balls," he said when asked for a few words. "I dropped Dykes' fly in the fifth and put Root in a hole because I was late in locating it. Miller's fly in the seventh was short, and when I got a line on it I was too far back. Haas' ball later in the seventh never was in my vision until it was almost to the ground. I stuck out my bare hand to get it, but it bounced past for a homer."

Hack then added that he was wearing sun glasses, but that the sun was so bright the darkened spectacles did him no good. The deep background of the grandstand didn't bother him. It was after the balls rose over the roof and passed into the sun's rays that he lost sight of them.

Root, who regardless of everything is a skilled hurler and who proved it by holding the Macks to three hits in six innings just as he did in seven rounds at Chicago, is the man who should have complained. Like McCarthy, he attributed everything to bad luck.

Root said afterward that he never felt better in his life. When the seventh started with Simmons hitting a homer on a high inside ball such as he likes, the Cub infielders rushed over to the ace hurler to ask whether he was tiring. He assured them he wasn't. They came back again to ask the same question when Foxx, the next hitter, looped a single into right. Root still insisted to them he would get out of the inning with a big lead.

"Looks like I'm the big chump of the series," Wilson said when seen for the only time during the day. "I play good all season, and in the most important game I'm ever in, I blow up. The bugs will have all winter in which to think up wise cracks to hand me next season, and I won't be able to do anything except tip my cap to the greetings.

216

"They'll be calling me a long lost brother of Snodgrass and Merkle, and to think that the weather man promised we'd have a cloudy day! If he'd only been right."

The few fellow players who saw him when he showed up this morning for breakfast gave him the same greeting they'd have given him if the game hadn't turned into the biggest upset in World Series history. Hack, however, knew they were just trying to make him feel good.

Wilson's indignities even included a mocking song that was written and published in the papers, to the tune of "My Old Kentucky Home."

"The sun shone bright in our great Hack Wilson's eyes. 'Tis Sunday, the Mack men are gay. The third game's won and Cub pitching's gone astray. As our series title fades far away. Weep no more, Dear Cub fan. Oh, weep no more today; for we'll sing one song for the game and fighting Cubs. For the record whiffing Cubs far away." [155]

Reporters called Wrigley "the most disappointed man connected with the Chicago club." He had his heart, mind and money set on a pennant winner and could see it slipping away.

He already was looking to next year.

"We'll have new strength next year and probably will win a pennant and also a series," he said.

Privately, he was upset about McCarthy leaving Root in too long in Game Four and taking him out too soon in Game One.

Burns wrote that even the happy trio wasn't so happy.

> One of the most striking effects of the Saturday flop has been seen in the attitude of the vaudevillians. The team of Grimm, Cuyler and Heathcote had been planning to make certain changes in their act in the event of the loss of the series, but the spectacular character of the Saturday collapse has caused them to fear raucous comment from the galleries.
>
> Led by Cuyler, they have sought to get out of their contract, but the holders of their contract are insistent that they stick, figuring, perhaps, that they will be as interesting as wounded veterans as they would be as conquering heroes.

---

[155] *The World Series: A Complete Pictorial History.*

Blowing an eight-run lead is harsh enough. Instead of tying the series at two games apiece, the Cubs now face elimination. The Cubs must win Game Five on Monday, Oct. 14, or they go back to Chicago for the winter.

Catalina Island Museum Collection

Charlie Grimm performs with the banjo
for KFWB Radio in Hollywood, California.

Game Five

Pat Malone led the National League with 161 strikeouts and was the only Cub who could walk to the mound with confidence after the Game Four debacle. He had retired both of the hitters he faced in the 10-run explosion with consecutive strikeouts.

Connie Mack decides to start Howard Ehmke one more time, but the strikeout magic is gone. The Cubs knock him out in the fourth when Cuyler doubles, Stephenson walks and Grimm and Taylor both single. Walberg, in relief of Ehmke, allows only two hits and stops any more runs for the remainder of the game.

Going into the bottom of the ninth, Malone has allowed only two singles to the 26 batters he has faced and is leading 2-0. Only two others have reached base, on a walk and an error.

President Herbert Hoover had traveled from Washington, D.C., to see the game. Schools were off and people lined Lehigh Avenue to see the president, even if they didn't have tickets.

Hoover's presence unquestionably added to the pomp and ceremony surrounding the Series. But his attendance also gave a lot of fans the chance to sound off about Prohibition.

As Hoover made his way to his box seat, the fans began chanting, "Beer! Beer! We want beer!"

Al Capone was very much on the mind of President Hoover who had asked for FBI updates ever since the Valentine's Day Massacre.

Chicago leaders, embarrassed by worldwide publicity about all of the mob murders during the year, raised money and opened a crime lab at Northwestern University specializing in forensics and ballistics tests.

The ineffective Prohibition Unit in the Treasury Department was reorganized and transferred to Justice. Elliott Ness, a 26-year-old University of Chicago graduate, was named its head just before the World Series began. They would become famous as "The Untouchables."

Capone would learn later that desk-bound accountants at the FBI would do him in, not gun-toting agents, as they methodically reviewed his network of businesses, his income and his failure to pay the necessary taxes.[156]

The chants about beer embarrassed Connie Mack who complained later to reporters about the fans' disrespect for Hoover, saying every president is owed respect regardless of party or politics.

With one out in the ninth inning, the crowds in Shibe Park begin walking to the exits, watching the game over their shoulders.

With two strikes on him, Max Bishop singles over third, and some in the crowd of 30,000 begin returning to their seats.

Even President Hoover, who had buttoned his overcoat while his wife Lou donned her suede gloves, pauses in his bunting-wreathed box down the third-base line.

Mule Haas plants him there with a two-run, game-tying homer over the right-field wall. Mayor Mackey plunges from the stands and embraces Haas as he is mobbed by teammates.[157]

Cochrane grounds into the second out, but Simmons doubles and Foxx is intentionally walked. Miller looks for a curve that he can hit and gets a fastball instead, doubling to the scoreboard.

As Simmons and Foxx score, the Cubs have blown the lead, the game and the 1929 World Series, 3-2.

In the Athletics clubhouse, Commissioner Landis offers his congratulations to all but Cochrane.

Earlier in the Series, Commissioner Judge Kenesaw Mountain Landis had warned the teams about the obscenities and bench jockey-

---

[156] Capone sources include pages 222-252 in Schoenberg's *Capone* and pages 258-260 in Kobler's *Capone*.
[157] Kaplan, Jim, *Lefty Grove: American Original*.

ing. "If the vulgarities continue," he told both managers, "the culprits will be fined their full World Series' share."

Cochrane's sarcastic reply was, "After the game, we'll serve tea in the clubhouse!"

Landis, clearly within earshot, was not amused. But rather than acknowledge it, he stared straight ahead as if he had heard nothing. [158]

Before he leaves the winners' locker room, Landis elbows his way to the Athletics catcher and, with a straight face, says, "Hello, Sweetheart, I came in after my tea. Will you pour?"

As all of Philadelphia celebrates, Mack quietly retreats to his private office in the Shibe Park Tower. When they see him entering, three secretaries rush toward the 66-year-old manager, fighting to plant a kiss on him. But graciously refusing them the privilege, he closes the door, lies down on his battered couch, and falls sound asleep.

He has captured his fourth world championship, placing him above all other managers in the history of the game at that time. It proves that he still has the touch as a baseball manager and knows how to win. It also proves that the so-called advanced ideas ushered in by the lively ball era did not belong solely to younger men.

As the train returns to Chicago with the Cubs, families and reporters, there is sadness about how they missed this opportunity.

But there is optimism about next year.

And there is plenty of blame to go around, although it is only discussed in the reporters' car on the train. The Cubs struck out 50 times in five games, scored 17 runs and made seven errors.

Hornsby hit an uncharacteristically low .238 with only one RBI during the five games of the World Series.

Wilson's .471 batting average was the best of any player, but there were no homers. He had seven singles and a triple. Wilson's misplays are what Cub fans would remember.

As the train clatters along, teammates hear a strange drumming sound in the middle of the night.

---

[158] Kashatus.

Peering out from behind curtains in their sleeping berths, some of the Cubs witness Wilson in the aisle on his knees, cursing and pounding the floor with his fists.

He looks like a little boy who has disappointed someone he cared much about.[159]

When the train arrives in Chicago, the *Associated Press* reports that Wilson "forced his way out of a crowd of admirers with tears streaming down his face."

"Let me alone now, fellows," he said as he choked and sobbed. "I haven't anything to say except that I am heartbroken and that we did get some awful breaks."

Root family archives

Lewis "Hack" Wilson autographed his
photo to his "pal" Charlie Root.

---

[159] Parker, Clifton Blue, *Fouled Away,* pg. 87.

Heading for Home

"They give me hell with their razzing when I'm going good, but now, when I deserve it, they give me cheers instead."
—Hack Wilson, amazed by the warm reception of Cub fans treating him like a winner, *Chicago Tribune*, Oct. 16, 1929.

Like Hack Wilson, Charlie Root is amazed at how loyal Cub fans are even after such an embarrassing collapse.

Root's next reception from fans is even more personal when he visits his hometown before returning to Los Angeles for the winter. The *Middletown Journal* seizes the chance to honor its homegrown hero, hosting "Charlie Root Day."

Root is more nervous about stepping out on the front steps of the newspaper office, where about 250 friends, family and fans are waiting, than any trip to the mound in a sold-out ballpark.

He hates public speaking but needs to say a few words to the Middletown crowd.

He is surprised at how many people left church early this Sunday morning just to see him.

Even former antagonists wait in the crowd.

Charlie tells how it all started at Armco, pitching as a teen-ager against men as hardened as the steel they produced.

He gets more comfortable as he recalls those happy days, his big break with the St. Louis Browns and then this great Cubs team.

He doesn't linger long. He steps into the crowd and shakes hands with every one of the people who came to see him.

The childhood bully is there, with apologies and a story about why his attacks stopped suddenly.

When Charlie started grade school, he was very frail and an easy target. He was near death with diphtheria when he was six years old.

His mother held him in her arms as he gasped for breath. The punishing disease was cutting off his airway. A local doctor provided the only comfort that was known, placing a silver tube down his throat.

The Roots learned of a Cincinnati doctor who was experimenting with a new drug, and they volunteered to expose Charlie to the shot and the risk. "He's going to die," Charlie's mom tells the doctor. "Yes, try anything."

The shot works and DPT immunizations later become a childhood standard nationwide to fight diphtheria, pertussis (whooping cough) and tetanus.

After his weight loss and frail condition, the bully starts pushing Charlie around in school. Roy Bailey becomes Charlie's personal friend and body guard.

Bailey served later as a Marine in World War II and was a champion welterweight boxer, but Charlie didn't realize how early his friend's career really started.

"Roy Bailey beat the hell out of me for pushing you around," the bully tells Charlie. "I bet you wondered why I suddenly left you alone."

Also in the crowd are two guys who had told Charlie that the major leagues would "eat him for breakfast." They were here today to eat their words.

As Charlie shakes hands with the final well-wishers, he notices Mr. and Mrs. Wills, the black family who lived next door to the Roots while Charlie was growing up.

"Mrs. Wills, I still remember your cow and chickens and the butter and eggs you brought us. How were your green beans and tomatoes this year?"

"We would love for you to come over and find out, Cholly. Please come to our home for dinner," Mrs. Wills said, "And bring Dorothy and Della and little Cholly."

There was time for lunch before Charlie's afternoon exhibition game.

"Mr. and Mrs. Wills waited on us like royalty in their very plain kitchen, and despite Mom and Dad's insistence that they sit down with us, they wouldn't do it," Della recalled.

"Cholly, I know you remember Lenore," Mrs. Wills said after the meal. "Well, she married a doctor and they named their first child, Cholly, after you. And he has the same naturally curly hair, just like you."

The Wills were friendly neighbors, but Charlie's parents didn't socialize with them; it just wasn't proper then. Root had no such reluctance.

Charlie got everyone laughing as he recalled how he almost killed the Wills' son, Homer, when they were kids. They used to throw rocks at knotholes in fences until Homer decided to throw one at Charlie.

"Homer jumped behind a tree so I couldn't get him," Charlie said. "But I knew he'd stick that head out sooner or later and I nailed him right between the eyes."

"You knocked him out cold. We thought he was dead," Mr. Wills said. "Then you went high-tailing home and hid under your bed."

"Do you remember what you did, Mrs. Wills? You came running over in front of our house, yelling, 'The debbil gonna gitcha, Cholly Root. The debbil gonna gitcha.'"

"It's a wonder any of you children grew up," Mrs. Wills said, laughing and wiping her hands on her apron as she started to clear the table.

"They're going to have to lift me up on the mound, I've had so much to eat," Charlie said, as all the Roots and Wills got ready to go to Charlie's exhibition.

A boys' orphanage in Middletown asked Charlie to pitch at a fund-raiser while he was there. The stands were packed and the game was delayed for a ceremony in which orphaned boys of about 8 years old gave Charlie flowers.

As Charlie approached the mound amid cheers from the crowd, a tall man carrying a Bible burst from the stand and ran to the mound, Della recalled.

"Good God," cried one of the fans. "It's Chal."

Chal Brewer was married to Charlie's oldest sister, Sarah, and he was very active in the Methodist Church. He was trying to read to Charlie from the Bible and pull him from the mound at the same time. "I am sure he had found a new commandment that said, 'Thou shalt not pitch on Sunday,'" Della said.

Charlie asked Chal to return to the stands, but Chal tried to pull Charlie from the mound. There was no contest. The police came and hauled Chal away, which Della found exciting but her family saw as appalling.

Immediately after the game, Charlie went to his sister's house and Chal was there. It was quite evident that Chal had not mentioned the incident to his wife. Charlie said nothing to Sarah.

There was no way to spoil the day.

Charlie couldn't help thinking about the "Kaiser," wishing that his dad could see how all of Middletown turned out for him because of baseball.

He could show his dad that he didn't throw his life away with something as frivolous as a game of baseball.

Jacob Root died in 1925 and missed his son's best season in professional baseball. He died the year that Charlie was sent back to the minors by St. Louis and the year before he made it big with the Cubs.

Charlie never heard a compliment or witnessed his father's pride.

"Jacob Henry no longer derided Charlie's career, but neither did he wish him well or brag about him leading the Pacific Coast League," Della said.

There was another side that the tough Kaiser never let his son see and Joe Day is the one who delivers the surprise and highlight of "Charlie Root Day."

Charlie had started working at Day's grocery store when he was 10. The store was at the corner of Fleming and Grimes in Middletown, just a couple of houses away from where Root was born.

Day jokes that Charlie spent more time playing baseball on the vacant lot next to his home than he did on his job sweeping the floors and working in the grocery store.

"Well, Jake Root always bragged about his Charlie," Day says.

"What are you talking about?" Charlie asks.

"Every time he came into the store, he was telling the latest baseball news involving his boy," Day replies.

"You didn't know how much he was bragging about you?" [160]

Photo from Root family archives

Charlie Root, behind the counter, started work at Joe Day's grocery store in Middletown, Ohio, at age 10.

---

[160] All details come from author's interviews with, and journal of, Della Root Arnold.

227

Epilogue

"If that big fat guy had pointed, you'd think we would have seen it."
—Della Root Arnold, 2004, about the myth, legend and hype
of Babe Ruth's 1932 World Series homer off her dad.

In the Cubs' final move of the 1929 season, they voted to divide the loser's share of World Series money. Each Cub on the final roster was entitled to $4,002.

The Cubs voted for Berly Horne to get $2,000 and also to include shares for McCarthy and the coaches.

The final split was $3,500 for the active players.[161]

The bonus doubled the pay of almost everyone except the stars like Hornsby, Wilson and Root. Root was the highest-paid pitcher in all of baseball, at $22,000, in a year when bread was 10 cents, hamburger 20 cents a pound, and there was no income tax. Ten gallons of gas cost $1.

Ruth was easily the highest paid of all players. His pay topped $70,000 two years earlier when he hit 60 homers in 1927.

By 1931, only five other players made as much as Root and Ruth.

Player salaries were five times the average income of an American laborer, but far below the profits that owners were making. By 1929, major league payrolls had climbed to $3.75 million, still only 35 percent of overall club expenses, one of the lowest ratios of labor cost to overall expense in American business.[162]

---

[161] *Chicago Tribune*, Oct. 17, 1929.

[162] House Judiciary Committee, Organized Baseball: Report of the Subcommittee on the Study of Monopoly Power, 1610-12, as cited on pg. 23 in the book, "Much More Than A Game: Players, Owners and American Baseball since 1921," by Robert F. Burk, University of North Carolina Press, 2001.

Just days after the Cubs' colossal crash in the World Series, an even larger crash rocked the entire United States.

The stock market hit a historic low, ultimately destroying the finances of millions of Americans, ushering in the Great Depression and creating bank runs as never before. Baseball nearly died in the process.

When it was clear that the crash was long-term, William Wrigley Jr. handed Root a personal check for $3,000.

Wrigley had talked Root into investing in the market for the first time, hoping he could build a nest egg for when his baseball days were over. Wrigley suggested putting the money on Yellow Cab back in the spring when the Cubs were at Catalina Island.

"When the crash came, Mr. Wrigley called him back to the office," Della said. "'Charlie, I gave you a real bum steer. Here, please take my check.'" [163]

Hornsby also took a pounding with the crash. Back in 1926, on the advice of stockbroker Mark Steinburg, his St. Louis friend and admirer, Hornsby had bought 1,000 shares in Radio Corporation of America, obtaining most of it on margin at $52 per share.

Within two years RCA had soared to 276½, but Steinberg predicted the stock would continue to rise, so Hornsby still held his 1,000 shares when the Crash came.

"I lost a lot more money in Wall Street than I ever did on the race track," Hornsby said. "Those sanctimonious cusses with side whiskers can take your money faster than the bookmakers, and leave you less for it." [164]

After Charlie Grimm's injury, Horne had taken the train to California to join the Los Angeles Angels, the Cubs' minor league team. The day Horne arrived, he was on the mound, losing a tough 2-1 game in 13 innings.

Horne spent the rest of his baseball career in the minors, mostly the Pacific Coast, playing for Los Angeles, Hollywood, San Diego and Seattle. His career spanned from 1917 in Jacksonville, Florida, to 1938

---

[163] Della Root Arnold.

in Yakima, Washington. He won 229 games in the minors, pitching in 676 games and piling up 3,726 innings.

Even in his final season, at age 39, Horne had a winning season of 12-8. His career ERA was 3.87.

Horne used the Series bonus to buy a new 1930 Chrysler. He drove it until it was a rusted heap, and his wife joked that she would divorce him if he didn't get rid of it. He didn't want to part with what he called his "World Series car." [165]

Horne never made it back to the majors, but he played in the minors with future major leaguers like Joe and Vince Dimaggio, Bobby Doerr, George Myatt and Ted Williams.

In a personal journal, Horne wrote about when Williams joined their San Diego team, straight out of high school as a pitcher.

"Frank Shellenbach, our manager, made an outfielder of Ted," Horne said. "He always had a bat in his hand and carried a bat on the train on our trips in the Coast League.

"He liked to eat and wanted to go eat with the older players so he could get our desserts, three or four extra desserts after our evening meals."

Horne worked as a carpenter, building sets for Paramount's movie studios, and later was an accountant in Los Angeles. After his wife died in the 1950s, Horne came back to Arcanum, Ohio, and later cared for his ailing mother, who died in 1976.

He stayed in Arcanum until an arthritic hip began to bother him. He moved to Franklin, Ohio, in June 1980, and finally had to give up playing golf.

Horne finally got a chance to go to a World Series in 1981 when a Springboro, Ohio, bank awarded him two tickets as part of a contest. Once again, an injury blocked him from his first World Series, this time a bad hip due to old age.

Horne wore his Cubs warm-up jacket to the bank and opted for a 19-inch color TV instead so he could watch the Series at home.

---

[164] Alexander, Charles C., *Rogers Hornsby*, pg. 158-159.
[165] Murray Horne, son of Berly Horne, author's interview, October 2001.

On February 9, 1983, *Franklin Chronicle* sports editor Terry Baver wrote one final story about Horne who had died on February 3 at age 84.

"Although he only played one year in the major leagues, baseball player Berly Horne never lost his love and enthusiasm for the sport.

"That love for the game continued during a 20-year span as a professional baseball player and lasted an additional 64 years until his death…"

Nephew Andrew Kopp flew over Bachman, Ohio, where Horne was born, and scattered Berly's ashes from a plane. He sent a postcard to his family.

"I took Berly on his last flight…He wanted me to tell you that he is resting peacefully," Kopp wrote.

The card was postmarked February 14, 1983—exactly 64 years from the day when an excited Berly hopped on the train in Chicago's Union Station bound for spring training at Catalina Island.

Finding Root's daughter, Della, was the greatest thrill of all in the pursuit of this story. But the greatest surprise came after the manuscript was completed.

The day after the Boston Red Sox won the 2004 World Series, Anne Bernini called me from her home in Sonoma, Calif., responding to an ad and Web posting that I placed as a member of the Society for American Baseball Research (SABR).

I was trying to solve the mystery of whatever happened to Eddie Lautenbacher, the 21-year-old kid at Catalina Island who nearly unseated Berly Horne for the final spot on the 1929 Chicago Cubs roster. In fact, the last story by Ed Burns in the *Chicago Tribune* was that Lautenbacher actually made the team.

No subsequent story ever said what happened and the *Baseball Encyclopedia* witnessed that Lautenbacher never pitched a game in the major leagues.

"I understand you're looking for information about my father," Bernini said in her phone call.

I could not believe her next words, "Would you like to speak to him?"

At 97, Lautenbacher was the only surviving member of that exclusive club—a player invited to spring training at Catalina Island in 1929. Three quarters of a century later, his hearing was diminished but not his memory.

Do you regret coming so close and not making it in the majors? "Every day. I'm sure I even thought about it this morning," Lautenbacher said, laughing. "If I'd only had just a little better curveball."

He knew Berly Horne by his nickname, "Sonny," and remembered him as a very tough competitor in the minors when Horne was pitching for Jersey City and Lautenbacher for Reading.

"There was good competition between Reading and Jersey City. We played against him, with both teams trying for the championship and both being near the top," Lautenbacher said.

Lautenbacher thought he had made the 1929 roster. But on the final day, Manager Joe McCarthy decided that he needed an extra catcher on the roster to back up the aging Cuban, Mike Gonzales, and to compensate for the likely loss of Gabby Hartnett for the season.

Lautenbacher was told by one of the coaches that he would return to Reading and the minor league team where he started in 1928 in his senior year at Columbia University.

Lautenbacher kept pitching in the minors. He was invited back to Catalina in 1930. For the rest of the 1930s, he pitched semi-pro ball for the East River Savings Bank in downtown Manhattan. He started as a bank clerk and rose to vice president.

"The crowds came to those semi-pro games," Lautenbacher said. "I did fine because I was just pitching on weekends."

"Baseball was such a wonderful life. I just wish I could have lasted longer."

Lautenbacher was born Oct. 1, 1907, and settled in Napa, Calif. "I give thanks every day," he said during that October 2004 interview.

The Red Sox were on his mind, having won the World Series when Lautenbacher was 11 years old, and then again when he was 97. He spoke in admiration of Curt Schilling as someone an old-timer could

232

admire, grinding out his Game Two win in the 2004 World Series with an injured tendon and blood staining his sock.[166]

Lautenbacher died several months after my interview, in the summer of 2005. His daughter, Anne Bernini, asked a *Newsday* reporter to call me for a final tribute, a story about his life.[167]

His passing closed the chapter on the final cast of characters who were so full of hope at Catalina Island during that spring training in 1929.

Hack Wilson was surprised by how warmly Cub fans treated him after the disastrous World Series blunders. He repaid them during the 1930 season, driving in 191 runs, a single-season RBI record that still stands today.

His 56 homers in the same season stood as a National League record for decades, until Mark McGwire came along. Wilson's .356 batting average in 1930 stood as his personal career high.

The Elgin Co. made the costly promotional decision of awarding Wilson with a new watch for every homer that season. In the end, Wilson asked for one watch, studded with diamonds, for his wife.[168]

Wilson's short career, his rapid rise and rapid fall are frequently blamed on "old man barleycorn," as Horne described the boozing problems of Wilson in his personal journal years later.

But his career stats show another interesting detail.

Wilson hit over .300 only from 1926 to 1930. His home run and RBI production were off the charts in those seasons.

Significantly, those seasons match exactly when Joe McCarthy was his manager. Wilson never played better before or after the span when McCarthy was watching over him.

Without McCarthy, Wilson's life ended as sadly as it began. He was alone. His drinking worsened and baseball ended for him in 1934. In 1938, Virginia finally gave up and divorced him.

---

[166] Eddie Lautenbacher, telephone interview from his home in Napa, Calif., Oct. 28, 2004.

[167] *Newsday,* By Indrani Sen, Aug. 10, 2005.

[168] Della Root Arnold, letter with editing notes, Oct. 30, 2004.

He died in 1948, when he was 48 without a penny to his name. His body lay unclaimed for three days until National League President Ford Frick paid $350 for a proper funeral.[169]

Ten months later, McCarthy went to Wilson's hometown of Martinsburg, W. Va., for a final farewell, a memorial attended by about a thousand.

"May God rest his soul," McCarthy said of the tortured kid he understood.

William Wrigley Jr. never got over the 10-run inning in the World Series and held McCarthy responsible for not capturing the crown. Wrigley was done with McCarthy when the Cubs didn't win the pennant in 1930.

Rogers Hornsby could be ingratiating when he wanted to be and he won Wrigley over. Hornsby's sniping from the wings made it easier for Wrigley to cut McCarthy loose.

It was a big mistake for the Cubs but a real career boost for McCarthy who would win seven World Series championships with the New York Yankees and become the fourth greatest manager in baseball history with 2,126 wins.

The players hated Hornsby and weren't even close to a pennant race in 1931, finishing third and 17 games back. Hornsby didn't survive the 1932 season as popular Charlie Grimm took over as manager. The Cubs won 20 of their first 25 games with Grimm and immediately were back in the race. The Cubs returned to the World Series, triggering the match-up between Charlie Root and Babe Ruth.

Wrigley didn't live to see it. He died just before spring training on January 26, 1932, of a stroke in his Phoenix winter home.

Hornsby's last great season was 1929. He would stand alone as the greatest offensive second baseman in history.

---

[169] Parker, Clifton Blue, *Fouled Away*, pg. 193.

Al Capone was never implicated in the Valentine's Day Massacre. Instead, he was brought down by newly trained accountants at the FBI who documented his ill-gotten gains.

On June 16, 1931, Capone pled guilty to tax evasion and Prohibition charges. When he found out the judge wasn't going for a 2 ½-year sentence, he asked for a trial and was convicted on Oct. 18, 1931 and sentenced to 11 years in federal prison.

In 1933, Prohibition was repealed.

Capone was transferred to Alcatraz prison in 1934 and remained there until 1939 when he was so disoriented by syphilis that he was released and remained in a Baltimore hospital until 1940.

He died of a heart attack at his Palm Island palace on January 25, 1947, one week after Andrew Volstead, the author of Prohibition, died.

Catcher Gabby Hartnett returned to greatness in 1930, recovering from his 1929 arm injury and making up in large measure for Hornsby's decline.

He never lost his sense of humor and instigation of practical jokes. After a game in the 1930s, a Cub coach was drunk on the train and asked the team to wake him when they got to Indianapolis where his family was meeting him.

Before the train even got all the way out of Chicago, Hartnett yelled at the sleeping coach, "Indianapolis!"

The coach raged, "Why didn't you give me more time?" Not stopping for an answer, the coach jumped off the car, hailed a taxi and rattled off an Indianapolis address. That's when he realized he was still in Chicago.[170]

By 1933 and 1934, Hartnett was the best catcher in baseball, setting a major league record by going 452 consecutive chances without an error.[171]

---

[170] Grimm, Charlie, *Jolly Cholly.*

[171] Feldmann, Doug, *September Streak: The 1935 Chicago Cubs Chase the Pennant,* McFarland & Co. Inc., Jefferson, North Carolina, and London, 2003.

Charlie Root and Gabby Hartnett stood alone as the only battery to be together in four World Series, until Yogi Berra and Whitey Ford topped that with five in the 1950s and 1960s.[172]

Hartnett reached the Hall of Fame as one of the great catchers in baseball history.

For a game so precise about its stats, baseball has its share of exaggerations—like Abner Doubleday as baseball's founder, and Babe Ruth's "called shot" off Charlie Root in the 1932 World Series.

Woody English said the Cubs were fired up because Ruth had called them "cheap" and "penny pinching" before the World Series began. Former Yankee Mark Koenig was playing shortstop for the Cubs during the 1932 season, but the Cubs had voted to only give him a half share of the World Series money.

"I roomed with Charlie Root," English said. "He was a nice guy, but when he was out on that mound, don't take too big a toe-hold on him. You'll get one right behind your ear. He was a sidearm pitcher, threw hard, had a good curve ball, and was a competitor all the way."

"That day Ruth and Gehrig each had homered," English said. "Ruth got up again, and it was funny. He had two strikes on him. I was playing third base. I was right close to it. He's got two strikes on him. The guys are yelling at him from our dugout. He's looking right in our dugout, and he holds up two fingers. He said, 'That's only two strikes.'

"But the press box was way back on top of Wrigley Field, and to the people in the press, it looked like he pointed to center field. But he was looking right into our dugout and holding two fingers up. That is the true story. I've been asked the question five hundred times." [173]

"Ruth would never do a thing like that, point," English said. "Charlie Root would have murdered him."

Second baseman Billy Herman said, "I hate to explode one of baseball's great legends, but I was there and saw what happened. Sure, he made a gesture, he pointed—but it wasn't to call his shot.

---

[172] Della Root Arnold and the *Baseball Encyclopedia*.
[173] Golenbock, Peter, *Wrigleyville*, pg. 234-239.

"What Ruth did then was hold up his hand, telling them that was only two strikes, that he still had another one coming and that he wasn't out yet. When he held up his hand, that's where the pointing came in. But he was pointing out toward Charlie Root when he did that, not toward the center-field bleachers.

"Then the legend started that he had called his shot, and Babe went along with it. Why not?

"But he didn't point. Don't kid yourself. I can tell you just what would have happened if Ruth had tried that—he would never have got a pitch to hit. Root would have had him with his feet up in the air." [174]

First baseman Charlie Grimm said Guy Bush was leading the jockeying from the bench, calling Ruth by the names he hated, such as "Big Monkey."

Grimm also said that Ruth was pointing out to Root that he had one more pitch.

Grimm wrote in his autobiography, *Jolly Cholly*:

> I hesitate to spoil a good story, one that has been built up to such proportions down the years that millions of people have insisted they saw the gesture, but the Babe actually was pointing to the mound. As he pointed, I heard Ruth growl, "You'll be out there tomorrow, so we'll see what you can do with me, you so-and-so tightwad."
>
> Root never squawked as the legend grew that Ruth had called his shot for baseball's most celebrated home run. But he did balk when he was offered a chunk of money to recreate the scene in the Babe Ruth movie made later in Hollywood. If old Chinski could have called back any one of the thousands of pitches he made for the Cubs, the one Ruth picked on would have been his choice. Let's face it, though, a great guy hit that homer, the greatest slugger of all time. And if you want to believe he really planned it that way, you just go right ahead.

Ed Froelich was the trainer for the Brooklyn Dodgers in 1938 when Ruth was a coach for the Dodgers. Froelich asked Ruth for the truth.

"You tell those people for Baby that Baby says they're full of crap right up to their eyeballs," Ruth replied. "I'm not that dumb. I'm going

---

[174] Ibid., pg. 234-239.

to point to the center-field bleachers with a barracuda like Root out there? On the next pitch they'd be picking it out of my ear with a pair of tweezers."

When Ken Burns took on the daunting task of documenting the history of baseball for PBS-TV, Burns discovered a fan's 16 mm home movie of the 1932 game. [175]

Sure enough, Ruth appears to be gesturing toward the Cub dugout, matching most of the eyewitness accounts.

This only known record of the home run is held today by Kirk M. Kandle, an ad copywriter for the same Louisville *Courier-Journal* where William Veeck began his career. I viewed the film in Kandle's home with *Kentucky Monthly* publisher Stephen Vest and the friend who edited this manuscript, Ted Sloan.[176]

In less than two minutes, Kandle's great-grandfather, Matt Sr., captured one of baseball's greatest controversies and the most painful moment in Root's career.

Kandle's film does not completely resolve the dispute. The surprisingly clear images match most closely what Cub catcher Gabby Hartnett repeated for years.

After taking a strike, Root gestures noticeably toward the Cub dugout. Hartnett, the closest to Ruth, said Ruth yelled, "It only takes one to hit it." [177]

After a second called strike, Ruth points a finger twice toward Root, almost as if he is poking a pistol at him. The gesture is rapid and not as aggressive as his earlier move toward the Cubs dugout. It may not have been obvious in the press box or to fans directly behind the

[175] Ward, Geoffrey C., and Burns, Ken, *Baseball: An Illustrated History*, Alfred A. Knopf, 1994, pg. 210.

[176] Author's interview with Kirk M. Kandle, published in *Kentucky Monthly*, October 2005.

[177] Murphy, James M., *The Gabby Hartnett Story: From a Mill Town to Cooperstown*, Exposition Press, 1983, pg. 35-36; Creamer, Robert, *Babe: The Legend Comes to Life*, Simon & Schuster, 1974, pg. 362.

plate because Ruth raises his hand only about chest-high, and Hartnett and the umpire are standing.

Yankees first baseman Lou Gehrig was the next closest, at the on-deck circle. He said Root yelled something to Ruth from the mound. Gehrig said Ruth yelled back, "I'm going to knock the next pitch down your goddamned throat." [178]

The film confirms Root's claim that he tried to waste an outside pitch with two strikes on Ruth. Ruth reaches out and golfs the ball over the center field scoreboard, the longest shot ever hit at Wrigley up to that time.

On the film, a dejected Root takes one quick glance over his shoulder. Root's head drops and he looks at his feet as he walks almost to second base while Ruth begins his home run trot.

"We enjoy a great legend or myth and we don't like to have that demystified," Kirk Kandle said. "I'm happier that the film is not absolutely conclusive as forensic evidence. That keeps this alive and feeds the ongoing great debate."

The film refutes the exaggeration of Ruth standing defiantly at the plate, pointing toward the fence, obviously calling his shot. Instead, it is more obvious that Ruth was yelling back to the heckling Cubs that he was going to get even. His bat did the rest.

Years later, Root refused to recreate the moment in the movie, *The Babe Ruth Story,* "Not if you're going to show him pointing," he said.

Sifting through all the accounts, the catcher, first baseman, second baseman, third baseman and pitcher all agreed that Ruth pointed first at the Cub dugout and then gestured to Root that he had one more chance.

Della, who was seated about a dozen rows behind the plate, said, "If that big fat guy had pointed, you'd think we would have seen it."

From the hitter himself, "Ruth was evasive when asked if he really had called his shot. 'Why don't you read the papers?' he said. 'It's all right there in the papers.'" [179]

---

[178] Creamer, Robert W., *Babe,* pg. 362.
[179] Ibid., pg. 210.

Ruth was right. The newspapers had all versions, from no mention of an incident at all to the most exaggerated, and the truth is sprinkled somewhere among all of them.

Ruth was just as responsible for the myth, at first denying that he would have been as foolish as to try to show Root up and then embellishing the story years later about how defiantly he stood at the plate and called his shot.

Della said the lies began several days later and did not originate from the actual sportswriters who sat in the press box and wrote their game accounts on deadline Saturday, Oct. 1.

Della challenged whether any sportswriter in the press box that day wrote anything about a called shot in his game-day story.

Stories from the two largest newspapers, *The New York Times* and the *Chicago Tribune,* match what Della recalled.

The New York Times highlighted how many balls were flying out of windy Wrigley, including two homers each by Ruth and Gehrig. No mention was made of any sort of confrontation.

Della said in a 2004 interview:

> Immediately after the Series, we went on a cruise to Australia and never heard a word until we came back. The story came later from a young reporter from New York and his name was Meany, which was a pretty good name for a guy like that. It was four days later, check the newspaper morgue.
>
> There is not one word on that October day about anyone pointing. Dad threw a strike and Ruth held up one finger and second strike and two fingers. He would not have pointed. That would have been bush league and Babe Ruth was no bush leaguer.
>
> For a long time, Babe Ruth denied it. Then the Yankees hired Christy Walsh to manage Ruth's money and actions; such a good story, too good to keep denying. How it kept growing and growing. At first, he said, "I would have been a damn fool to point on a pitcher like Root."
>
> He hollered at the dugout and made a gesture to Guy Bush that I'll have you tomorrow.

But nothing about Ruth's homer off Root is so simply explained. There was at least one same-day, on-deadline news report of Ruth pointing and calling his shot, according to author Robert Creamer.

Creamer found the story by Joe Williams, sports editor for Scripps-Howard newspapers. In late editions that same afternoon of the game, Oct. 1, the *New York World-Telegram* carried Williams' story under the headline, "Ruth Calls Shot as He Puts Homer No. 2 in Side Pocket." [180]

Williams wrote, "In the fifth, with the Cubs riding him unmercifully from the bench, Ruth pointed to center and punched a screaming liner to a spot where no ball had ever been hit before."

Williams noted that Ruth pointed one finger to the Cub dugout after Root's first strike.

Creamer said that Williams is the only same-day reporter who mentions Ruth pointing to center field.

Another same-day report happened just before the game even started, as Richards Vidmer wrote for the *New York Herald Tribune.* Ruth already was sparring with the Cubs and pointed to right field and grinned, making it obvious that he was going to get even, Vidmer said. [181]

He hit nine towering homers in batting practice and yelled at the Cub bench, "I'd play for half my salary if I could hit in this dump all the time."

Ruth said he could take the razzing from the Cubs, but hearing loud heckling from their trainer was a bit much. "Andy Lotshaw yelled, 'If I had you, I'd hitch you to a wagon, you potbelly.'"

Ruth said afterwards, "I didn't mind no ballplayers yelling at me, but the trainer cutting in—that made me sore." [182]

The exaggerations started coming within days, Creamer said, when Paul Gallico of the *New York Daily News* wrote, "He pointed like a duelist to the spot where he expected to send his rapier home."

What annoyed Della most, she said, was that Gallico was not at the game.

---

[180] Creamer, pg. 363.
[181] Ibid., pg. 360.

Three days later, Bill Corum of Hearst newspapers wrote that Ruth "pointed out where he was going to hit the next one, and hit it there." Corum reported no such dramatics when he wrote his Saturday story from the press box, Creamer said.

Tom Meany, who worked for Williams, wrote the story that Della referred to the following week and kept fanning the flames of the called shot.

Meany's biography about Ruth in 1947 resurrected the "called shot" stories, although Creamer said that Meany reported both sides, saying Ruth pointed in the direction of center field, while "some say it was merely a gesture toward Root." [183]

There was even uncertainty over the pitch count when Ruth hit the homer. Everyone agreed Ruth was down to his last strike, but varying accounts say there were no balls, two balls and three balls.

Conflicting accounts are given about whether Root was trying to waste the pitch and strike Ruth out on a changeup curve.

"Ruth did not point at the fence before he swung," Root said. "If he had made a gesture like that, well, anybody who knows me knows that Ruth would have ended up on his ass."

"I fed him a changeup curve. It wasn't a foot off the ground and it was three or four inches outside, certainly not a good pitch to hit. But that was the one he smacked." [184]

This matches what Della recalls her dad saying.

But Root was quoted at a high school assembly in Los Angeles as saying, "Sure, Babe gestured to me. We had been riding him, calling him 'Grandpop' and kidding him about not getting to be manager of the Yankees. We wanted to get him mad, and he was when he came to bat. As he stepped up, he challenged me to lay the ball in. After I had gotten the first strike over, Babe pointed to me and yelled, 'That's only one strike.'

---

[182] Ibid., pg. 360.
[183] Ibid., pg. 364-365.
[184] Ibid., pg. 366-367

"Maybe I had a smug grin on my face after he took the second strike. Babe stepped out of the box again, pointed his finger in my direction and yelled, 'You still need one more, kid.'

"I guess I should have wasted the next pitch, and I thought Ruth figured I would, too. I decided to try to cross him and came in with it. The ball was gone as soon as Ruth swung. It never occurred to me then that the people in the stands would think he had been pointing to the bleachers." [185]

"THE CALLED SHOT" by Matt Kandle, Sr. © Kirk Kandle 1992

Ruth gesturing to Root, to the dugout, or toward
the fence, depending on who is telling the story

For all the conflict and controversy, the basic facts surrounding the confrontation are undisputed. The Cubs angered Ruth, and he got even. Ruth launched one of the longest blasts ever seen at Wrigley up to that

---

[185] Golenbock, Peter, *Wrigleyville,* pg. 234-239.

time. Root, who respected Ruth's greatness as a hitter, couldn't believe that he killed a pitch in that location.

The blow was Ruth's last World Series home run in a record-setting post-season career.

For Della, there is one other sad and unfair result. One pitch made her dad a footnote in almost every baseball history book.

The exaggerated reporting by columnists who weren't at the game made it even worse. The horrible William Bendix movie showed Ruth theatrically and defiantly pointing toward center field, author Creamer said.

Forgotten is that Root was the greatest pitcher to wear a Cub uniform, with the most wins, games and innings pitched in franchise history. All three franchise records stand today.

The Root family's attempt to forget Ruth's homer and remember Charlie's career continues quite visibly for a third generation. Della's brother, Charlie Jr., was the first family member to have a "Babe Who" license plate in California two decades ago. His daughter now has the license plate on her car and a "babewho" e-mail address.

Something quieter and far more personal happened to Charlie Root in 1932. It wasn't another World Series appearance or the annoying and growing myth of Babe Ruth's "called shot."

Root was very self-conscious about being thrust into the limelight and being asked to give speeches, fearing that his lack of education would be too obvious.

During the off-season, Charlie and Dorothy went to night school together for an English grammar class so Charlie could make up for the school years that he missed while working at Armco.

"I had a grammar teacher who was very strict and really worked me when I was in seventh grade," Della said. "I can remember being at the dinner table when Dad said, 'He don't...' and I corrected him and said, 'He doesn't...'"

"As I look back on that, I would have smacked me," Della said. "Instead, Mom and Dad took a night English course together. I was thirteen. This was 1932."

"He could do the most remarkable things," Della said. "When I got into algebra, he would work the problem backwards through math and could get it every time."

"He had an incredible head for numbers and could remember the pitch count on every batter and what happened."

Also quietly and behind the scenes, Charlie supported all nine siblings through the Depression. "He was so strong," Della said. "He didn't care whether people liked him or not. The friends at the beginning of his life were still his friends at the end."

Root wasn't haunted by the "called shot" legend, but several incidents indicated how he felt about it, even when it involved his own family and a "friendly" wiffle ball game.

The first incident occured in Milwaukee in the 1950s. Warren Spahn mocked Root by pointing to center field while Root was pitching batting practice. Root stunned everyone by sizzling a fast ball right at their top star's head. No Brave was brave enough to mock Root again.

In 1961, during a Cub tryout, a young player did the same thing while instructor Root was pitching spring training batting practice.

Root knocked the kid flat with the first pitch and then unloaded all of the balls in his pockets to keep him pinned on his back in the dirt at home plate.

"OK, he didn't point," the kid yelled so he could get back up.

During a family outing, Charlie Junior's wife defiantly pointed her wiffle ball bat toward center. Root hissed the wiffle ball right at his daughter-in-law, hitting her neck.[186]

Charlie Grimm brought his close friend Charlie Root along as pitching coach when he became manager of the Milwaukee Braves in the 1950s. Grimm was gone in 1957 when Milwaukee beat the Yankees in the World Series, but Root was still there as pitching coach. As a result, Root finally got his only World Series championship ring. Della said he never wore it because he didn't win it as a player. Grimm never

---

[186] Della.

got his ring, despite reaching the Series as a player or manager in 1929, 1932, 1935, and 1945.

Grimm was the player who coined Root's nickname of "Chinski," which lives on in the *Baseball Encyclopedia.* "Root would stick out his chin and battle you," Grimm said in his autobiography.[187]

Root pitched in the majors until 1941, when he was 42, followed up by seven more years in the minors as a player-manager. Root still holds all of the Chicago Cub franchise records for wins (201), games (605) and innings pitched (3,138).

Many nights, Root would dream and play games over in his head from years before.

"He would slip out to the porch to sleep when it was really hot, since there was no air conditioning," nephew Robert Gorman said.

"During the night, he would dream of a game, pitch by pitch, and cuss just like he did during the game," Gorman said. "You would hear him, very vociferous, yelling 'bullshit' at the umpire."

Photo from Root family archives

Charlie Root, pitching coach for the Braves

"In the morning, a family member asked if they heard that man cussing all night long, not knowing it was Charlie."

Phil Cavarretta describes the Charlie Root of 1935 as a greater pitcher, the Old Bear, who never beat himself, who taught the younger pitchers, a true pitcher's coach.[188]

In the 1960s, Grimm and Root both had coaching or instructional roles with the Cubs for a time.

---

[187] Grimm, Charlie, *Jolly Cholly,* pg. 108.
[188] Golenbock, pg. 255.

In the Roots' retirement years, Dorothy's hobby at their California ranch was searching for gold. She found small slivers here and there in rocks along the creek bed and the hilly areas of their property.

One weekend, when Della was visiting at the ranch, "Mom asked if I'd seen Dad—and about that time he came running across the backyard hollering, 'I've found it, I've found it.'"

"Mom was so excited and Dad couldn't hold back his laughter," Della said.

In yet another of his practical jokes, Charlie had patiently used a soldering iron and soldered a copper collar button into a quartz rock. He did a remarkable job of making the rock look like gold.[189]

The Swanville rookies and Catalina kids never lost touch. Grimm and Dizzy Dean stayed in contact by phone as Root faded away in the final six weeks of his life from leukemia.

In a telegram that Della saved, Grimm wrote, "I have lost a very dear friend and I'm sorry."

"Mom said we had to go over to the undertaker, who obviously was no baseball fan," Della said. When he asked in which newspaper to place the obit, Mom said, "The Associated Press will take care of that."

"He looked at poor, dear old Mother," Della said. "My brother and I got the giggles. He just didn't understand why the Associated Press would care."

News of Root's death at age 71 on November 5, 1970, traveled the world, even appearing in Paris newspapers, Della said.

The second paragraph of his obituary by United Press, said, "He was probably best known in baseball lore for one pitch he threw to Babe Ruth. Ruth hit the ball over the center field fence in Wrigley Field, Chicago, just after he supposedly had pointed to the distant grandstand, calling his shot."

Three umpires wrote about what a gentleman he was, including these words from Charley Moran: "Charlie was a ballplayer's ballplayer, a gentleman without peer, the word 'quit' was not in his

---

[189] Della Root Arnold, letter with editing notes, Oct. 30, 2004.

vocabulary. He was a great credit to baseball and the Cubs. I'm glad I knew him." [190]

Grimm died November 15, 1983, and his family scattered his ashes under first base at Wrigley Field, abiding by his final wish. [191]

Clyde Beck was the last of the friends to depart. On his last visit to the Root ranch, he was 88 and told Dorothy, "If I'd known I was going to live this long, I'd taken better care of myself." [192]

Nearly a year after her Charles died, Dorothy told Della, "I took your dad's ashes today and sprinkled them on top of the mountain where he liked to drive the Jeep."

Until the end, Dorothy enjoyed a drink or two every evening before meals.

"How many drinks are you having?" her doctor asked.

"As many as I want," Dorothy snapped, without hesitation.

When the doctor persisted, Dorothy said, "I don't know why you're making such a fuss. There are a lot more old drunks than old doctors."

Dorothy, 89, died on May 14, 1988. "She said she was going to go down swinging, just like Charlie always said," Della said.

Dorothy's ashes were sprinkled in the same spot as her beloved husband's at their final resting place together at the Hollister ranch.

Not so many years ago, Della returned to Catalina Island and was disappointed to find little mention of the Chicago Cubs.

Cub fans insist on keeping Della's memories alive, however.

Every week, tourists wander from cruise ships docked near the harbor at Avalon and ask about the Cubs and want to stand on the old ball field, said Catalina natives and brothers Joe and Lolo Saldana.

The eucalyptus trees still shade the left field line and chalk marks the boundaries just as 80 years ago, but this time for soccer and football, not for baseball.

---

[190] Della, pg. 108.
[191] Feldmann, Doug, *September Streak: The 1935 Chicago Cubs Chase the Pennant.* Della mentions specifically that it was under first base.
[192] As told to Della by her mother.

The stands are gone. The field is in disrepair, with construction barriers and materials cluttering the territory once roamed by Hack Wilson, Riggs Stephenson and Kiki Cuyler.

At the Country Club, where the Cubs had their locker room and got the Andy Lotshaw rubdowns and treatments, there is a photo hanging over the bar of Charlie Root, Pat Malone and Gabby Hartnett. A uniform on the wall is from the 1929 team.

At the Casino, the beautiful ballroom where Dorothy and Charlie Root danced is still in perfect condition. Downstairs in the museum is a wall devoted to the Cubs and spring training. The only team photo displayed is of the 1929 team, with rookie Berly Horne smiling in the back row and Charlie Root hiding the secret about his hurting arm.

Joe Saldana showed me all of this, opening doors all over the island in February 2009, exactly 80 years after Berly Horne and Charlie Root stood or danced in the same spots.

When the Cubs spent their last days in spring training here in 1951, Joe, then 11, dove for coins in the harbor and shagged flies in the outfield. Joe owns Coyote Joe's restaurant on the island, and his brother, Lolo, is the barber of Avalon.

The Saldanas hope, and the mayor promised during my visit, to restore the plaque that once marked the ball field and keep the story alive about how significant Catalina is to Cub fans, history lovers and baseball in general.

The unofficial museum of Catalina is in Lolo's barbershop. He has used every square inch of his walls for old photos and a Cub ball cap, so a large picture of the old ballpark has now spilled to a shelf in the middle of the barbershop.

Photo by Roger Snell

Joe Saldana, owner of Coyote Joe's Restaurant on Catalina Island, shagged flies in the outfield during the Cubs last season at Catalina in 1951 when he was 11.

Photo by Roger Snell

This sign still hangs in the Country Club where the Cubs had their lockers and training room just a short walk from left field of the Catalina ball field.

Photo by Roger Snell

The unofficial Cub museum of Catalina Island is found in Lolo
Saldana's barbershop at Avalon. Cub fans from all over the
world find their way to the Saldana brothers seeking baseball
history. All four walls are filled with photos and memorabilia.

Photo by Roger Snell

The old Cub ball field is nearly forgotten, but the eucalyptus trees down the left field boundary remain. The mayor of Avalon promises to restore a Wrigley plaque as tourists on cruise ships weekly stop to ask where the field is. The white line today marks the edge of a soccer field.

If you want to hear the real history of the Cubs at Catalina, pull up a chair at Coyote Joe's restaurant or stop in for a trim at Lolo's barbershop.

Or listen to the stories of innkeeper Susan Griffin at The Inn on Mt. Ada as she talks lovingly of William Wrigley Jr. and his wife. Susan watches over the remarkable preservation of the Wrigley home, now a bed and breakfast, overlooking the harbor, the remnants of the ballfield and the Casino.

"The grand, old beautiful St. Catherine Hotel is missing from our Avalon," Della said. "The ball park is gone, the steamer, *S.S. Catalina,* replaced by jet boats.

"The lovely Casino ballroom, where every year we had the Chicago Cub dances to the music of the famous big bands, is closed except to special summer parties," Della said.

Della misses those dances with her dad.

"He always danced with Mom first and then would dance with me," Della said. "He was so smooth in his moves."

"What a happy life," Della said.

She wishes baseball history would remember her dad for so much more than one pitch.

But Charlie was realistic even moments before his death.

In his final words to Della before slipping into a coma, her father said, "Isn't it funny? I gave my whole life to baseball, and I'll be remembered for something that never happened."

Charlie Root Career Pitching Statistics

17 year won/loss record = .557

Year	Ag	Tm	Lg	W	L	G	GS	CG	SHO	GF	SV	IP	H	R	ER	HR	BB	SO	HBP	WP	BFP	IBB	BK	ERA	*lgERA	*ERA+	WHIP
1923	24	SLB	AL	0	4	27	2	0	0	15	0	60.0	68	45	38	4	18	27	6	1	263		0	5.70	4.18	73	1.433
1926	27	CHC	NL	18	17	42	32	21	2	7	2	271.3	267	104	85	10	62	127	6	1	1110		1	2.82	3.86	137	1.213
1927	28	CHC	NL	26	15	48	36	21	4	12	2	309.0	296	148	129	16	117	145	9	3	1316		1	3.76	3.87	103	1.337
1928	29	CHC	NL	14	18	40	30	13	1	6	2	237.0	214	109	94	15	73	122	7	0	992		0	3.57	3.86	108	1.211
1929	30	CHC	NL	19	6	43	31	19	4	9	5	272.0	286	120	105	12	83	124	3	1	1158		0	3.47	4.62	133	1.357
1930	31	CHC	NL	16	14	37	30	15	3	6	3	220.3	247	122	106	17	63	124	7	1	967		0	4.33	4.87	113	1.407
1931	32	CHC	NL	17	14	39	31	19	3	6	2	251.0	240	109	97	7	71	131	7	1	1043		0	3.48	3.86	111	1.239
1932	33	CHC	NL	15	10	39	23	11	0	9	3	216.3	211	99	86	10	55	96	5	4	908		0	3.58	3.76	105	1.230
1933	34	CHC	NL	15	10	35	30	20	2	4	0	242.3	232	85	70	14	61	86	10	3	1008		0	2.60	3.27	126	1.209
1934	35	CHC	NL	4	7	34	9	2	0	14	0	117.7	141	62	56	8	53	46	5	2	538		0	4.28	3.90	91	1.649
1935	36	CHC	NL	15	8	38	18	11	1	16	2	201.3	193	85	69	15	47	94	3	2	826		0	3.08	3.94	128	1.192
1936	37	CHC	NL	3	6	33	4	0	0	15	1	73.7	81	34	34	3	20	32	2	0	315		0	4.15	3.98	96	1.371
1937	38	CHC	NL	13	5	43	15	5	0	20	5	178.7	173	71	67	18	32	74	4	2	729		0	3.38	3.99	118	1.147
1938	39	CHC	NL	8	7	44	11	5	0	20	8	160.7	163	62	51	10	30	70	2	0	673		0	2.86	3.82	134	1.201
1939	40	CHC	NL	8	8	35	16	8	0	12	4	167.3	189	83	75	11	34	66	2	0	709		1	4.03	3.96	98	1.333
1940	41	CHC	NL	2	4	36	8	1	0	10	1	112.0	118	61	48	9	33	50	1	0	490		0	3.86	3.77	98	1.348
1941	42	CHC	NL	8	7	19	15	6	0	4	0	106.7	133	68	64	8	37	46	0	1	484		0	5.40	3.52	65	1.594
Total				201	160	632	341	177	21	185	40	3197.3	3252	1467	1274	187	889	1459	79	22	13529	0	3	3.59	3.96	110	1.295
Average				14	11	44	23	12	1	12	2	223.3	227	102	89	13	62	101	5	1	945	0	0	3.59	3.96	110	1.295
High				26	18	48	36	21	4	20	8	309.0	296	148	129	18	117	145	10	4	1316	0	1	4.87	3.96	137	1.147

Team Pitching Statistics   1929 Chicago Cubs

	Player	Age	G	ERA	W	L	SV	GS	GF	CG	SHO	IP	H	R	ER	HR	BB	SO	BFP	WP	HBP	BK	ERA+
SP	Charley Root	30	43	3.47	19	6	5	31	9	19	4	272.0	286	120	105	12	83	124	1158	1	3	0	133
SP	Sheriff Blake	29	35	4.29	14	13	1	30	3	13	1	218.3	244	122	104	8	103	70	962	4	2	0	108
SP	Pat Malone	26	40	3.57	22	10	2	30	7	19	5	267.0	283	120	106	12	102	166	1152	6	6	1	129
SP	Guy Bush	27	50	3.66	18	7	8	29	15	18	2	270.7	277	135	110	16	107	82	1176	7	4	0	126
RP	*Mike Cvengros	28	32	4.64	5	4	2	4	15	0	0	64.0	82	39	33	2	29	23	294	2	1	1	99
RP	Hal Carlson	37	31	5.16	11	5	2	14	9	6	2	111.7	131	71	64	8	31	35	492	0	1	0	90
RP	*Art Nehf	36	32	5.59	8	5	1	15	8	4	0	120.7	148	85	75	11	39	27	529	1	2	0	83
RP	Trader Horne	30	11	5.09	1	1	0	1	4	0	0	23.0	24	20	13	3	21	6	111	2	0	0	91
	Claude Jonnard	31	12	7.48	0	1	0	2	4	0	0	27.7	41	27	23	4	11	11	142	0	1	0	62
	Ken Penner	33	5	2.84	0	1	0	0	2	0	0	12.7	14	11	4	1	6	3	58	0	0	0	162
	Bob Osborn	26	3	3.00	0	0	0	1	2	0	0	9.0	8	3	3	0	2	1	36	0	0	0	154
	Hank Grampp	25	1	27.00	0	1	0	1	0	0	0	2.0	4	6	6	0	3	0	13	0	1	0	17
	Average or Total		156	4.16	98	54	21	156	77	79	14	1398.0	1542	758	646	77	537	548	6123	23	21	2	111
	Rank among 8 NL teams			2		1		8	2	2	1		3			2	6	2					

* - throws left-handed

255

1929 Chicago Cubs Batting Statistics (pitchers omitted)

Pos	Player	Ag	G	AB	R	H	2B	3B	HR	RBI	BB	SO	BA	OBP	SLG	CS	HBP	SH	OPS+
C	Zack Taylor	30	64	215	29	59	16	3	1	31	19	18	0.274	0.336	0.391	0	1	3	79
1B	* Charlie Grimm	30	120	463	66	138	28	3	10	91	42	25	0.298	0.358	0.436	3	1	10	96
2B	Rogers Hornsby	33	156	602	156	229	47	8	39	149	87	65	0.380	0.459	0.679	2	1	22	178
3B	Norm McMillan	33	124	495	77	134	35	5	5	55	36	43	0.271	0.324	0.392	13	3	7	76
SS	Woody English	23	144	608	131	168	29	3	1	52	68	50	0.276	0.352	0.339	13	3	21	72
OF	Hack Wilson	29	150	574	135	198	30	5	39	159	78	83	0.345	0.425	0.618	3	2	16	155
OF	Riggs Stephenson	31	136	495	91	179	36	6	17	110	67	21	0.362	0.445	0.562	10	7	13	147
OF	Kiki Cuyler	30	139	509	111	183	29	7	15	102	66	56	0.360	0.438	0.532	43	5	16	139
	* Cliff Heathcote	31	82	224	45	70	17	0	2	31	25	17	0.313	0.384	0.415	9	1	7	98
	Clyde Beck	29	54	190	28	40	7	0	0	9	19	24	0.211	0.282	0.247	3	0	4	32
	Mike Gonzalez	38	60	167	15	40	3	0	0	18	18	14	0.240	0.317	0.257	1	1	3	44
	Chick Tolson	30	32	109	13	28	5	0	1	19	9	16	0.257	0.325	0.330	0	2	3	63
	* Earl Grace	22	27	80	7	20	1	0	2	17	9	7	0.250	0.333	0.338	0	1	4	67
	* Footsie Blair	28	26	72	10	23	5	0	1	8	3	4	0.319	0.347	0.431	1	0	2	91
	* Johnny Schulte	32	31	69	6	18	3	0	0	9	7	11	0.261	0.329	0.304	0	0	2	58
	* Johnny Moore	27	37	63	13	18	1	0	2	8	4	6	0.286	0.338	0.397	0	1	1	81
	* Gabby Hartnett	28	25	22	2	6	2	1	1	9	5	5	0.273	0.407	0.591	1	0	1	144
	* Tom Angley	24	5	16	1	4	1	0	0	6	2	2	0.250	0.333	0.313	0	0	3	61
	Danny Taylor	28	2	3	0	0	0	0	0	0	1	1	0.000	0.250	0.000	0	0	0	-32

* Bats Left-handed

Index

Q

Quinn, John, 210

R

Root, Charlie, 1, 6, 25, 57, 70, 73, 78, 81, 83, 86, 89, 94, 104, 113, 115, 124, 128, 129, 141, 158, 162, 167, 171, 181, 193, 196, 199, 203, 209, 210, 215, 216, 223
  "called shot", 236–45
  1929 opening day, 98, 114
  30th birthday, 90
  a bad season, 65
  and his family, 86
  arm problems, 93
  as newspaper columnist, 169
  becomes the ace in 1926, 58
  birthplace, v
  career in danger, 9
  Charlie Root Day, 223
  competitive nature, 214
  demonstrates pitching accuracy, 81
  evaluation of Series line-ups, 169
  family photo, 26
  first pro contract, 108
  first start for Cubs, 184
  gold prank on Dorothy, 247
  his sidearm delivery, 192
  ill as child, 224
  investments in stock market, 180
  leads NL pitchers in 1927, 62
  leukemia, 248
  makes the team, 58
  math ability, 245
  Milwaukee pitching coach, 246
  nickname Chinski,, 246
  pennant race, 135
  practical joke, 82
  racial attitude, 224
  replay games in dream, 247
  retirement years, 247
  rookie breaks ankle, 110
  saves Horne's first win, 140
  Spahn "called shot", 246
  spring training, 5
  strikes out Cobb, 183

  traded to Los Angeles, 110
  wiffle ball "called shot", 246
Root, Charlie, Jr.
  fifth birthday, 84
  misbehaves at the ball park, 99
Root, Della, iii, v, 1, 3, 25, 87, 93, 108, 114, 127, 183, 185, 202, 203, 248
  discovery by author Snell, 231
  tenth birthday, 85
  watches fights, 154
Root, Della and Junior, 12
Root, Dorothy, 7, 25, 60, 85, 99, 105, 109, 106–13
  and children, 87
  antics, 134
  death of her mother, 106
  defies the Kaiser, 108
  drives to San Francisco, 113
  first date with Charlie, 107
  gold prank, 247
  learns to drive, 112
  packing for Catalina, 12
  plays piano, 130
  traveled with Charlie, 132
Root, Dorothy and Charlie, 8, 23, 83, 108, 130, 204
  dancing, 133
  go to night school, 245
  host rookies, 131
  learning the Charleston, 84
  retirement years, 247
Root, Dorothy and Della, 102, 103, 104, 169, 187
  massage Charlie's shoulder, 99
  shopping in Avalon, 80
Root, Jacob, 107, 108, 109, 111, 226
  The Kaiser, 8
Ruth, Babe, 46, 50, 67, 115, 122, 143, 163, 187, 193
  "called shot", 3, 236–45
  comments on "called shot", 238
  picks Cubs to win NL, 101
  picks Cubs to win Series, 179
  salary, 228
  suspected heart attack, 178

Z

About the Author

Roger Snell won top investigative journalism awards throughout his 18-year newspaper career, including the Pulitzer Prize and Silver Gavel.

Snell wrote more than 3,000 articles while working for newspapers in Ohio and Missouri and was state capital bureau chief in both states for three news organizations. He won the Pulitzer Prize in 1994 as a member of the Akron (Ohio) Beacon Journal staff.

Snell and Michael J. Berens won several awards in 1990 at the Columbus Dispatch, exposing cops who owned crack houses, a police informant who committed murder and other major irregularities in the city's anti-drug war.

Snell's investigations of ethical abuses on the Ohio Supreme Court won the American Bar Association's top national journalism award in 1992, the Silver Gavel.

The Ohio Academy of Trial Lawyers named Snell the Ohio Reporter of the Year in 1992 and 1993, the only reporter ever to win in consecutive years.

Snell lives in Frankfort, Ky., with his wife Linda and daughters Rachel and Hannah. His lifelong baseball passion extends beyond this book. He is a member of the Society for American Baseball Research (SABR) and is now volunteering his fourth season as a software beta tester for Out of the Park Baseball.

This book was inspired by the first newspaper article that Snell ever wrote as an Ohio State freshman, about the neighbor who lived five doors away in Arcanum, Ohio. Berly "Trader" Horne only made it to the majors for one season—the 1929 Chicago Cubs. He told his story to the author on his front porch in 1978. Horne became Snell's own personal Moonlight Graham, just like the character in the movie "Field of Dreams."

Author Roger Snell,
standing outside
Wrigley Field

CPSIA information can be obtained
at www.ICGtesting.com
Printed in the USA
BVOW08s1920121217
502602BV00002B/131/P